NO LONGER PROPERTY OF
FALVEY MEMORIAL LIBRARY

Engdahl, Const'l Fed., 2nd Ed., NS—1

Nutshell Series

of

WEST PUBLISHING COMPANY

P.O. Box 64526

St. Paul, Minnesota 55164-0526

Accounting—Law and, 1984, 377 pages, by E. McGruder Faris, Late Professor of Law, Stetson University.

Administrative Law and Process, 2nd Ed., 1981, 445 pages, by Ernest Gellhorn, Former Dean and Professor of Law, Case Western Reserve University and Barry B. Boyer, Professor of Law, SUNY, Buffalo.

Admiralty, 1983, 390 pages, by Frank L. Maraist, Professor of Law, Louisiana State University.

Agency-Partnership, 1977, 364 pages, by Roscoe T. Steffen, Late Professor of Law, University of Chicago.

American Indian Law, 1981, 288 pages, by William C. Canby, Jr., Adjunct Professor of Law, Arizona State University.

Antitrust Law and Economics, 3rd Ed., 1986, 472 pages, by Ernest Gellhorn, Former Dean and Professor of Law, Case Western Reserve University.

Appellate Advocacy, 1984, 325 pages, by Alan D. Hornstein, Professor of Law, University of Maryland.

Art Law, 1984, 335 pages, by Leonard D. DuBoff, Professor of Law, Lewis and Clark College, Northwestern School of Law.

Banking and Financial Institutions, 1984, 409 pages, by William A. Lovett, Professor of Law, Tulane University.

Church-State Relations—Law of, 1981, 305 pages, by Leonard F. Manning, Late Professor of Law, Fordham University.

List current as of February, 1987

NUTSHELL SERIES

Civil Procedure, 2nd Ed., 1986, 306 pages, by Mary Kay Kane, Professor of Law, University of California, Hastings College of the Law.

Civil Rights, 1978, 279 pages, by Norman Vieira, Professor of Law, Southern Illinois University.

Commercial Paper, 3rd Ed., 1982, 404 pages, by Charles M. Weber, Professor of Business Law, University of Arizona and Richard E. Speidel, Professor of Law, Northwestern University.

Community Property, 1982, 447 pages, by Robert L. Mennell, Former Professor of Law, Hamline University.

Comparative Legal Traditions, 1982, 402 pages, by Mary Ann Glendon, Professor of Law, Harvard University, Michael Wallace Gordon, Professor of Law, University of Florida and Christopher Osakwe, Professor of Law, Tulane University.

Conflicts, 1982, 470 pages, by David D. Siegel, Professor of Law, St. John's University.

Constitutional Analysis, 1979, 388 pages, by Jerre S. Williams, Professor of Law Emeritus, University of Texas.

Constitutional Federalism, 2nd Ed., 1987, about 360 pages, by David E. Engdahl, Professor of Law, University of Puget Sound.

Constitutional Law, 1986, 389 pages, by Jerome A. Barron, Dean and Professor of Law, George Washington University and C. Thomas Dienes, Professor of Law, George Washington University.

Consumer Law, 2nd Ed., 1981, 418 pages, by David G. Epstein, Dean and Professor of Law, Emory University and Steve H. Nickles, Professor of Law, University of Minnesota.

Contract Remedies, 1981, 323 pages, by Jane M. Friedman, Professor of Law, Wayne State University.

Contracts, 2nd Ed., 1984, 425 pages, by Gordon D. Schaber, Dean and Professor of Law, McGeorge School of Law and Claude D. Rohwer, Professor of Law, McGeorge School of Law.

NUTSHELL SERIES

Corporations—Law of, 2nd Ed., 1987, 515 pages, by Robert W. Hamilton, Professor of Law, University of Texas.

Corrections and Prisoners' Rights—Law of, 2nd Ed., 1983, 386 pages, by Sheldon Krantz, Dean and Professor of Law, University of San Diego.

Criminal Law, 2nd Ed., 1987, about 300 pages, by Arnold H. Loewy, Professor of Law, University of North Carolina.

Criminal Procedure—Constitutional Limitations, 3rd Ed., 1980, 438 pages, by Jerold H. Israel, Professor of Law, University of Michigan and Wayne R. LaFave, Professor of Law, University of Illinois.

Debtor-Creditor Law, 3rd Ed., 1986, 383 pages, by David G. Epstein, Dean and Professor of Law, Emory University.

Employment Discrimination—Federal Law of, 2nd Ed., 1981, 402 pages, by Mack A. Player, Professor of Law, University of Georgia.

Energy Law, 1981, 338 pages, by Joseph P. Tomain, Professor of Law, University of Cincinnatti.

Environmental Law, 1983, 343 pages by Roger W. Findley, Professor of Law, University of Illinois and Daniel A. Farber, Professor of Law, University of Minnesota.

Estate and Gift Taxation, Federal, 3rd Ed., 1983, 509 pages, by John K. McNulty, Professor of Law, University of California, Berkeley.

Estate Planning—Introduction to, 3rd Ed., 1983, 370 pages, by Robert J. Lynn, Professor of Law, Ohio State University.

Evidence, Federal Rules of, 2nd Ed., 1987, 473 pages, by Michael H. Graham, Professor of Law, University of Miami.

Evidence, State and Federal Rules, 2nd Ed., 1981, 514 pages, by Paul F. Rothstein, Professor of Law, Georgetown University.

Family Law, 2nd Ed., 1986, 444 pages, by Harry D. Krause, Professor of Law, University of Illinois.

Federal Jurisdiction, 2nd Ed., 1981, 258 pages, by David P. Currie, Professor of Law, University of Chicago.

Future Interests, 1981, 361 pages, by Lawrence W. Waggoner, Professor of Law, University of Michigan.

NUTSHELL SERIES

Government Contracts, 1979, 423 pages, by W. Noel Keyes, Professor of Law, Pepperdine University.

Historical Introduction to Anglo-American Law, 2nd Ed., 1973, 280 pages, by Frederick G. Kempin, Jr., Professor of Business Law, Wharton School of Finance and Commerce, University of Pennsylvania.

Immigration Law and Procedure, 1984, 345 pages, by David Weissbrodt, Professor of Law, University of Minnesota.

Injunctions, 1974, 264 pages, by John F. Dobbyn, Professor of Law, Villanova University.

Insurance Law, 1981, 281 pages, by John F. Dobbyn, Professor of Law, Villanova University.

Intellectual Property—Patents, Trademarks and Copyright, 1983, 428 pages, by Arthur R. Miller, Professor of Law, Harvard University, and Michael H. Davis, Professor of Law, Cleveland State University, Cleveland-Marshall College of Law.

International Business Transactions, 2nd Ed., 1984, 476 pages, by Donald T. Wilson, Late Professor of Law, Loyola University, Los Angeles.

International Law (Public), 1985, 262 pages, by Thomas Buergenthal, Professor of Law, Emory University and Harold G. Maier, Professor of Law, Vanderbilt University.

Introduction to the Study and Practice of Law, 1983, 418 pages, by Kenney F. Hegland, Professor of Law, University of Arizona.

Judicial Process, 1980, 292 pages, by William L. Reynolds, Professor of Law, University of Maryland.

Jurisdiction, 4th Ed., 1980, 232 pages, by Albert A. Ehrenzweig, Late Professor of Law, University of California, Berkeley, David W. Louisell, Late Professor of Law, University of California, Berkeley and Geoffrey C. Hazard, Jr., Professor of Law, Yale Law School.

Juvenile Courts, 3rd Ed., 1984, 291 pages, by Sanford J. Fox, Professor of Law, Boston College.

NUTSHELL SERIES

Labor Arbitration Law and Practice, 1979, 358 pages, by Dennis R. Nolan, Professor of Law, University of South Carolina.

Labor Law, 2nd Ed., 1986, 397 pages, by Douglas L. Leslie, Professor of Law, University of Virginia.

Land Use, 2nd Ed., 1985, 356 pages, by Robert R. Wright, Professor of Law, University of Arkansas, Little Rock and Susan Webber Wright, Professor of Law, University of Arkansas, Little Rock.

Landlord and Tenant Law, 2nd Ed., 1986, 311 pages, by David S. Hill, Professor of Law, University of Colorado.

Law Study and Law Examinations—Introduction to, 1971, 389 pages, by Stanley V. Kinyon, Late Professor of Law, University of Minnesota.

Legal Interviewing and Counseling, 2nd Ed., 1987, about 472 pages, by Thomas L. Shaffer, Professor of Law, Washington and Lee University and James R. Elkins, Professor of Law, West Virginia University.

Legal Research, 4th Ed., 1985, 452 pages, by Morris L. Cohen, Professor of Law and Law Librarian, Yale University.

Legal Writing, 1982, 294 pages, by Lynn B. Squires and Marjorie Dick Rombauer, Professor of Law, University of Washington.

Legislative Law and Process, 2nd Ed., 1986, 346 pages, by Jack Davies, Professor of Law, William Mitchell College of Law.

Local Government Law, 2nd Ed., 1983, 404 pages, by David J. McCarthy, Jr., Professor of Law, Georgetown University.

Mass Communications Law, 2nd Ed., 1983, 473 pages, by Harvey L. Zuckman, Professor of Law, Catholic University and Martin J. Gaynes, Lecturer in Law, Temple University.

Medical Malpractice—The Law of, 2nd Ed., 1986, 342 pages, by Joseph H. King, Professor of Law, University of Tennessee.

Military Law, 1980, 378 pages, by Charles A. Shanor, Professor of Law, Emory University and Timothy P. Terrell, Professor of Law, Emory University.

Oil and Gas Law, 1983, 443 pages, by John S. Lowe, Professor of Law, University of Tulsa.

NUTSHELL SERIES

Personal Property, 1983, 322 pages, by Barlow Burke, Jr., Professor of Law, American University.

Post-Conviction Remedies, 1978, 360 pages, by Robert Popper, Dean and Professor of Law, University of Missouri, Kansas City.

Presidential Power, 1977, 328 pages, by Arthur Selwyn Miller, Professor of Law Emeritus, George Washington University.

Products Liability, 2nd Ed., 1981, 341 pages, by Dix W. Noel, Late Professor of Law, University of Tennessee and Jerry J. Phillips, Professor of Law, University of Tennessee.

Professional Responsibility, 1980, 399 pages, by Robert H. Aronson, Professor of Law, University of Washington, and Donald T. Weckstein, Professor of Law, University of San Diego.

Real Estate Finance, 2nd Ed., 1985, 262 pages, by Jon W. Bruce, Professor of Law, Vanderbilt University.

Real Property, 2nd Ed., 1981, 448 pages, by Roger H. Bernhardt, Professor of Law, Golden Gate University.

Regulated Industries, 2nd Ed., 1987, 389 pages, by Ernest Gellhorn, Former Dean and Professor of Law, Case Western Reserve University, and Richard J. Pierce, Professor of Law, Southern Methodist University.

Remedies, 2nd Ed., 1985, 320 pages, by John F. O'Connell, Professor of Law, University of La Verne College of Law.

Res Judicata, 1976, 310 pages, by Robert C. Casad, Professor of Law, University of Kansas.

Sales, 2nd Ed., 1981, 370 pages, by John M. Stockton, Professor of Business Law, Wharton School of Finance and Commerce, University of Pennsylvania.

Schools, Students and Teachers—Law of, 1984, 409 pages, by Kern Alexander, President, Western Kentucky University and M. David Alexander, Professor, Virginia Tech University.

Sea—Law of, 1984, 264 pages, by Louis B. Sohn, Professor of Law, University of Georgia and Kristen Gustafson.

Secured Transactions, 2nd Ed., 1981, 391 pages, by Henry J. Bailey, Professor of Law Emeritus, Willamette University.

NUTSHELL SERIES

Securities Regulation, 2nd Ed., 1982, 322 pages, by David L. Ratner, Dean and Professor of Law, University of San Francisco.

Sex Discrimination, 1982, 399 pages, by Claire Sherman Thomas, Lecturer, University of Washington, Women's Studies Department.

Taxation and Finance, State and Local, 1986, 309 pages, by M. David Gelfand, Professor of Law, Tulane University and Peter W. Salsich, Professor of Law, St. Louis University.

Taxation of Corporations and Stockholders, Federal Income, 2nd Ed., 1981, 362 pages, by Jonathan Sobeloff, Late Professor of Law, Georgetown University and Peter P. Weidenbruch, Jr., Professor of Law, Georgetown University.

Taxation of Individuals, Federal Income, 3rd Ed., 1983, 487 pages, by John K. McNulty, Professor of Law, University of California, Berkeley.

Torts—Injuries to Persons and Property, 1977, 434 pages, by Edward J. Kionka, Professor of Law, Southern Illinois University.

Torts—Injuries to Family, Social and Trade Relations, 1979, 358 pages, by Wex S. Malone, Professor of Law Emeritus, Louisiana State University.

Trial Advocacy, 1979, 402 pages, by Paul B. Bergman, Adjunct Professor of Law, University of California, Los Angeles.

Trial and Practice Skills, 1978, 346 pages, by Kenney F. Hegland, Professor of Law, University of Arizona.

Trial, The First—Where Do I Sit? What Do I Say?, 1982, 396 pages, by Steven H. Goldberg, Professor of Law, University of Minnesota.

Unfair Trade Practices, 1982, 445 pages, by Charles R. McManis, Professor of Law, Washington University.

Uniform Commercial Code, 2nd Ed., 1984, 516 pages, by Bradford Stone, Professor of Law, Detroit College of Law.

Uniform Probate Code, 2nd Ed., 1987, about 418 pages, by Lawrence H. Averill, Jr., Dean and Professor of Law, University of Arkansas, Little Rock.

NUTSHELL SERIES

Water Law, 1984, 439 pages, by David H. Getches, Professor of Law, University of Colorado.

Welfare Law—Structure and Entitlement, 1979, 455 pages, by Arthur B. LaFrance, Professor of Law, Lewis and Clark College, Northwestern School of Law.

Wills and Trusts, 1979, 392 pages, by Robert L. Mennell, Former Professor of Law, Hamline University.

Workers' Compensation and Employee Protection Laws, 1984, 274 pages, by Jack B. Hood, Former Professor of Law, Cumberland School of Law, Samford University and Benjamin A. Hardy, Former Professor of Law, Cumberland School of Law, Samford University.

Hornbook Series
and
Basic Legal Texts
of
WEST PUBLISHING COMPANY
P.O. Box 64526
St. Paul, Minnesota 55164-0526

Admiralty and Maritime Law, Schoenbaum's Hornbook on, 1987, about 550 pages, by Thomas J. Schoenbaum, Professor of Law, University of Georgia.

Agency and Partnership, Reuschlein & Gregory's Hornbook on the Law of, 1979 with 1981 Pocket Part, 625 pages, by Harold Gill Reuschlein, Professor of Law Emeritus, Villanova University and William A. Gregory, Professor of Law, Georgia State University.

Antitrust, Sullivan's Hornbook on the Law of, 1977, 886 pages, by Lawrence A. Sullivan, Professor of Law, University of California, Berkeley.

Civil Procedure, Friedenthal, Kane and Miller's Hornbook on, 1985, 876 pages, by Jack H. Friedental, Professor of Law, Stanford University, Mary Kay Kane, Professor of Law, University of California, Hastings College of the Law and Arthur R. Miller, Professor of Law, Harvard University.

Common Law Pleading, Koffler and Reppy's Hornbook on, 1969, 663 pages, by Joseph H. Koffler, Professor of Law, New York Law School and Alison Reppy, Late Dean and Professor of Law, New York Law School.

Conflict of Laws, Scoles and Hay's Hornbook on, 1982, with 1986 Pocket Part, 1085 pages, by Eugene F. Scoles, Professor of Law, University of Illinois and Peter Hay, Dean and Professor of Law, University of Illinois.

HORNBOOKS & BASIC TEXTS

Constitutional Law, Nowak, Rotunda and Young's Hornbook on, 3rd Ed., 1986, 1191 pages, by John E. Nowak, Professor of Law, University of Illinois, Ronald D. Rotunda, Professor of Law, University of Illinois, and J. Nelson Young, Late Professor of Law, University of North Carolina.

Contracts, Calamari and Perillo's Hornbook on, 3rd Ed., 1987, about 900 pages, by John D. Calamari, Professor of Law, Fordham University and Joseph M. Perillo, Professor of Law, Fordham University.

Contracts, Corbin's One Volume Student Ed., 1952, 1224 pages, by Arthur L. Corbin, Late Professor of Law, Yale University.

Corporations, Henn and Alexander's Hornbook on, 3rd Ed., 1983, with 1986 Pocket Part, 1371 pages, by Harry G. Henn, Professor of Law Emeritus, Cornell University and John R. Alexander.

Criminal Law, LaFave and Scott's Hornbook on, 2nd Ed., 1986, 918 pages, by Wayne R. LaFave, Professor of Law, University of Illinois, and Austin Scott, Jr., Late Professor of Law, University of Colorado.

Criminal Procedure, LaFave and Israel's Hornbook on, 1985 with 1986 pocket part, 1142 pages, by Wayne R. LaFave, Professor of Law, University of Illinois and Jerold H. Israel, Professor of Law University of Michigan.

Damages, McCormick's Hornbook on, 1935, 811 pages, by Charles T. McCormick, Late Dean and Professor of Law, University of Texas.

Domestic Relations, Clark's Hornbook on, 1968, 754 pages, by Homer H. Clark, Jr., Professor of Law, University of Colorado.

Economics and Federal Antitrust Law, Hovenkamp's Hornbook on, 1985, 414 pages, by Herbert Hovenkamp, Professor of Law, University of Iowa.

Environmental Law, Rodgers' Hornbook on, 1977 with 1984 Pocket Part, 956 pages, by William H. Rodgers, Jr., Professor of Law, University of Washington.

Evidence, Lilly's Introduction to, 1978, 490 pages, by Graham C. Lilly, Professor of Law, University of Virginia.

HORNBOOKS & BASIC TEXTS

Evidence, McCormick's Hornbook on, 3rd Ed., 1984 with 1987 Pocket Part, 1156 pages, General Editor, Edward W. Cleary, Professor of Law Emeritus, Arizona State University.

Federal Courts, Wright's Hornbook on, 4th Ed., 1983, 870 pages, by Charles Alan Wright, Professor of Law, University of Texas.

Federal Income Taxation of Individuals, Posin's Hornbook on, 1983 with 1985 Pocket Part, 491 pages, by Daniel Q. Posin, Jr., Professor of Law, Catholic University.

Future Interest, Simes' Hornbook on, 2nd Ed., 1966, 355 pages, by Lewis M. Simes, Late Professor of Law, University of Michigan.

Insurance, Keeton's Basic Text on, 1971, 712 pages, by Robert E. Keeton, Professor of Law Emeritus, Harvard University.

Labor Law, Gorman's Basic Text on, 1976, 914 pages, by Robert A. Gorman, Professor of Law, University of Pennsylvania.

Law Problems, Ballentine's, 5th Ed., 1975, 767 pages, General Editor, William E. Burby, Late Professor of Law, University of Southern California.

Legal Ethics, Wolfram's Hornbook on, 1986, 1120 pages, by Charles W. Wolfram, Professor of Law, Cornell University.

Legal Writing Style, Weihofen's, 2nd Ed., 1980, 332 pages, by Henry Weihofen, Professor of Law Emeritus, University of New Mexico.

Local Government Law, Reynolds' Hornbook on, 1982, 860 pages, by Osborne M. Reynolds, Professor of Law, University of Oklahoma.

New York Estate Administration, Turano and Radigan's Hornbook on, 1986, 676 pages, by Margaret V. Turano, Professor of Law, St. John's University and Raymond Radigan.

New York Practice, Siegel's Hornbook on, 1978 with 1985 Pocket Part, 1011 pages, by David D. Siegel, Professor of Law, St. John's University.

HORNBOOKS & BASIC TEXTS

Oil and Gas Law, Hemingway's Hornbook on, 2nd Ed., 1983, with 1986 Pocket Part, 543 pages, by Richard W. Hemingway, Professor of Law, University of Oklahoma.

Poor, Law of the, LaFrance, Schroeder, Bennett and Boyd's Hornbook on, 1973, 558 pages, by Arthur B. LaFrance, Professor of Law, Lewis and Clark College, Northwestern School of Law, Milton R. Schroeder, Professor of Law, Arizona State University, Robert W. Bennett, Dean and Professor of Law, Northwestern University and William E. Boyd, Professor of Law, University of Arizona.

Property, Boyer's Survey of, 3rd Ed., 1981, 766 pages, by Ralph E. Boyer, Professor of Law Emeritus, University of Miami.

Property, Law of, Cunningham, Whitman and Stoebuck's Hornbook on, 1984, with 1987 Pocket Part, 916 pages, by Roger A. Cunningham, Professor of Law, University of Michigan, Dale A. Whitman, Dean and Professor of Law, University of Missouri, Columbia and William B. Stoebuck, Professor of Law, University of Washington.

Real Estate Finance Law, Nelson and Whitman's Hornbook on, 1985, 941 pages, by Grant S. Nelson, Professor of Law, University of Missouri, Columbia and Dale A. Whitman, Dean and Professor of Law, University of Missouri, Columbia.

Real Property, Moynihan's Introduction to, 1962, 254 pages, by Cornelius J. Moynihan, Late Professor of Law, Suffolk University.

Remedies, Dobb's Hornbook on, 1973, 1067 pages, by Dan B. Dobbs, Professor of Law, University of Arizona.

Secured Transactions under the U.C.C., Henson's Hornbook on, 2nd Ed., 1979 with 1979 Pocket Part, 504 pages, by Ray D. Henson, Professor of Law, University of California, Hastings College of the Law.

Securities Regulation, Hazen's Hornbook on the Law of, 1985, with 1987 Pocket Part, 739 pages, by Thomas Lee Hazen, Professor of Law, University of North Carolina.

Sports Law, Schubert, Smith and Trentadue's, 1986, 395 pages, by George W. Schubert, Dean of University College, University of North Dakota, Rodney K. Smith, Professor of Law,

HORNBOOKS & BASIC TEXTS

Delaware Law School, Widener University, and Jesse C. Trentadue, Former Professor of Law, University of North Dakota.

Torts, Prosser and Keeton's Hornbook on, 5th Ed., 1984, 1286 pages, by William L. Prosser, Late Dean and Professor of Law, University of California, Berkeley, Page Keeton, Professor of Law Emeritus, University of Texas, Dan B. Dobbs, Professor of Law, University of Arizona, Robert E. Keeton, Professor of Law Emeritus, Harvard University and David G. Owen, Professor of Law, University of South Carolina.

Trial Advocacy, Jeans' Handbook on, Soft cover, 1975, 473 pages, by James W. Jeans, Professor of Law, University of Missouri, Kansas City.

Trusts, Bogert's Hornbook on, 6th Ed., 1987, about 700 pages, by George G. Bogert, Late Professor of Law, University of Chicago and George T. Bogert.

Uniform Commercial Code, White and Summers' Hornbook on, 2nd Ed., 1980, 1250 pages, by James J. White, Professor of Law, University of Michigan and Robert S. Summers, Professor of Law, Cornell University.

Urban Planning and Land Development Control Law, Hagman and Juergensmeyer's Hornbook on, 2nd Ed., 1986, 680 pages, by Donald G. Hagman, Late Professor of Law, University of California, Los Angeles and Julian C. Juergensmeyer, Professor of Law, University of Florida.

Wills, Atkinson's Hornbook on, 2nd Ed., 1953, 975 pages, by Thomas E. Atkinson, Late Professor of Law, New York University.

Advisory Board

Professor JOHN A. BAUMAN
University of California School of Law, Los Angeles

Professor CURTIS J. BERGER
Columbia University School of Law

Dean JESSE H. CHOPER
University of California School of Law, Berkeley

Professor DAVID P. CURRIE
University of Chicago Law School

Dean DAVID G. EPSTEIN
Emory University School of Law

Professor YALE KAMISAR
University of Michigan Law School

Professor MARY KAY KANE
University of California,
Hastings College of the Law

Professor WAYNE R. LaFAVE
University of Illinois College of Law

Professor RICHARD C. MAXWELL
Duke University School of Law

Professor ARTHUR R. MILLER
Harvard University Law School

Professor JAMES J. WHITE
University of Michigan Law School

Professor CHARLES ALAN WRIGHT
University of Texas School of Law

CONSTITUTIONAL FEDERALISM

IN A NUTSHELL

SECOND EDITION

By

DAVID E. ENGDAHL

Professor of Law

University of Puget Sound

Successor edition to
Constitutional Power: Federal and State

ST. PAUL, MINN.
WEST PUBLISHING CO.
1987

COPYRIGHT © 1974 By WEST PUBLISHING CO.
COPYRIGHT © 1987 By WEST PUBLISHING CO.
50 West Kellogg Boulevard
P.O. Box 64526
St. Paul, Minnesota 55164–0526

All rights reserved
Printed in the United States of America

Library of Congress Cataloging-in-Publication Data

Engdahl, David E.
  Constitutional federalism in a nutshell.

  (Nutshell series)
  Includes index.
  1. Federal government—United States. I. Title.
II. Series.
KF4600.Z9E49 1987   342.73'042   87–6188

ISBN 0–314–38329–8

Engdahl, Const'l Fed., 2nd Ed., NS

DEDICATION

The author dedicates this work to
HON. RICHARD D. LAMM,
Former three-term Governor of Colorado;
Respected friend, sometime client . . .
and
Inspiration;

and to
HON. SANDRA DAY O'CONNOR,
Associate Justice of the United States Supreme Court;
Sagacious judge, renascent federalist . . .
and
Hope.

Despite any differences, both recognize the importance to practical democracy of demarcations between central and decentralized power, and of grounding new steps of political invention upon clear comprehension of what has gone before.

*

PREFACE

This book is not entirely typical of the Nutshell series. It is a mini-treatise on that part of Constitutional Law passed over most quickly in the typical academic course. It challenges the seemingly prevalent impression that *legal* issues of federalism have little substance (and less importance) today. It is not a summary digest of what is taught in most Constitutional Law classes; instead, it is a sorely needed supplement thereto.

Most readers will find the book difficult, even though revealing; and at least it will require careful and attentive study. The subject is treated here with more sophistication than even in available "hornbook" texts; the Nutshell format has been used in order to make it less expensive, and thus more easily available to students.

Yet its target audience is not current students alone; for few members of today's legal profession—whether in academia, or in practice, or on the bench—have given to this part of Constitutional Law the serious and systematic attention it deserves. Among the unfortunate consequences are inept analysis, inadequate briefs, and dysfunctional opinions in fields as diverse as civil rights enforcement, the legal consequences of federal funding, and interstate compact law. This book is an introduction to critical thinking in these fields;

PREFACE

and as such it is designed no less for practicing lawyers and judges than for law students and others who desire to grasp the coherent complex of federalism law concepts.

Although denominated a "second edition," it is more accurately described as a successor to the author's *Constitutional Power: Federal and State, In A Nutshell,* published in 1974. The basic structure of concepts remains the same; but the author's thoughts have matured considerably in thirteen years. The book therefore has been completely rewritten; the presentation and most of the substance have changed so dramatically that, in essence, it is a different work. The new title is more apt to the real focus of the book.

Supreme Court decisions through the end of the Term in July, 1986, are taken into account. Relevant opinions will have been delivered since; but as the reader gets more deeply into this book it will become evident why the most recent utterances are neither indispensable, nor necessarily useful, in the effort to master this branch of Constitutional Law.

The author credits and thanks two very capable young lawyers whose assistance while students helped materially in the preparation of this work, particularly Chapter Eleven: Ms. Brenda Turner and Mr. Barnett Kalikow.

D.E.E.

Tacoma, Washington
February, 1987

OUTLINE

	Page
PREFACE	XIX
TABLE OF CASES	XXXI

Chapter One. The Winds of Doctrine and Federalism Law ... 1
 § 1.01 What Distinguishes Federalism Law? ... 1
 § 1.02 Why Study Federalism Law? ... 3

Chapter Two. The Starting Point for Federalism Analysis: The Doctrine of Enumerated Powers ... 7
 § 2.01 The Concept and Misconceptions of "Enumerated Powers" ... 7
 § 2.02 An Aid to Analysis ... 14
   FIGURE 1 ... 14

Chapter Three. The Necessary and Proper Clause ... 16
 § 3.01 The Concept and Misconceptions of the Clause ... 16
   FIGURE 2 ... 19
 § 3.02 Erroneous Restraints on the Necessary and Proper Clause Power ... 20
   FIGURE 3 ... 21
 § 3.03 Statutes Leaving Telic Determinations to Courts or Agencies ... 24
 § 3.04 The "Particularity" Feature of the Necessary and Proper Clause ... 27
   FIGURE 4 ... 30

OUTLINE

		Page
Chapter Three.	**The Necessary and Proper Clause**—Continued	
§ 3.05	The Class Basis Principle	32
§ 3.06	Enforcible Limits of the Necessary and Proper Clause: Introduction	33
§ 3.07	The "Substantiality" Requirement	34
§ 3.08	The "Rational Basis" Requirement	35
§ 3.09	Congressional Determination of Telic Relation	39
§ 3.10	The Difficulty of Ascertaining Purpose	43
§ 3.11	Change of Circumstances	48
§ 3.12	The Dangers of Imprecise Expression	49
§ 3.13	Congress Alone Has This Power	50
Chapter Four.	**Enumerated Powers and Extraneous Ends**	52
§ 4.01	The Mischievous *McCulloch* Dictum	52
	FIGURE 5	52
§ 4.02	Progress Through Confusion: Emergence of the So-Called "Federal Police Power" (a Misnomer)	53
§ 4.03	The *Dagenhart* Error: Taking the *McCulloch* Dictum Seriously	57
§ 4.04	Demise of the *McCulloch* Dictum and Affirmation of Sound Principle	59
§ 4.05	Extraneous Ends of Necessary and Proper Clause Measures	62
	FIGURE 6	63
§ 4.06	Avoiding the "Bootstrap" Error	65

OUTLINE

		Page
Chapter Four.	**Enumerated Powers and Extraneous Ends**—Continued	
	FIGURE 7	66
	FIGURE 8	69
	FIGURE 9	70
	FIGURE 10	71
Chapter Five.	**Preemptive Capability**	74
§ 5.01	The Concept of Preemptive Capability	74
§ 5.02	Preemptive Capability and Matters Within the Circle of Legitimate Federal Concerns	77
§ 5.03	Preemptive Capability and the Necessary and Proper Clause	77
§ 5.04	Preemptive Capability as to "Matters" Not Touched by Congress	78
§ 5.05	*No* Preemptive Capability With Respect to Extraneous Ends	79
§ 5.06	Cases Illustrating the Lack of Preemptive Capability	82
§ 5.07	Circuitous Means to Legitimate Ends	85
	FIGURE 11	87
§ 5.08	Particularized Analysis for Preemptive Capability	90
	FIGURE 12	90
Chapter Six.	**Congress' Power Over Interstate Commerce**	93
§ 6.01	The Terms of the Commerce Clause	93
§ 6.02	Non-Commercial Interstate "Commerce"	99
§ 6.03	Interstate Commerce Without Discernible Line-Crossing	102
§ 6.04	The Importance of Caution in Characterization	108

OUTLINE

Chapter Six. Congress' Power Over Interstate Commerce—Continued

		Page
§ 6.05	Putting the Old Cases in Their Place	110
§ 6.06	Congress and Competition in Interstate Commerce	114
§ 6.07	The "Scarlet Letter" Error	117
§ 6.08	Confusion From Imprecise Expression	122
§ 6.09	Immaterial Predominant Ends	127
§ 6.10	Navigable Waters: A Peculiar Case	128
§ 6.11	Navigable Waters and Preemptive Capability	134
§ 6.12	International Commerce	135

Chapter Seven. Congress' Power to Tax 138

§ 7.01	"Direct" Taxes and "Apportionment"	138
§ 7.02	"Indirect" Taxes and "Uniformity"	141
§ 7.03	Other Limits On Federal Taxes	143
§ 7.04	Taxes and Non-Revenue Objectives	144
	FIGURE 13	145
§ 7.05	"Taxes" That Are Not Taxes, and Taxes That Really Are	147
§ 7.06	Necessary and Proper Means to Revenue Ends	154
§ 7.07	"Provisions Extraneous to Any Tax Need"	156
§ 7.08	Preemptive Capability and the Taxing Power	161

OUTLINE

		Page
Chapter Eight.	Congress' Spending and Borrowing Powers	162
§ 8.01	Source of the Power to Spend	162
§ 8.02	The "General Welfare" Limitation	164
§ 8.03	The Classic Dispute Over the Spending Power: Madison, Hamilton, and Monroe	166
§ 8.04	The Dim Dawning of Awareness: *Butler* and the Social Security Act Cases	170
§ 8.05	Modern Use of the Spending Power to Promote Extraneous Ends	174
§ 8.06	Preemptive Capability and the Spending Power	179
§ 8.07	Congress' Power Over Recipients: The Contractual Character of Spending Conditions	185
§ 8.08	Enforcement of Spending Conditions	189
§ 8.09	The Necessary and Proper Clause and Spending	197
§ 8.10	The Source and Uses of Congress' Borrowing Power	199
Chapter Nine.	Exceptions and Qualifications to Enumerated Powers Doctrine: The Foreign Affairs and Property Powers	203
§ 9.01	National Powers and Foreign Affairs	203
§ 9.02	Foreign Affairs and the Necessary and Proper Clause	207
§ 9.03	Treaties and Federal Laws	210

OUTLINE

		Page
Chapter Nine.	**Exceptions and Qualifications to Enumerated Powers Doctrine: The Foreign Affairs and Property Powers**—Continued	
§ 9.04	State Law and Foreign Affairs	212
§ 9.05	Classic Doctrine Regarding Federal Enclaves Within States	213
§ 9.06	Classic Doctrine Regarding Territory Outside Any State	218
§ 9.07	Classic Doctrine Regarding Other Federal Property	221
§ 9.08	The Scrambled Egg: Enclave and Property Clause Doctrine in Disarray	226
Chapter Ten.	**Congress' Enforcement Power**	233
§ 10.01	The Enforcement Clauses of Certain Amendments	233
§ 10.02	The Necessary and Proper Clause Analogy	234
§ 10.03	Much Ado About Nothing: The Furor Over *Morgan's* Second (or "Substantive") Rationale	239
§ 10.04	Enforcement of Rights Not Derived From Amendments	244
Chapter Eleven.	**Negative Implications of Federal Power**	248
§ 11.01	Exclusivity *Vel Non*	248
§ 11.02	The Dormant Commerce Clause From 1789 to *Cooley*	250
§ 11.03	Evolution Under *Cooley*	257
§ 11.04	The (Justice) Stone Foundations of the Modern Approach	262
§ 11.05	Aside: The Market Participant Doctrine	269

OUTLINE

Chapter Eleven. Negative Implications of Federal Power—Continued

		Page
§ 11.06	Aside: Alcoholic Beverages	271
§ 11.07	The Modern Approach: Preface	272
§ 11.08	The Modern Approach: Stage One	276
§ 11.09	The Modern Approach: Stage Two	280
§ 11.10	The Modern Approach: Stage Three	287
§ 11.11	Critique of the Modern Approach	292
§ 11.12	Negative Implications for State Taxes: Preface	298
§ 11.13	The Tax Cases Before 1977	299
§ 11.14	The Tax Cases Since 1977	309
§ 11.15	Critique of the Current Approach in Tax Cases	323
§ 11.16	State Taxes and International Commerce	326

Chapter Twelve. Preemption 334

§ 12.01	Introduction	334
§ 12.02	Evolution of Preemption Doctrine	334
§ 12.03	Modern Preemption Methodology	341
§ 12.04	"Express" Preemptive Intent	350
§ 12.05	Preemption and Federal Administrative Agencies	351
§ 12.06	Permissive Licensure and Preemption	353
§ 12.07	A Reminder About Preemptive Capability	354

Chapter Thirteen. Congressional Enlargement of State Power 357

§ 13.01	State Actions Contingent Upon Federal Consent	357

OUTLINE

Chapter Thirteen. Congressional Enlargement of State Power—Continued

		Page
§ 13.02	Congressional Enlargement of State Power Over Interstate and Foreign Commerce	358
§ 13.03	Recent Cases on Congressional Consent to State Regulation and Taxation of Commerce	364

Chapter Fourteen. Intergovernmental Immunities 368

§ 14.01	Introduction	368
§ 14.02	Constitutional Immunity for the United States and Its Instrumentalities: The *McCulloch* Rational	369
§ 14.03	Constitutional Federal Immunity Dehors *McCulloch*	376
§ 14.04	Federal Immunity for Private Entities	377
§ 14.05	Federal Immunity Governed by Statute	381
§ 14.06	State Immunity Before 1976	383
§ 14.07	State Immunity: *Usery, Garcia,* and Beyond	386

Chapter Fifteen. Intergovernmental Cooperation 391

§ 15.01	Some Methods of Federal-State Cooperation	391
§ 15.02	Miscellaneous Methods of Interstate Cooperation	393
§ 15.03	Interstate Agreements and Compacts: The Requirement of Congressional Consent	394
§ 15.04	How Congress' "Consent" Is Given	399

OUTLINE

Chapter Fifteen. Intergovernmental Cooperation—Continued

§ 15.05 The Consequences of Consent, and the "Law of the Union" Doctrine 400

INDEX 407

TABLE OF CASES

References are to Pages

Acker, United States v., 155
Adams Mfg. Co., J.D. v. Storen, 324
Adamson v. California, 122
Addyston Pipe & Steel Co. v. United States, 25, 109
AFL & CIO v. Kahn, 178
Alabama v. King & Boozer, 378, 379
Alaska v. Troy, 148
Allen v. Pullman's Palace Car Co., 301
Allenberg Cotton Co., Inc. v. Pittman, 114, 279, 287
Allgeyer v. Louisiana, 259
American Insurance Co. v. Canter, 218
American Power Co. v. SEC, 126
Appalachian Electric Power Co., United States v., 59, 60, 129, 130, 132, 172, 177
Arizona v. California, 129, 131
Arizona Train Limit Case, 361
Arkansas Electric Cooperative Corp. v. Arkansas Public Comm'n, 288, 289
Arlington Hts. v. Metropolitan Housing Development Corp., 47
Armco Inc. v. Hardesty, 311, 321
Asakura v. Seattle, 212
Asarco Inc. v. Idaho State Tax Comm'n, 320, 321
Ashwander v. TVA, 59
Atascadero State Hosp. v. Scanlon, 193, 194
Atchison, Topeka & Santa Fe Ry. v. Railroad Comm'n, 336
Auto Transit, Inc. v. Brady, 309, 310, 321, 331

Bailey v. Drexel Furniture Co., 148, 149, 152, 153, 155
Baker v. General Motors Corp., 345
Baldwin v. Franks, 212
Baldwin v. G.A.F. Seelig, Inc., 261, 276, 277
Bank of Augusta v. Earle, 298

TABLE OF CASES

Bass, United States v., 45
Belmont, United States v., 213
Bevans, United States v., 217
Bibb v. Navajo Freight Lines, 290, 291
Bishop Processing Co., United States v., 100
Bob-Lo Excursion Co. v. Michigan, 290
Boyd, United States v., 379
Bradley v. Public Utilities Comm'n, 261, 278
Braniff Airways, Inc. v. Nebraska State Board of Equalization, 307
Breard v. Alexandria, 278
Brolan v. United States, 137
Brotherhood of Locomotive Firemen & Enginemen v. Chicago, R.I. & Pac. RR Co., 49, 280
Brotherhood of Railroad Trainmen v. Jacksonville Terminal Co., 344
Brown v. Maryland, 117, 118, 328, 330
Brown-Forman Distillers Corp. v. New York Liquor Auth., 272, 274, 275, 277
Brushaber v. Union Pac. R.R. Co., 142, 144
Buck v. Kuykendall, 261
Buckley v. Valeo, 166, 198, 199
Burbank v. Lockheed Air Terminal, 341, 348
Burnet v. Brooks, 204
Burnison, United States v., 80
Burroughs v. United States, 245
Butler, United States v., 81, 83, 164, 170–173, 175, 182, 183, 199, 356
Butte City Water Co. v. Baker, 224

California v. Zook, 339, 340, 341, 347
California Coastal Comm'n v. Granite Rock Co., 354
California Dept. of Human Res. v. Java, 193
Camfield v. United States, 225
Caminetti v. United States, 56, 100
Campbell v. Hussey, 339, 345, 348
Cannon v. University of Chicago, 191
Carleson v. Remillard, 185
Carolene Prod. Co., United States v., 96, 294
Carson v. Roane-Anderson Co., 382, 383
Carter v. Carter Coal Co., 23–25, 34, 112, 339
Case v. Bowles, 386
Central R.R. Co. v. Pennsylvania, 308
Chae Chan Ping v. United States, 206, 211

TABLE OF CASES

Champion v. Ames, 18, 55, 56, 80, 101, 392
Chandler-Dunbar Water Power Co., United States v., 129
Chapman v. Public Utilities Dist., 135
Charleston & Western Carolina Ry. v. Varnville Furniture Co., 336, 337, 341
Chastelton Corp. v. Sinclair, 48
Cherokee Tobacco, The, 211
Chicago Board of Trade v. Olsen, 22, 44
Chirac v. Chirac, 212, 249
Cincinnati Soap Co. v. United States, 144
Cities Service Gas Co. v. Peerless Oil & Gas Co., 278
Civil Rights Cases, 233, 235, 237
Clark v. Allen, 249
Clark Distilling Co. v. Western Maryland Ry. Co., 392
Classic, United States v., 245
Clearfield Trust Co. v. United States, 76, 180, 197, 198, 202
Cloverleaf Butter Co. v. Patterson, 351
Collector v. Day, 384
Colorado v. Toll, 224
Colorado Anti-Discrimination Comm'n v. Continental Air Lines, 289, 340, 341
Commonwealth Edison Co. v. Montana, 309, 311, 316, 317, 324
Compco Corp. v. Day-Brite Lighting, Inc., 344
Consolidated Rail Corp. v. Darrone, 188, 191
Constantine, United States v., 149, 151, 152
Consumer Mail Order Ass'n v. McGrath, 393
Container Corp. of America v. Franchise Tax Board, 318, 322, 332
Cooley v. Board of Wardens, 250, 254, 256, 257, 260, 263, 290, 300, 324, 334, 335, 340, 358, 359
Corn Products Refining Co. v. Eddy, 337
Cornell v. Coyne, 143
Cornell, United States v., 217
Covington & Cincinnati Bridge Co. v. Kentucky, 100
Cunningham v. Neagle, 371
Currin v. Wallace, 64
Curtiss-Wright Export Corp., United States v., 204, 206
Cuyler v. Adams, 398, 400, 402, 403

Dahnke-Walker Milling Co. v. Bondurant, 113
Daniel Ball, The, 104, 112, 131
Darby, United States v., 23, 50, 59, 61, 72, 96, 115, 173, 182, 371–373, 375
Davis, Helvering v., 59, 165, 172, 173, 184

TABLE OF CASES

de Geofroy v. Riggs, 212
Dean Milk Co. v. Madison, 283
Delaware River Joint Toll Bridge Comm'n v. Colburn, 403, 404
Department of Employment v. United States, 376
Detroit v. Murray Corp., 378–380
Detroit, United States v., 378, 379
Dewitt, United States v., 40, 41, 54
Dion, United States v., 211
DiSanto v. Pennsylvania, 262, 263
Dooley v. United States, 143
Doremus, United States v., 56, 64, 156, 159, 392
DOT v. Paralyzed Veterans of America, 165
Duckworth v. Arkansas, 266

Edelman v. Jordan, 193
Edgar v. Mite Corp., 277, 289
Edye v. Robertson (The Head Money Case), 211
EEOC v. Wyoming, 239, 388
Electric Bond & Share Co. v. SEC, 59, 124
Employers Liability Cases, 110, 125
Erie R.R. Co. v. Tompkins, 51, 75
Evans v. Cornman, 227, 228
Ex parte (see name of party)
Exxon Corp. v. Hunt, 350
Exxon Corp. v. Maryland, 286
Exxon Corp. v. Wisconsin Dept. of Revenue, 312–315, 317, 320, 322

Farmers Educational & Co-op Union v. WDAY, 351
Federal Land Bank v. Bismarck Lumber Co., 374, 375
Federal Radio Comm'n v. Nelson Bros. Bond & Mtge. Co., 100
Felsenheld v. United States, 157
FERC v. Mississippi, 388
Fernandez v. Wiener, 142, 143
Fidelity Federal Sav. & Loan Ass'n v. de la Cuesta, 342, 352
First Agricultural National Bank v. State Tax Comm'n, 376, 381
First Iowa Hydro-Electric Coop. v. FPC, 135
Fitzpatrick v. Bitzer, 194
Five Gambling Devices, United States v., 37
Flemming v. Nestor, 47
Florida Lime & Avocado Growers, Inc. v. Paul, 340
Fong Yue Ting v. United States, 206
Fort Leavenworth Railroad Co. v. Lowe, 223, 371
Foster-Fountain Packing Co. v. Haydel, 261, 277

TABLE OF CASES

FPC v. Florida Power & Light Co., 100
Freed, United States v., 157, 158
Freeman v. Hewit, 299, 301
Fry v. United States, 33
Fullilove v. Klutznick, 46

Galveston v. Mexican Petrol. Corp., 118
Garcia v. San Antonio Metro. Transit Auth., 31, 386, 388–390
Geer v. Connecticut, 277
Georgia Pub. Serv. Comm'n, United States v., 382
Gerlach Live Stock Co., United States v., 183
Gibbons v. Ogden, 53, 94–97, 107, 108, 117, 128, 248, 251–253
Gilman v. Philadelphia, 128
Gloucester Ferry Co. v. Pennsylvania, 99
Golden State Transit v. Los Angeles, 344
Goldstein v. California, 263, 342
Graves v. New York ex rel. O'Keefe, 372–375
Great A & P Tea Co. v. Cottrell, 281, 283, 288, 365
Green v. Biddle, 400
Green v. Mansour, 185, 193, 194
Griffin v. Breckenridge, 238, 245
Grimaud, United States v., 225
Grosso v. United States, 155
Grove City College v. Bell, 178, 187
Guaranty Trust Co. v. United States, 213
Gwin, White & Prince, Inc. v. Henneford, 323

Hall v. DeCuir, 260, 290
Hammer v. Dagenhart (Child Labor Case), 18, 57–59, 96, 114, 115
Hampton, Jr. & Co. v. United States, 145
Hans v. Louisiana, 192–196
Hauenstein v. Lynham, 212
Haynes v. United States, 155, 157
Hays v. Pacific Mail Steamship Co., 303–307
Head v. New Mexico Board of Examiners, 340, 341, 351
Head Money Cases, 144
Heart of Atlanta Motel, Inc. v. United States, 35, 44, 65
Heisler v. Thomas Colliery Co., 301
Helvering v. _____ (see opposing party)
Hicklin v. Orbeck, 277
Hill v. Wallace, 44
Hill, United States v., 56, 100

TABLE OF CASES

Hillsborough County v. Automated Medical Laboratories, 343, 349, 352, 354
Hinderlider v. LaPlata River & Cherry Creek Ditch Co., 76, 404, 406
Hines v. Davidowitz, 340, 348
Hipolite Egg Co. v. United States, 56
Hodel v. Indiana, 30
Hodel v. Virginia Surface Mining & Reclam. Ass'n, 30, 34, 387
Hoke v. United States, 56, 100
Holmes v. Jennison, 396
Hood & Sons, H.P. v. DuMond, 276
Hope Natural Gas v. Hall, 301
Hopkirk v. Bell, 212
Houston, E. & W. Tex. Ry. v. United States, 50
Howard v. Comm'rs, 227
Hudson County Water Co. v. McCarter, 277
Hughes v. Alexandria Scrap Corp., 270
Hughes v. Oklahoma, 277, 282, 283
Hulbert v. Twin Falls County, 386
Hunt v. Washington State Apple Advertising Comm'n, 282–285
Huron Portland Cement Co. v. Detroit, 278, 290
Hylton v. United States, 139

Illinois v. Milwaukee, 100
International Shoe Co. v. Washington, 293, 303, 305, 361
Ivanhoe Irrig. Dist. v. McCracken, 177

James v. Dravo Contracting Co., 217, 378, 379
Japan Line, Ltd. v. Los Angeles, 136, 263, 306, 317, 324, 330–332
Johnson v. Maryland, 372
Jones v. Alfred H. Mayer Co., 237, 238
Jones v. Rath Packing Co., 341
Jones v. United States, 206

Kahriger, United States v., 146–148, 150–153, 160, 392
Kassel v. Consolidated Freightways, 48, 285, 289–291, 296
Katzenbach v. McClung, 33, 35, 44, 50, 65, 119
Katzenbach v. Morgan, 236–239, 240–242
Kelley v. Rhoads, 100
Kentucky v. Dennison, 393
Kentucky Whip & Collar Co. v. Illinois Central RR Co., 392
Kern-Limerick, Inc. v. Scurlock, 379
Kidd v. Pearson, 104
King v. Smith, 60, 181, 193

TABLE OF CASES

Kleppe v. New Mexico, 228–232
Knight Co., E.C., United States v., 25, 112
Knowlton v. Moore, 143
Kohl v. United States, 223

Lake Country Estates, Inc. v. Tahoe Regional Planning Agency, 405
Lawrence County v. Lead-Deadwood School District, 354, 356
Leary v. United States, 48
Leisy v. Hardin, 118, 258, 300, 359, 360, 365, 367
Leloup v. Port of Mobile, 258, 301
Lewis v. BT Investment Managers, Inc., 279, 282, 366
License Tax Cases, 144, 161, 253, 256, 262, 272, 304, 367
Linder v. United States, 59, 155, 157
Local 174, Teamsters v. Lucas Flour Co., 79, 344
Lochner v. New York, 259
Logan v. Zimmerman Brush Co, 37
Long v. Rockwood, 378
Louisiana Public Service Comm'n v. FCC, 346
Low v. Austin, 329

McCall v. California, 105
McCarroll v. Dixie Greyhound Lines, Inc., 323
McCray v. United States, 55, 146
McCready v. Virginia, 112
McCulloch v. Maryland, 8, 13, 19–22, 24, 25, 27, 34, 44, 46, 52, 53, 55–57, 59, 61, 68, 106, 111, 124, 146, 157, 198, 234, 369, 370, 375, 376, 383, 389
McDermott v. Wisconsin, 50, 78, 121
McGowan v. Maryland, 244
Mackenzie v. Hare, 206
Maine v. Taylor, 274, 275, 278, 282–284, 366, 367
Maine v. Thiboutot, 195, 196
Marchetti v. United States, 155
Marigold, United States v., 54
Maryland v. Louisiana, 309, 311, 342
Maryland v. Wirtz, 33, 35, 45, 116, 386, 387
Massachusetts v. Mellon, 84, 180
Massachusetts v. United States, 389
Mayo v. United States, 375
Mayor of New York v. Miln, 252–254
Michelin Tire Corp. v. Wages, 118, 329–331
Midatlantic National Bank v. New Jersey Dept. of Environmental Protection, 348

TABLE OF CASES

Milk Control Board v. Eisenberg Farm Products, 265–267
Miller v. Arkansas, 372
Minnesota v. Barber, 283
Minnesota v. Clover Leaf Creamery Co., 283–286, 289
Minor v. United States, 154, 158
Mintz v. Baldwin, 261, 278, 338, 339, 351
Mississippi Tax Comm'n, United States v., 227
Mississippi University for Women v. Hogan, 242
Missouri v. Holland, 208
Missouri Pacific Ry. Co. v. Porter, 337, 341
Mobil Oil Corp. v. Commissioner of Taxes, 299, 308, 309, 313, 314, 317–320, 322, 325
Mondou v. New York, N.H. & Hartford R.R. Co., 106, 111
Monell v. Department of Soc. Services, 195
Montana v. Blackfeet Tribe, 94
Moorman Mfg. Co. v. Bair, 313, 317, 320–322, 324
Morgan v. Virginia, 257, 261, 287, 290–292, 294
Munn v. Illinois, 258
Muskegon, United States v., 379

NAACP v. Wallace, 87–90
Napier v. Atlantic Coast Line RR, 336, 337
National Geographic Society v. California Board of Equalization, 314, 315
National League of Cities v. Usery, 387–389
Nebbia v. New York, 264
New England Power Co. v. New Hampshire, 276, 365, 366
New Hampshire v. Maine, 397, 398
New Mexico, United States v., 377, 380, 381, 389
New Orleans v. United States, 221–223
New York v. Miln, 101
New York v. O'Neill, 394
New York v. United States, 385, 387–389
New York State Dept. of Social Serv. v. Dublino, 185, 341, 348, 351
New York Telephone Co. v. New York Labor Dept., 345
Newport v. Facts Concerts, Inc., 195
Nigro v. United States, 156, 159
NLRB v. Fainblatt, 26
NLRB v. Friedman-Harry Marks Clothing Co., 26
NLRB v. Fruehauf Trailer Co., 26
NLRB v. Jones & Laughlin Steel Corp., 23, 24–26, 34, 50, 110, 111, 264
Norfolk & Western Ry. v. Missouri State Tax Comm'n, 308

TABLE OF CASES

North American Co. v. SEC, 125
Northeast Bancorp v. Board of Gov. of Fed. Reserve System, 293, 365, 367, 393, 398
Northwestern States Portland Cement Co. v. Minnesota, 299, 319, 323, 325

Offshore Logistics v. Tallentire, 350
Ogden v. Saunders, 249
Ohio v. Thomas, 372
Oklahoma v. United States Civil Service Comm'n, 61, 84, 177, 181
Oklahoma ex rel. Phillips v. Guy F. Atkinson Co., 50, 64, 130
Omaechevarria v. Idaho, 224
Oregon v. Corvallis Sand & Gravel Co., 231
Oregon v. Mitchell, 241, 242, 245
Oregon-Washington RR & Navig. Co. v. Washington, 336
Owen v. Independence, 195

Pacific Gas & Electric Co. v. State Energy Resources Comm'n, 346, 349, 354
Pacific Insurance Co. v. Soule, 138, 140, 141
Papasan v. Allain, 193, 194
Parker v. Brown, 266, 278, 351
Passenger Cases, 254
Paul v. United States, 227
Paul v. Virginia, 107, 298
Peck v. Lowe, 143
Penn Dairies v. Milk Control Comm'n, 378
Pennhurst State School & Hosp. v. Halderman, 187, 188, 196, 239
Pennoyer v. Neff, 304
Pennsylvania v. Nelson, 348
Pennsylvania v. New Jersey, 277
Pennsylvania v. West Virginia, 277
Pennsylvania v. Wheeling & Belmont Bridge Co., 401
Pennsylvania RR v. Public Serv. Comm'n, 336, 337
Pensacola Tel. Co. v. Western Union Tel. Co., 99, 105
Perez v. Brownell, 36
Perez v. Campbell, 344
Perez v. United States, 33, 34, 50
Pervear v. Commonwealth, 248
Petty v. Tennessee-Missouri Bridge Comm'n, 404
Philadelphia v. New Jersey, 281, 282
Philadelphia, B. & W.R.R. Co. v. Smith, 105

TABLE OF CASES

Phillips v. Martin Marietta Corp., 36
Phillips Chemical Co. v. Dumas Independent School Dist., 379
Philpott v. Essex Co. Welfare Bd., 185
Pickard v. Pullman Co., 301
Pike v. Bruce Church, Inc., 273, 274, 276, 278, 282
Pink, United States v., 213
Pipe Line Cases, 100
Pittman v. Home Owners' Loan Corp., 372, 375, 382, 383
Polar Ice Cream & Creamery Co. v. Andrews, 276
Pollard v. Hagan, 221–223
Pollock v. Farmers' Loan & Trust Co., 140, 142
Popper, United States v., 56
Port Authority Bondholders Protective Committee v. Port of New York Authority, 404
Postal Telegraph-Cable Co. v. Richmond, 302
Prudential Insurance Co. v. Benjamin, 97, 361, 362, 364, 365, 402
Ptasynski, United States v., 142, 143
Public Util. Comm'n of Calif. v. United States, 382
Public Utilities Dist. v. FPC, 135
Pullman's Palace Car Co. v. Pennsylvania, 304–307, 318, 321

Quarles, United States ex rel. Toth v., 36

Railroad Comm'n of Wisconsin v. Chicago B. & Q. R.R. Co., 112
Railroad Retirement Board v. Alton RR Co., 22, 25
Railway Express Agency, Inc. v. New York, 244
Ramsay Co. v. Associated Billposters, 106
Ray v. Atlantic Richfield Co., 263, 289
Raymond Motor Transportation, Inc. v. Rice, 287, 289, 290
Rearick v. Pennsylvania, 105
Reeves, Inc. v. Stake, 270
Regents v. Carroll, 82, 83, 134, 135
Reid v. Covert, 37
Reily v. Lamar, 217
Rice v. Santa Fe Elevator Corp., 340, 348
Riverside Bayview Homes, Inc., United States v., 133
Rivoli Trucking Corp. v. American Export Lines, Inc., 404
Robbins v. Shelby County, 105, 258, 260, 300, 302
Rogers v. Lodge, 47
Rogers v. United States, 148
Rome v. United States, 49, 234–238
Rosado v. Wyman, 193

TABLE OF CASES

S.R.A. v. Minnesota, 217
San Diego Building Trades Council v. Garmon, 341, 351
San Francisco, United States v., 59, 60, 172
Sanchez, United States v., 150, 392
Savage v. Jones, 336, 337
Scarborough v. United States, 45, 50
Schechter Poultry Corp., A.L.A., v. United States, 22, 111
Schwartz v. Texas, 341
Scripto, Inc. v. Carson, 325
Seaboard Airline Ry. v. Blackwell, 262
Sears, Roebuck & Co. v. Stiffel Co., 344
Shreveport Case, The, 112
Silkwood v. Kerr-McGee Corp., 345, 349
Simpson, United States v., 100
Slaughter-House Cases, 246
Smith, United States v., 154
Sonzinsky v. United States, 150, 157, 392
South Carolina v. Katzenbach, 234, 236, 238
South Carolina v. United States, 385
South Carolina State Highway Dept. v. Barnwell Bros., 263–269, 275, 276, 280, 284, 291, 294
South-Central Timber Devel. Co. v. Wunnicke, 48, 270, 271, 276, 366
South Dakota v. Adams, 177
South-Eastern Underwriters Ass'n, United States v., 107–109, 361
Southern Pacific Co. v. Arizona, 266, 268, 269, 275, 284, 287, 293, 361, 362
Southern Pacific Terminal Co. v. ICC, 112
Southern Ry. v. King, 262
Southern Ry. v. Railroad Comm'n of Indiana, 336
Southern Ry. v. Reid & Beam, 337, 338
Southern Ry. Co. v. United States, 46, 112
Spalding & Bros., A.G. v. Edwards, 143
Spector Motor Service v. O'Connor, 301
Sporhase v. Nebraska ex rel. Douglas, 101, 277, 281, 365
Springer v. United States, 140, 154
Stafford v. Wallace, 22, 35, 44, 112
Standard Oil Co. v. Peck, 308
Standard Pressed Steel Co. v. Washington Dept. of Revenue, 317, 323
State Freight Tax, Case of 299
Steward Machine Co., Chas. C. v. Davis, 84, 143, 144, 171–173, 176

TABLE OF CASES

Sturges v. Crowninshield, 249
Sullivan, United States v., 120–122
Sunshine Anthracite Coal Co. v. Adkins, 148
Surplus Trading Co. v. Cook, 217
Swift & Co. v. United States, 108–110

Texas v. New Mexico, 403
Texas v. White, 8
Textile Workers Union v. Lincoln Mills, 76
Thornton v. United States, 55, 100
Toomer v. Witsell, 276
Tot v. United States, 37
Toth, United States ex rel. v. Quarles, 36
Townsend v. Swank, 85, 193
Trade-Mark Cases, 54
Transcontinental Gas Pipe Line Corp. v. State Oil & Gas Bd., 348
Trop v. Dulles, 36

United Fuel Gas Co. v. Hallanan, 113
United States v. _____ (see opposing party)
United States Dept. of Transp. v. Paralyzed Veterans of America, 178, 186, 188
United States ex rel. v. _____ (see opposing party and relator)
United States Railroad Retirement Bd. v. Fritz, 47
United States Steel Corp. v. Multistate Tax Comm'n, 325, 397, 398
United Transp. Union v. Long Island RR Co., 388
Utah v. United States, 132

Van Brocklin v. Tennessee, 372
Veazie Bank v. Fenno, 145
Ventura County v. Gulf Oil Corp., 231
Virginia, Ex parte, 234, 236
Virginia v. Tennessee, 397, 398, 400

Wabash, St. L. & P.R. Ry. Co. v. Illinois, 258, 259
Ward v. Race Horse, 224
Wardair Canada, Inc. v. Florida Dept. of Rev., 273, 275, 309, 324, 332, 347, 349, 367
Ware v. Hylton, 213
Washington v. Davis, 46, 47

TABLE OF CASES

Washington Dept. of Revenue v. Association of Washington Stevedoring Companies, 309, 316, 317, 321, 322, 324
Weber v. Freed, 56
Weeks v. United States, 56
Welton v. Missouri, 258, 260, 300, 302
West Virginia ex rel. Dyer v. Sims, 405
Western Live Stock v. Bureau of Revenue, 288, 302, 307
Western Union Tel. Co. v. Texas, 99
Wharton v. Wise, 400
White v. Massachusetts Council of Construction Employers, 270, 292, 294, 364
Whitfield v. Ohio, 360
Whitney v. Robertson, 211
Wickard v. Filburn, 28, 33, 50, 185
Wilkerson v. Rahrer, 360, 365
Williamson v. Lee Optical Co., 244
Willson v. Black Bird Creek Marsh Co., 251
Wilson v. Cook, 224
Wilson v. New, 46, 112
Wisconsin Dept. of Industry v. Gould, Inc., 344
Woodruff v. Parham, 302
Woolworth Co., F.W. v. New Mexico Tax. & Rev. Dept., 320, 321

Yarbrough, Ex parte, 245
Young, Ex parte, 192, 193
Youngstown Sheet & Tube Co. v. Sawyer, 51

Zobel v. Williams, 37
Zschernig v. Miller, 249

*

CONSTITUTIONAL FEDERALISM
IN A NUTSHELL
SECOND EDITION

*

CHAPTER ONE

THE WINDS OF DOCTRINE AND FEDERALISM LAW

§ 1.01 What Distinguishes Federalism Law?

Most of the issues discussed in this book—issues concerning the allocation of governing power between the nation and the states—typically receive less attention in law school than those aspects of constitutional law having to do, for example, with equality of treatment, liberty claims and morality constraints, and aspects of criminal procedure. This has been true for about thirty years. It seems now, however, that the Zeitgeist is changing; and if that is true, issues of "organic" constitutional law—federalism and the separation of powers—should receive increasing attention during the coming years.

Disputes over liberty, equality, and rights are heavily value-loaded, and often emotion-charged. The judiciary's willing and even eager involvement with such topics has emphasized moral reasoning and resolve, and without doubt has placed the Supreme Court in the thick of political debate. Perhaps as a consequence of this, a new style of writing about constitutional law has emerged, pretending to superior critical skill but hardly distinguishable from philosophical and political debate.

The discourse among "noninterpretivists" with their various theories, and between them and others whom they disparagingly describe as "interpretivists," often is quite warm and usually is quite arid; but it has rendered untenable almost any claim that contemplated elaborations, refinements, or retrenchments of theory in such constitutionalized fields as privacy, expression, police restraint, and equality can be founded on articulable premises universally or even very widely shared. This in turn has made it difficult to deny that authoritarianism (however benign) is evident when judges attribute to the Constitution controverted value choices never actually pursued to public consensus, and still subject to vigorous debate. (At least this seems evident so long as the judicial structure remains hierarchical on the points involved.)

The subject matter of this book, however, significantly differs. For one thing, the issues treated here are less value-laden. Certainly they are not totally free of value-based disagreement, but by comparison with other constitutional topics they are remote from factional strife. We deal here with aspects of government organization or structure, with parts of "organic constitutional law:" This is the framework of role allocation within which the political struggles take place.

Most of the issues discussed in this book also differ in that, as to them, the text of the Constitution has much more to say. Instead of isolated clauses or phrases vague and general enough that, despite unresolved value conflicts, differing factions each could subscribe, we deal here with organizing principles labored to a substantial degree of agreement at one point in time, and pervading an instrument designed and adopted deliberately to change the structure of government under which the nation had operated before. We deal with abstractions, but abstractions which correlate with one another to comprise a logically integrated conceptual scheme.

We thus deal indubitably in the realm of ideas, but not of ideology. The "noninterpretivist" has less latitude here. There is more logical structure, a generic core of concepts, the possibility of true confusion as distinguished from mere disagreement, and a basis for judging statements not merely undesirable or impolitic, but wrong.

§ 1.02 Why Study Federalism Law?

Of the constitutional law casebooks in general use today, none devotes as much as 20% of its bulk to the gamut of federalism issues. Most devote about 15%, and one of the most widely used only 7%. A newly published Nutshell surveying the whole of Constitutional Law devotes about 10%. (Forty years ago, by contrast, the typical proportion was about 48%, quite apart from space devoted to the separation of powers and elaboration of the judicial role.)

These figures do more than reflect the explosion of judicial and academic interest in enhancing liberty, rights, and equality through constitutional theory: They suggest that federalism issues have suffered relative neglect in the training of a generation (and more) of lawyers.

The consequences might not be apparent to those who have fostered or experienced this neglect; but they are quite profound. One is the persistence of mythology about the New Deal—particularly the legend that dramatically in the late 1930's some ancient doctrinal dragons restraining the national government were slain, the gound rules of federalism changed, and a new script engrossed for the future (which misguided anachronists periodically set out to redact). The realities of the intellectual phenomena are far more complex than that. (See, e.g., §§ 3.02–3.03.)

More important than some exaggeration of the New Deal's significance, however, are several changes in judicial doctrine (and consequently in political structure) that have occurred without policy choice, and even without awareness of viable options, largely because of negligent inattention to the fine points of federalism law analysis. These inadvertent changes have been dysfunctional as often as they have been responsive to "the felt needs of the time." Some remarkable examples are brought forward in the course of this book.

Potentially the most significant consequence of the neglect of federalism law, however, is a weakening of the defenses of liberty. Law as we know it is an artificial construct of mind, adhered to or enforced as an alternate to the rule of force. The organic principles of our particular government do not derive from nature; they are human contrivances by which we hope to forestall the dominance of the willful and strong. But with regard, for example, to the Constitution's conceptual complex combining cross-checks, commingling, and separation of powers (a topic beyond the scope of this book), misunderstanding of principles today is enhancing the concentration of power in the executive branch—as if power had a propensity, when the mental constructs designed to prevent this fail, to poise where it can be most expeditiously invoked. Likewise, now that the real risk of national disintegration is more than a century past, misunderstanding of the concepts of federalism law is increasing the concentration of power in the central government, where it can be utilized more efficiently and with more sweeping effects. Most often, liberty is ill-served by concentrations of power.

Fortunately, nothing in human experience seems so tenacious, resurgent, and powerful as an idea that makes sense. The concepts of American federalism law, contrived to facilitate national coordination and union while preserving sub-national centers of political control and choice, cohere as a sensible whole. There has been some evolution in these concepts as conditions have changed; but it would be inaccurate to visualize the development of federalism law as a linear process. The imagery of a pendulum is no better, for it suggests vacillation between extremes with periodic even though fleeting passes over center. The history of American federalism law has conformed to neither model.

What that history does show is that federalism law has an intellectual center of gravity, from which various of its elements might be impelled by various forces, for various periods, from time to time, but toward which there is a tendency always to return. Thus, for example, we can trace necessary and proper clause doctrine through successive periods of distortion and confusion and always see the same concept eventually emerge. (See especially Chapters Three & Four.) That also is why certain thoughts of Hamilton and Monroe prototype concepts regarding Congress' spending power which the Justices are just beginning to rediscover in the 1980's. (See §§ 8.03 & 8.06.) For the same reason, one can predict the eventual demise (though one ought not say when) of various aberrational propositions incompatible with the mainline of federalism law. (See, e.g., § 9.08.)

At any given time one should expect that various elements of federalism law will be in disarray: Doctrinal purity exists only in theorists' minds. The center of gravity, nonetheless, shows the direction in which opinion most easily can be turned, and those which probably will require more strenuous effort even for temporary success.

CHAPTER TWO

THE STARTING POINT FOR FEDERALISM ANALYSIS: THE DOCTRINE OF ENUMERATED POWERS

§ 2.01 The Concept and Misconceptions of "Enumerated Powers"

The United States originally was composed of states substantially autonomous as to internal affairs. For years before the Constitution it already was established that the Union, not any state, was "sovereign" on the international plane. The Constitution did not change that; but it did reallocate governing authority over internal matters.

The Convention of 1787 resolved that the new national government have authority to act for the general interests of the Union and where the states separately were incompetent or might disrupt the harmony of the whole. When the resolutions were referred to a Committee of Detail to prepare a coherent document, however, that Committee (as a member explained) restated this general principle as "an enumeration of particular instances, in which the application of the principle ought to take place * * *"—an enumeration he thought "safe and unexceptionable" and as "accurate" as could be expected. 2 Works of James Wilson at 76

(McCloskey ed., 1967). The Convention approved the Committee's innovation.

Wilson expressed the general principle in terms of "objects of government," not "powers." "Power," however, means the ability to do something; thus when the "objects" a government is to deal with are enumerated, it is convenient verbal shorthand to speak of an enumeration of "powers." This shorthand form of expression is used even in the Constitution itself.

Various "powers" (in this shorthand sense) are given to each branch of the federal government; and from the start it has been fundamental doctrine that this "government is * * * one of enumerated powers." McCulloch v. Maryland, 4 Wheat. (17 U.S.) 316, 405 (1819).

Sometimes this is called the doctrine of "delegated" powers; but that terminology is misleading. The first premise of traditional American political theory is that sovereignty resides ultimately in "the people," not in the organs of government they create. It was not the state *governments* that delegated authority to the nation. Rather, the "states" *in the sense of political communities* of people, see Texas v. White, 7 Wall. (74 U.S.) 700, 720 (1869), delegated some governing authority to the national government and some to the governments of their respective states. Thus, all are governments of "delegated" powers. The only difference is that the delegation to the federal government is explicit (except with regard to foreign

§ 2.01   *DOCTRINE OF ENUMERATED POWERS*

affairs, see § 9.01), while the "delegations" to state governments generally are figments of theory.

It is no contradiction, by this theory, to say the states have governments of "reserved" powers; that simply means that when "the people" delegated some powers to their common national government they "reserved" others to their respective state governments (and still others, perhaps, to themselves). This political theory is affirmed by the tenth amendment: "The powers not delegated to the United States by this Constitution, nor prohibited by it to the States, are reserved to the States respectively, or to the people."

The tenth amendment really does nothing more. In particular, it is not a "states' rights" provision. If any right is implicated, it is only the right of "the people" to allocate governing power as they will. Attempts to use the tenth amendment to restrict federal power are made from time to time; but in the long run such attempts always and inevitably fail. The reason is that the amendment begs the critical question: It affirms that what is not delegated to the United States is reserved, but says nothing to clarify what has been delegated and what has not been.

For these reasons the starting point for federalism analysis cannot be the tenth amendment or the concept of "reserved" powers. The starting point must be the doctrine of enumerated powers. This doctrine posits that the federal government does not have (in *any* of its branches) any "inherent" or "intrinsic" domestic governing power. Disregarding limitations imposed by the Constitution and exceptions made by their own organic laws, state governments are repositories of "general governmental jurisdiction;" but the federal government has only the "enumerated powers."

Yet one can be confused by this imprecise terminology. As noted previously, referring to various federal "powers" is really a shorthand way of saying that the national government is authorized to deal with what James Wilson called various "objects of government." The term "power" as so used denotes legal competence to take governmental action concerning some subject matter—some "object of government," to use Wilson's phrase. Speaking most precisely it is not governing "power," but rather the subject matter which governing power might concern, that is multifarious.

To be most precise, then, one would not say that the Constitution gives Congress something called "the commerce power," for example; instead one would say that it makes Congress competent to govern concerning the subject matter described as "commerce with foreign Nations, and among the several States, and with the Indian Tribes." The same is true of similar phrases like "the taxing power," "the war power," "the police power," etc.: To be most precise, one would say instead that a government is or is not legally competent to concern itself with the subject matter each of these shorthand terms contemplates.

§ 2.01   *DOCTRINE OF ENUMERATED POWERS*

Communication is encumbered, however, by constantly being so precise; therefore we all use (and will continue to use) the more convenient shorthand expressions. It is essential, however, to recognize that it is shorthand we are using; and it is essential to grasp clearly the concept to which this shorthand imprecisely refers.

To fail in this is to make oneself easy prey to the seductive "dual federalism" error, a corruption of constitutional theory which became dominant soon after the more perceptive Chief Justice Marshall was gone. Taking the shorthand terminology too literally, dual federalism conceives of governmental power itself as sliced into separate segments and parceled between nation and states. State and federal directives concerning the same subject matter then must be conceived as assertions of different "powers". A natural corollary of this pie-slice misconception is that national and state governments each are forbidden to nibble at the other's plate. Such erroneous dual federalism thinking still often recurs in constitutional jurisprudence.

The first step toward correct understanding is to recognize that saying the federal government is one of "enumerated powers" really means that it has legal competence to govern only concerning those subject matters which the Constitution designates for it.

This is only the *first* step toward understanding, however; for "subject matter" may be variously characterized. One might say that a "power" to coin money concerns the matter of stamping metal fragments to serve as media of exchange. But one could as well say that the subject matter concerned is commerce, or finance. A "power" to borrow money might be said to concern the funding of government operations; but if the debt is represented by negotiable paper, it might also concern currency and the "money" supply, the value of capital, and the economy at large. A quarantine of diseased cattle might be said to concern public health, but it might as easily be said to concern agricultural wealth; and insofar as it precludes their shipment across state lines, it could as well be said to concern interstate commerce. Probably *every* action of government could be said with equal accuracy to "concern" several different subject matters at once.

The practical men who framed the Constitution were not unaware of this. James Wilson, in his speech cited earlier, explained: "It is only in mathematical science, that a line can be described with mathematical precision." See also Madison, The Federalist No. 37. The terms of the Constitution do as much as short phrases can do to suggest distinctions among possible governmental concerns; but they do not dictate which of several arguable subject matters any particular government action should be held to "concern." At some point in assessing the constitutionality of any government action a choice must be made as to which possible characterization of the subject matter con-

§ 2.02 *DOCTRINE OF ENUMERATED POWERS* 13

cerned is to be given legal significance. That, essentially, is what Chief Justice Marshall said in McCulloch v. Maryland when, after affirming the doctrine of enumerated powers, he added that "the question respecting the extent of the powers actually granted, is perpetually arising, and will probably continue to arise, so long as our system shall exist." 4 Wheat. (17 U.S.) at 405.

Despite the fair room for argument in its concrete application, however, it is crucial to sound analysis that this doctrine of enumerated powers be understood accurately in the abstract. The confusion which results from failure in this regard will be made very apparent in the Chapters which follow.

§ 2.02 An Aid to Analysis

Sound analysis is facilitated by a simple diagram, see Figure 1. The large circle represents *all possible governmental concerns;* it comprehends, abstractly, all possible "objects of government" (in Wilson's words) or all of the subject matters (however variously described) concerning which a government possibly might act. The smaller circle represents those governmental concerns which the Constitution makes "legitimate" for the federal government.

The term "legitimate" as used in this diagram (and throughout this book) must not be misunderstood. It refers to those concerns which are designated by the enumerating clauses themselves.

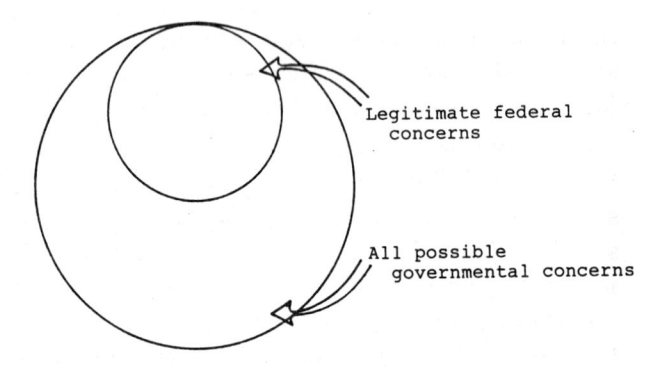

FIGURE 1

Thus, for example, "commerce among the several states" (whatever that is), "taxation" (whatever that is), "post offices" (whatever they are), and "bankruptcy" (whatever that is), are within this circle of "legitimate" federal concerns. But it is *not* necessarily "*il* legitimate," (in the sense of being forbidden) for the federal government to concern itself with matters *outside* this smaller circle. How and why it is perfectly constitutional (and thus "legitimate" in the quite different sense of being permitted) for the federal government to do exactly that, will be explained in Chapters Three and Four.

There are some matters of possible governmental concern with which the Constitution specially forbids the federal government to deal. It also excludes some matters from among the permitted concerns of states. (This is why the larger circle cannot be called that of *state* concerns.) For the sake of simplicity and clarity, however, Figure 1 leaves these complicating factors out of account.

Moreover, while some matters *are* excluded by the Constitution from among the concerns of states, this is *not* true of *all* matters within the small circle of legitimate federal concerns. The limitations on state authority derive from principles other than the doctrine of enumerated powers; therefore this diagram itself carries no necessary implication regarding possible concurrence of state and federal authority, or questions of federal supremacy and preemption. Those questions are dealt with in Chapters Eleven and Twelve.

In sum, the doctrine of enumerated powers means that federal competence extends only to matters which *either* are within the circle of legitimate federal concerns *or* are reached by virtue of one of the concepts to be discussed in Chapters Three and Four. This means that there *are* matters within the general principle first resolved by the Convention, which nonetheless the Constitution as ultimately adopted does *not* authorize the federal government to reach (unless by virtue of one of the concepts next to be discussed). In other words, the fact that a matter cries out for national attention or a nationwide solution does not necessarily mean that the federal government, without constitutional amendment, is legally competent to govern it.

CHAPTER THREE

THE NECESSARY AND PROPER CLAUSE

§ 3.01 The Concept and Misconceptions of the Clause

Ending the list of clauses in Article I, § 8, is one (cl. 18) giving Congress power "To make all laws which shall be necessary and proper for carrying into Execution the foregoing Powers [of Congress], and all other Powers vested by this Constitution in the Government of the United States, or in any Department or Officer thereof." No clause in the Constitution is more important than this, and none more frequently has been misconstrued.

This "necessary and proper" clause originated in the Committee of Detail, in part to enable Congress to legislate details of government organization which the Constitution itself did not fully prescribe. It is the source, for example, of Congress' power to structure the executive branch, and to implement Article III by fixing the size and arrangement of federal courts, defining the routes (if any) of appellate review, and vesting in one or another federal court all the subject matter jurisdiction contemplated by the Constitution. But this clause also does more.

§ 3.01   NECESSARY & PROPER CLAUSE

It first should be noted that Congress' power under this clause is an "enumerated power." The phrase "implied powers," commonly associated with this clause from the beginning, is an unfortunate and confusing misnomer. It is no more enlightening to speak of "ancillary" powers. It is true that, unique among the enumerated powers, this one concerns no particular subject matter but operates instead in conjunction with each of the other power-granting clauses. No single, familiar adjective is adequate, however, to explain precisely how.

Jefferson and other early critics labelled this the "sweeping clause," as if it gave Congress sweeping governmental jurisdiction in derogation of the doctrine of enumerated powers. That construction could have been credible, however, only if the clause had ended with a period after the word "proper."

Hamilton in The Federalist No. 33 gave the archetype of another misconception. Alluding to Congress' other "legislative" powers, he reasoned: "What are the MEANS to execute a LEGISLATIVE power, but LAWS? What is the power of laying and collecting taxes, but a LEGISLATIVE POWER, or a power of MAKING LAWS, to lay and collect taxes? What are the proper means of executing such a power, but NECESSARY and PROPER laws?" Under this misconception, the whole effect of this clause is to enable Congress, for example, to pass revenue *laws* as distinguished from dispatching its members on rounds as tax collectors. Certainly Hamilton was correct that on this view the clause, "though it may be chargeable with tautology or redundancy, is at least perfectly harmless." However, this view also completely ignores the operation of this clause in connection with the powers given to the two other branches. Hamilton himself had abandoned this misconception by the time he wrote his Opinion on the United States Bank; yet it has been reflected occasionally in judicial opinions. See, e.g., Champion v. Ames, 188 U.S. 321 at 355 (1903).

Another misconception of the necessary and proper clause underlay the majority opinion in the Child Labor case, Hammer v. Dagenhart, 247 U.S. 251 (1918), to be discussed more fully in Chapter Four. There the Court misconstrued this clause as a restraint against using enumerated powers to promote ends not themselves within the circle of legitimate federal concerns.

None of these misconceptions is supported by the main line of Supreme Court decisions; but their errors are subtle enough that they still occasionally are reflected in the language of lawyers, and even of courts.

The correct application of the necessary and proper clause is best illustrated by use of the diagram introduced earlier, and elaborated in Figure 2. This clause gives Congress power to deal with matters *outside* the circle of legitimate federal concerns, *insofar* as those "extraneous" matters

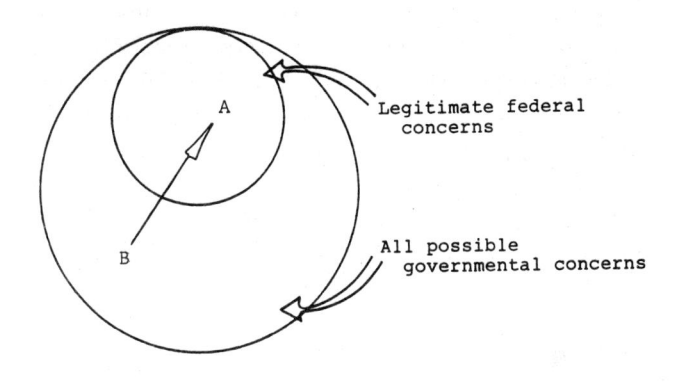

FIGURE 2

are dealt with as a means to effectuate federal policy with respect to some legitimate federal concern—i.e., as a means to effectuate some other enumerated power. For example: Creating corporations and establishing banks are not themselves matters within the circle of legitimate federal concerns. Collecting taxes, borrowing money, regulating interstate commerce, and supporting armed forces, however, certainly are; and incorporating a national bank might help the government deal with these concerns. Thus, as a means to the end of effectuating its policy with respect to these legitimate concerns, Congress by virtue of the necessary and proper clause may incorporate a bank. On this rationale the Bank of the United States was created, and later held valid in McCulloch v. Maryland, 4 Wheat. (17 U.S.) 316, 406–07 (1819).

The crucial requirement for validity under this clause is the telic (means to end) relation represented by the arrow in Figure 2 between an extraneous matter (employed as the means) and some legitimate federal concern (which is Congress' objective, or end). In the words of Chief Justice Marshall: "Let the end be legitimate, let it be within the scope of the constitution, and all means which are appropriate, which are plainly adapted to that end, * * * are constitutional." *McCulloch,* supra, 4 Wheat. (17 U.S.) at 421.

§ 3.02 Erroneous Restraints on the Necessary and Proper Clause Power

Early critics of the necessary and proper clause sought in two ways to restrict the power which it confers. First, they argued for a construction of the word "necessary" that would make it equivalent to "indispensable," so that extraneous matters could not be dealt with if there were other means available to achieve Congress' will for the targeted legitimate federal concern.

Second, they argued against the application of the necessary and proper clause to justify federal actions of the sort illustrated in Figure 3. For example, Jefferson ridiculed an 1800 proposal for federal incorporation of a copper mining company:

> Congress is authorized to defend the nation. Ships are necessary for defence; copper is necessary for ships; mines necessary for copper; a company necessary to work the mines; and who

§ 3.02   *NECESSARY & PROPER CLAUSE*   21

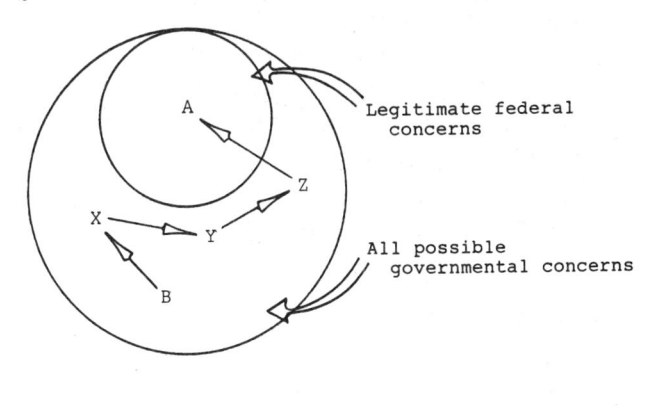

FIGURE 3

can doubt this reasoning who has ever played at 'This is the House that Jack Built'? Under such a process of filiation of necessities the sweeping clause makes clean work.

Quoted in 1 C. Warren, The Supreme Court in United States History 501 (rev. ed. 1926).

Both of these efforts to restrict the power conferred by the necessary and proper clause were rejected early by the Supreme Court. The word "necessary" was construed to include "any means calculated to produce the end, and not as being confined to those single means, without which the end would be entirely unattainable." *McCulloch,* supra, 4 Wheat. (17 U.S.) at 413–14. And the Court upheld incorporation of the second United States Bank on a "filiation of necessities" rationale like that diagrammed in Figure 3.

Thus, wide latitude was allowed to Congress when it acted under the necessary and proper clause. This did not mean that construction of the clause itself was given over to Congress; but the clause as judicially construed gave Congress discretion in choosing among possible means to effectuate federal concerns—even if the means chosen were manipulation of some extraneous matter. If Congress chose such a means (manipulating an extraneous matter), for a court "to inquire into the de[g]ree of its necessity [to achievement of the targeted end], would be to pass the line which circumscribes the judicial department, and to tread on legislative ground." *McCulloch,* supra, 4 Wheat. (17 U.S.) at 423.

This principle received repeated application well into the twentieth century. E.g., Chicago Board of Trade v. Olsen, 262 U.S. 1 (1923); Stafford v. Wallace, 258 U.S. 495, 521 (1922). When they confronted early New Deal legislation, however, some Justices became confused and for a time displaced classic necessary and proper clause doctrine with a more restrictive view. They demanded that the telic (means to end) necessity of a regulation applied to an extraneous matter be proved to the Court's own satisfaction. See, e.g., Railroad Retirement Board v. Alton RR Co., 295 U.S. 330 (1935). And they converted the "necessary and well-established distinction between direct and indirect," A.L.A. Schechter Poultry Corp. v. U.S. 295 U.S. 495, 546 (1935), into the same limitation upon

Congress that Jefferson had tried to impose more than a century before. Insisting that the clause authorized Congress to deal only with those extraneous matters having a "direct effect" upon enumerated federal concerns, the majority in Carter v. Carter Coal Co., 298 U.S. 238, 307–08 (1936) explained:

> The word "direct" implies that the activity or condition invoked or blamed shall operate proximately—not mediately, remotely, or collaterally—to produce the effect. It connotes the absence of an efficient intervening agency or condition. And the extent of the effect bears no logical relation to its character.

Justice Cardozo, dissenting in *Carter,* warned that "a great principle of constitutional law is not susceptible of comprehensive statement in an adjective. The underlying thought is merely this, that 'the law is not indifferent to considerations of degree.'" 298 U.S. at 327.

A few months after *Carter* the Court began to recover the classic view of Congress' power under the necessary and proper clause. Most commentators treat NLRB v. Jones & Laughlin Steel Corp., 301 U.S. 1 (1937), as a sudden about-face by the Supreme Court; this satisfies a thirst for drama, but it does not correspond to fact. (See the discussion of *Jones & Laughlin* in the next section.) The return to sound doctrine was not sudden, and it became manifest only later: See, e.g., that part of the opinion in U.S. v. Darby, 312 U.S. 100 (1941), dealing with the necessary and proper clause (p. 121). It is significant, however, that *Jones & Laughlin* expressed the telic requirement in terms less demanding than *Carter:* Instead of saying there must be no "intervening agency or condition," the Court found sufficient a "close and substantial relation * * *. The question is necessarily one of degree." 301 U.S. at 37. The Court also reaffirmed that whether a particular extraneous regulation promotes an end within the circle of legitimate federal concerns "is primarily for Congress to consider and decide * * *." 301 U.S. at 37.

§ 3.03 Statutes Leaving Telic Determinations to Courts or Agencies

In *McCulloch,* Congress itself had determined that incorporating a bank (an extraneous measure) would facilitate execution of various enumerated powers; and that telic determination by Congress was reviewed with deference by the Court. Sometimes, however, Congress makes no telic determination of its own, instead making a rule to be applied whenever a specified impact on some legitimate federal concern is found. For example, the Sherman Anti-Trust Act prohibited combinations which operated in restraint of interstate commerce, but left it to be ascertained case by case whether particular combinations in *non*-interstate activities (such as manufacturing) might so operate in effect, and thus come under the Act.

§ 3.03 NECESSARY & PROPER CLAUSE 25

In such circumstances, *McCulloch's* rule of latitude for congressional choice is not applicable; for instead of choosing which particular extraneous matters to reach as means to the targeted end, Congress has only specified the determination to be made. Therefore (unless some other body is given the task) the judiciary itself must determine whether the telic relation exists, from the evidence in each particular case. In the early years of the Sherman Act, prosecutors failed to show that a combination in sugar manufacture restrained interstate trade, while five years later a sufficient showing of such effect brought a combination in iron pipe manufacture under the Act. Compare U.S. v. E.C. Knight Co., 156 U.S. 1 (1895), with Addyston Pipe & Steel Co. v. U.S., 175 U.S. 211 (1899). In those cases and in others, the Court sometimes expressed its conclusions in terms of "direct" or "indirect" relation to the targeted legitimate end.

In early New Deal cases like *Alton* and *Carter Coal*, the Justices confounded these two distinct circumstances: Even where Congress *had* made a telic determination the Court wrongly required that the telic relation be shown, *to the judiciary's own satisfaction,* to be "direct." That requirement could have been proper only if (as by the Sherman Act) Congress had left the determination of telic relation to be made judicially, case by case.

This confounding of distinct circumstances still prevailed in *Jones & Laughlin.* Congress on the face of the NLRA had declared that labor relations in *all* of industry must be governed as a means to promote federal policy for interstate commerce (its legitimate concern). If the Court then had been ready to apply the classic necessary and proper clause doctrine, it could have upheld the NLRA as thus written; but it did not. Instead, declaring that the NLRA would be unconstitutional if given the scope which it claimed on its face, the Court ignored the congressional determination and construed the Act as reaching only those covered practices found to be either "in" or "affecting" interstate commerce. In that case (involving labor relations in a strike-prone basic industry), the requisite telic relation was easily found.

As thus misconstrued in *Jones & Laughlin*, the NLRA actually represented yet a third distinct circumstance: Instances in which Congress leaves the telic determination to be made, not by the courts, but by an administrative agency. Today, an agency determination that the application of federal requirements to some extraneous matter will help effectuate some legitimate federal concern ordinarily should be reviewed by a court under the standard of the Administrative Procedure Act: The agency determination should be set aside only if it is "unsupported by substantial evidence." 5 U.S.C. § 706(2)(E). Cf. NLRB v. Fruehauf Trailer Co., 301 U.S. 49, 57 (1937); NLRB v. Friedman-Harry Marks Clothing Co., 301 U.S. 58, 75 (1937); NLRB v. Fainblatt, 306 U.S. 601, 608 (1939).

§ 3.04   *NECESSARY & PROPER CLAUSE*   27

In sum: (1) When Congress has left the telic relation to be ascertained judicially case by case, requiring proof to the courts' satisfaction is appropriate; although earlier the Supreme Court had said a "direct" impact was necessary, today courts are satisfied with evidence of a "close and substantial" relation, being more sensitive to practical consequences and considerations of degree. (2) When Congress has left the telic relation to be ascertained by an administrative agency, the APA's "substantial evidence" test will be applied in judicial review. But (3) when Congress itself has made the telic determination, the role for the judiciary in reviewing that determination is recognized to be the very limited one classically described in *McCulloch,* and elaborated in the sections which follow:

§ 3.04   The "Particularity" Feature of the Necessary and Proper Clause

First in importance to the understanding of this clause is that it authorizes Congress to deal with matters outside the circle of legitimate federal concerns *only insofar* as that dealing is aimed at an end within the circle of legitimate federal concerns. The clause does not contemplate *general* legislative competence over an extraneous matter merely because some laws applied to that matter might conduce to a legitimate federal end; all it supports is those *particular* provisions having such telic effect: "Laws * * * necessary and proper for carrying into Execution" the federal will for legitimate federal concerns.

An example will illustrate this exceedingly important point: The production of grain is *not* a matter within the circle of legitimate federal concerns; but there are ways in which this extraneous matter might be regulated as a means to effectuate federal policy for *interstate trade* in grain—which *is* of legitimate federal concern. Thus, Congress imposed restraints on production of wheat (even for home consumption) as a means to stabilize the interstate wheat market, Wickard v. Filburn, 317 U.S. 111 (1942). But the fact that such production controls are valid on necessary and proper clause grounds carries no implication whatever for controls on grain storage, or crop rotation, or farm worker housing, etc. Every particular federal regulation of the extraneous matter must stand or fall on its own, depending on whether *that particular regulation* has a telic relation to some legitimate federal concern. It never is sufficient that it is a regulation of some matter, *other* regulations of which might promote some legitimate federal end.

Put another way, it is immaterial that *the matter regulated* impacts a legitimate federal concern; what is required is that the *particular regulation* in question be apt to effectuate Congress' policy regarding a legitimate federal concern.

This crucial point is obscured by the language unfortunately employed in very many cases. Especially notable are the scores of cases upholding federal controls on in*tra*state activities "affecting interstate commerce." Precisely stated, any such control is valid only if *that particular control* effects Congress' goal for interstate commerce; but the idiom commonly used suggests wrongly that the controls are valid because the *activities being controlled* affect interstate commerce.

Nothing in the necessary and proper clause—and nothing elsewhere in the Constitution—supports the proposition that Congress has general regulatory power over any extraneous matter because that matter affects interstate commerce. The valid proposition, rather, is that Congress may impose any *regulation* which promotes its goals for interstate commerce (or any other legitimate federal concern) regardless whether the matter to which that regulation applies is extraneous to the circle of legitimate federal concerns. Even though the extraneous *matter regulated* affects interstate commerce, any particular regulation of that matter lacks constitutional support unless *that particular regulation* bears a telic relation to some end within the circle of legitimate federal concerns.

For illustration, let the amoeba-like shape in Figure 4 represent "grain production," an extraneous activity. B1, B2, and B3 each represent particular regulations of that activity. B1 (e.g., production quotas) might be a regulation which Congress validly may impose because of its telic relation to Congress' policy for interstate grain marketing (A in the diagram); but B2 and B3 cannot be made

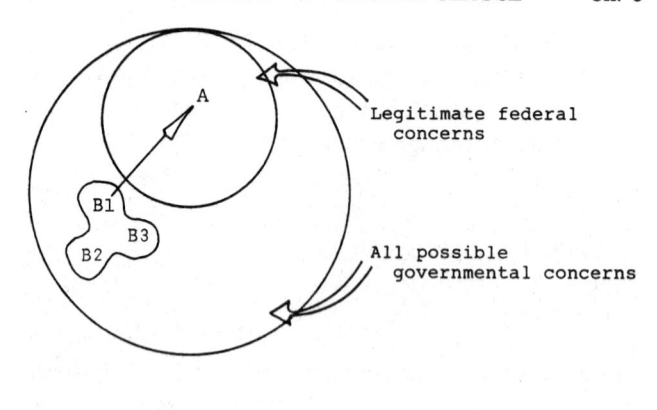

FIGURE 4

valid absent *their own* telic relation, if any, to some legitimate (i.e., enumerated) federal end. It is not sufficient that B2 and B3 are regulations of the same activity that B1 regulates; nor is it sufficient that some other conceivable regulations of that same activity (B4, B5, etc.) might conduce to legitimate federal ends.

Habits of imprecise expression, regrettably, often lead to failures in constitutional analysis. Such failure is illustrated by the rather recent companion cases, Hodel v. Virginia Surface Mining & Recl. Ass'n, 452 U.S. 264, and Hodel v. Indiana, 452 U.S. 314 (1981). There the Surface Mining Control and Reclamation Act of 1977, imposing a multitude of regulations on diverse extraneous aspects of the surface mining industry, was upheld on its face because surface mining "affects interstate commerce" in many ways. Some concurring Justices were deeply troubled by the decision, but none could identify the critical error in analysis. The point they overlooked was that each of the multifarious regulations imposed must stand or fall on its own telic relation: The fact that surface mining affects interstate commerce, or that many of the regulations imposed upon it might effect federal policy for interstate commerce, is not sufficient to sustain any *particular* regulation as to which such a telic relation is lacking. See Engdahl, "Some Observations on State and Federal Control of Natural Resources," 15 Houston L. Rev. 1201, 1214 et seq. (1978), reprinted in 16 Pub. Land & Res. L. Digest 230, 243 et seq. (1979); Engdahl, "The Federal Lands Program Under SMCRA," 26 Proceedings, Rocky Mt. Min. L. Fnd'n Ann. Institute 117, 143 et seq. (1981).

This error persists in large part because, at least since the early 1950's, Congress' power to reach extraneous matters for interstate commerce policy ends frequently has been misconceived as a function of the "commerce clause" itself, rather than of the necessary and proper clause: Hence the common assertion that Congress can regulate activities affecting interstate commerce "under the commerce clause." The fact that this familiar assertion inaptly states what really is the *necessary and proper clause's* function, was noted at last by three of the Justices in Garcia v. San Antonio Metro. Transit Auth., 469 U.S. 528 at 583–585 (1985) (O'Connor, with Powell and Rehnquist, dissenting).

See Engdahl, "Sense and Nonsense About State Immunity," 2 Const. Comm. 93, at 93, 107, 109–10 (1985); Engdahl, "Preemptive Capability of Federal Power," 45 U. Colo. L. Rev. 51, at 59–62 (1973).

As this judicial recognition matures, it may be expected that judicial language on the point will again become more precise, and perhaps that the sharper analysis entailed will alter results in various cases. If this occurs, those who persist in sloppy constitutional thinking might mistake the consequences for a departure from modern "commerce clause" doctrine; but in fact it will be a reaffirmation of classic necessary and proper clause doctrine, earlier affirmed by the enlightened decisions during and after the late New Deal era but since clouded by imprecise expression for some forty years.

§ 3.05 The Class Basis Principle

The "particularity" feature of the necessary and proper clause is not inconsistent with the "class basis" principle. In order to promote an end within the circle of legitimate federal concerns, Congress might apply a particular regulation to a whole class of extraneous activities—the class being defined in such terms or by such characteristics that application of the regulation to the class as a whole appears conducive to the legitimate end. In that event, the fact that imperfections in classification might result in the inclusion within that class of some individuals, application of the regulation to which in fact is *not* conducive to the end, is constitutionally immaterial. So long as the class is defined in such terms that it appears the regulation as applied to that class will conduce to a legitimate federal end, the only material question remaining is whether the individual is a member of the defined class. See *Wickard,* supra; Maryland v. Wirtz, 392 U.S. 183, 193, 197 n.27 (1968). See also Fry v. United States, 421 U.S. 542 (1975); Perez v. United States, 402 U.S. 146 (1971); Katzenbach v. McClung, 379 U.S. 294 (1964). This is fully consistent with the particularity feature of the necessary and proper clause, so long as the telic relation is present as to each particular regulation imposed by Congress on the class.

§ 3.06 Enforceable Limits of the Necessary and Proper Clause: Introduction

It sometimes is said that this clause is a "grant," not a "limitation," of power; and this statement is true, so long as it is not misunderstood. No grant of power in the Constitution is "unlimited" in the sense of comprehending authority to govern everything. Quite apart from limitations separately imposed (for example, by the Bill of Rights), each grant of power is circumscribed by the granting terms: Giving Congress power to establish post offices, for example, hardly made it competent to govern marriage, or inheritance. In this sense the necessary and proper clause, like every other power granting clause, has inherent limitations.

The essential requisite for invoking this clause is the telic relation between the extraneous regulation in question and some legitimate federal end; and there are several ways this requirement is, or can be, enforced.

§ 3.07 The "Substantiality" Requirement

Hamilton in his Opinion on the Bank of the United States said the telic relation should be "natural" or "obvious". Marshall wrote in *McCulloch* that the means must be "plainly adapted," or "really calculated" to accomplish the end. *Carter Coal's* rigorous requirement of "direct" relation, of course, has been repudiated, *Jones & Laughlin* declaring that "close and substantial" is enough. Justice Stewart, dissenting in Perez v. United States, 402 U.S. 146 at 157 (1971), found this "substantiality" requirement unsatisfied; but the other Justices disagreed. Chief Justice Burger and Justice Rehnquist, concurring in the *Hodel* Surface Mining Act cases, emphasized this requirement but found it satisfied.

"Substantiality" is a matter of judgment, not a litmus paper test; yet the requirement that the telic relation be "substantial" remains a basis on which courts might restrain abuse of the latitude for congressional choice of means which this clause affords. Justice Harlan once observed that the Court never has countenanced a "relatively trivial impact" on legitimate federal concerns "as an excuse for broad general regulation" of extraneous matters. Maryland v. Wirtz, 392 U.S. 183, at 197 n.27 (1968).

§ 3.08 The "Rational Basis" Requirement

Where Congress has dealt with a matter on its own determination of telic relation (rather than leaving it to be determined by courts or agencies, see § 3.03), the requirement that latitude be left for congressional judgment entails restraint on the part of reviewing courts. If the judiciary is not to tread on legislative ground, it must be possible for Congress' judgment of telic effect to control the validity of an enactment even if the courts are convinced Congress' judgment was wrong. It is not necessary, however, for the judiciary to defer to congressional judgments that are irrational or defy common sense. Hence the courts *do* require that the congressional judgment at least have a "rational basis." See, e.g., Heart of Atlanta Motel, Inc. v. U.S., 379 U.S. 241, 261–62 (1964); Katzenbach v. McClung, 379 U.S. 294, 303–04 (1964); Stafford v. Wallace, 258 U.S. 495, 521 (1922).

The requirement is not merely that Congress act rationally, or impose a rule that makes sense; it is not equivalent to the prohibition of "arbitrariness" sometimes associated with the fifth amendment's "due process" clause. The requirement, rather, is that Congress' determination that the regulation it imposes on some extraneous matter will conduce to some legitimate federal end be a determination that is rationally based.

On the other hand, the requirement does not mean that empirical data must be mustered to prove that Congress' determination was sound. What is required is not a "factual" basis, but only a "rational" one; sometimes, indeed, Congress' determination might be based on reasonable conjecture.

Consequently, evidence showing the telic relation to be absent in fact, tendered in court but never placed before Congress, ordinarily is immaterial to the issue; for at most such evidence might indicate that Congress could not rationally have made the determination it made had it been better informed. People make judgments rationally under the handicap of ignorance all the time; the remedy for any factual oversights is to make the overlooked facts known to Congress, not to the courts.

Skeptics so long have ridiculed the rational basis requirement as meaningless that lawyers frequently fail to challenge measures on this basis even where such a challenge probably could have prevailed. See, e.g., Phillips v. Martin Marietta Corp., 400 U.S. 542 (1971). But there are cases where a majority has found the requirement unfulfilled. One is U.S. ex rel. Toth v. Quarles, 350 U.S. 11 (1955). Justice Brennan's opinion that the requirement was satisfied in one case but not in the other accounts for the contrasting outcomes in Perez v. Brownell, 356 U.S. 44 (1958), and Trop v. Dulles,

356 U.S. 86 (1958). See also Reid v. Covert, 354 U.S. 1, 46–47 (1957) (Frankfurter, concurring).

Cases in which federal statutes have been given an artificially narrow construction to avoid ruling on a dubious telic relation claimed to support their literal application give further insight into the meaning of "rational basis." See, e.g., U.S. v. Five Gambling Devices, 346 U.S. 441, 447–49, 452 (1953); Tot v. U.S., 319 U.S. 463, 467–68, 472 (1943). Furthermore, a "rational basis" test is used in constitutional contexts other than the necessary and proper clause; and decisions in such contexts are enlightening by analogy here. See, e.g., Zobel v. Williams, 457 U.S. 55 (1982). As Justice Blackmun observed in a different context, what is required is "something more than the exercise of a strained imagination * * *." Logan v. Zimmerman Brush Co., 455 U.S. 422, 442 (1982) (concurring opinion).

One may conclude from a study of the holdings on "rational basis" issues that the congressional determination of telic relation must be consistent with the expectations of probability gleaned from common experience, and must not defy common sense. Unlike where Congress has left the determination to be made by courts or agencies case by case (see § 3.03), nothing approaching a "preponderance of the evidence" or a "substantial evidence" test can be applied; Congress is entitled to more deference than that. Its determination must be respected even if made without factual inquiry, on the basis of preconceptions which are not patently absurd. But if Congress' determination is irreconcilable with the data considered by Congress itself, it seems that a court could rightly pronounce that determination irrational. It also would seem that, whether or not Congress had considered factual data, a court could find that Congress' determination of telic relation lacks a rational basis if it is contrary to facts or phenomena so fully and widely understood as properly to be within the scope of judicial notice: A judgment in defiance of human experience must derive from other than rational grounds. (To respect the latitude for congressional judgment contemplated by this clause, however, the narrowest of horizons for judicial notice ought to be observed.)

The "class basis" principle (see § 3.05) is entirely consistent with this rational basis requirement. If Congress has determined that some particular regulation imposed upon a class of activities will conduce to a legitimate federal end, that determination is not necessarily irrational merely because the practical difficulties of class description result in some imprecision or overinclusiveness, embracing some particulars whose regulation in that manner will contribute nothing toward the targeted end. Since in any event Congress' judgment can be quite rational without necessarily being correct, a rational telic determination as to a class can hardly be impeached by showing it incorrect as to particular members of the class.

However, if the class is so poorly tailored that it contains a large number or a preponderance of members as to whose regulation in that manner no sufficient telic effect can be shown, a court properly might conclude that the bounds of rationality have been overreached: The more serious the defects in classification, the less rational it might seem to assert that the challenged regulation applied to that class will promote the targeted legitimate end.

§ 3.09 Congressional Determination of Telic Relation

One important factor implicit in the "rational basis" requirement deserves separate emphasis. "Rational basis" is the standard only for determinations of telic relation *which Congress itself makes;* when Congress instead prescribes a rule aimed at effecting a legitimate federal end but leaves it for courts or an administrative agency to determine whether application of that rule to one or another extraneous matter will contribute to that effect, the applicable standards are higher; see § 3.03. The reason for the lower standard is to leave Congress latitude to judge for itself (if it chooses to do so) whether governing a designated extraneous matter in a particular way will promote Congress' desired end. Therefore, unless Congress *does* make a telic judgment any discussion of "rational basis" is inappropos; it can make no difference whether bases are present for determinations which Congress has made.

In other words, the precondition for applying the rational basis test in reviewing a measure under the necessary and proper clause, is that Congress have targeted some legitimate objective and fashioned the particular measure with that end in view. Unless such a congressional judgment has been made, there is nothing to which the rational basis standard can be applied by way of review.

In this respect, Congress' power under the necessary and proper clause is almost unique among the enumerated powers. Generally, when governing power is exercised the purpose motivating the particular measure is constitutionally immaterial (unless that purpose runs afoul of some individual rights guarantee, beyond the scope of this book). Telic purpose, however, is the indispensable condition of Congress' power under this clause.

An example will help make the point. In 1867 Congress prohibited the sale of dangerously flammable illuminating oil. From all that appeared, the Act grew out of concern for consumer safety; but neither consumer safety nor local merchandising is within any enumerated power. The Act was declared beyond Congress' power in U.S. v. Dewitt, 9 Wall. (76 U.S.) 41 (1870). The result could have been different, however, had it appeared that Congress considered such oil a hazard to other cargo, and prohibited its sale to discourage its distribution so as to diminish the threat to Congress' goal of safe interstate commerce. The crucial question under the necessary and proper clause then would have been whether it was rational to conclude that prohibiting sales would tend to make interstate shipping safer; and the chain of reasoning just outlined certainly seems rational enough. (Of course it could not matter that other measures might have been equally or more effective toward that end; for Congress may choose the means it prefers.) There was no occasion to discuss this in *DeWitt,* however; for there was no indication that Congress had anything more than consumer safety in mind.

It is fair to ask: If regardless of purpose the sale prohibition would (or might) have the effect of making interstate cargo shipments safer, why should it matter whether Congress had that goal in mind? A sufficient answer is that consumer protection is not among Congress' enumerated powers, so that a regulation of local merchandising (also an extraneous matter) for no end other than consumer protection would be inconsistent with the doctrine of enumerated powers; but a more satisfactory explanation can be given.

An important function of constitutional doctrine is to make the political process do its work. It erects conceptual hurdles—deliberately artificial obstacles—to impede precipitous majoritarian action by multiplying (and isolating from transient issues) the points on which majority agreement must be reached. If we maintain that Congress has no consumer protection power per se, yet acknowledge that it may do what it will with interstate commerce, the *essential* questions remitted to the political processes of investigation, debate, collective judgment, bargaining of interests, and compromise become, not how to benefit consumers, but rather what policy for interstate commerce should be preferred, how it might be advanced, and at what price (in economic and in other terms) it should be pursued.

If sales of illuminating oil, for example, then are banned for reasons having nothing to do with any consequences for interstate commerce, the impediments to precipitous action have been circumvented: It is much easier to reach agreement that consumers should be protected from exploding lamps than to carry a majority on each step of the argument that interstate cargoes should be kept safe, that some illuminating oil (however packaged) endangers them, that such oil will not be shipped if it can find no market, and that sales of such oil therefore should be banned as the method of choice for protecting other interstate cargoes from harm. It is no consolation for the circumvention of this important function of constitutional doctrine that some good result (not itself one for which federal action was authorized or needed) might have been achieved.

Because it similarly countenances circumvention of steps in the political mechanics of legislating, it is no less intrusive into Congress' domain for judges to speculate as to what legitimate end Congress might have had in view, or how some enacted

§ 3.10   *NECESSARY & PROPER CLAUSE*   43

regulation of an extraneous activity might help to achieve that imagined objective, than for judges to override a manifest finding by Congress which they find unpersuasive. To do *either* arrogates to the judiciary a function which classic necessary and proper clause doctrine reserves to Congress.

Imaginative persons, cynical of federalism law, can hypothesize chains of telic connections tying virtually any regulation of extraneous matters to some postulated legitimate federal objective; but such entertaining fantasies are not the stuff of which sound necessary and proper clause arguments are made. The issue is not, "can we imagine that this regulation might promote some objective within the circle of legitimate federal concerns," but rather, "did Congress determine that it does?"

§ 3.10   The Difficulty of Ascertaining Purpose

Certainly any inquiry into "legislative purpose" presents problems. Occasionally Congress articulates a telic finding in a preamble or on the face of an act; but more often it does not, and there certainly is no requirement that it do so. Often Congress' determination is apparent from the text of significant committee reports or other legislative materials, or from the bulk of hearing testimony or other information known to have been considered by Congress and presumed to have had some influence. Thus, in several leading cases turning on the necessary and proper clause, the Supreme

Court has mustered legislative history to show that the telic finding reviewed on the rational basis standard actually was made by Congress. E.g., Heart of Atlanta Motel, Inc. v. United States, 379 U.S. 241, 246, 252–53, 265–66 (1964); Katzenbach v. McClung, 379 U.S. 294, 299–301 (1964); Chicago Board of Trade v. Olsen, 262 U.S. 1, 11–5, 37–8 (1923) (especially significant in light of Hill v. Wallace, 259 U.S. 44, 68–9 (1922)); Stafford v. Wallace, 258 U.S. 495, 499–502 (1922); *McCulloch,* 4 Wheat. (17 U.S.) at 402, 423–24 (1819).

Complicating the problem of ascertaining whether Congress has made a material telic finding is the fact that occasionally such a finding is articulated on the face of an act when in fact Congress has made no real gesture at determination at all. An example is Title VII of the 1968 Omnibus Crime Control and Safe Streets Act, which (inter alia) prohibits possession of firearms by convicted felons on the express premise that such possession constitutes "a burden on [interstate] commerce or a threat affecting the free flow of commerce." This Title was a last minute Senate floor amendment to the overall bill. There was no hearing, no committee report, and very little floor discussion concerning the amendment. Several Senators suggested "further thought" and "study;" but unexpectedly there was a call for a vote, and Title VII passed without modification. In the House, Title VII received no committee consideration or study, and only casual mention in debate; but it passed with

§ 3.10   NECESSARY & PROPER CLAUSE

the rest of the comprehensive bill. Is it fair to say that Congress indeed made the telic finding stated on the face of Title VII? Was there anything to which the "rational basis" test could be applied?

In U.S. v. Bass, 404 U.S. 336 (1971), the Supreme Court was so troubled by the dubious character of this purported "finding" that it gave Title VII a narrow construction to avoid the constitutional question. Inexplicably, however, just a few years later (and with no discussion whatever on the material point) the Court construed it more broadly and upheld a conviction (on particularly attenuated facts) as if the constitutional question which had seemed so troublesome in *Bass* were not even colorably a question at all; it was as though a merely hocus pocus incantation of purported effect upon interstate commerce were enough. Scarborough v. U.S., 431 U.S. 563 (1977).

Once Congress has made quite clear its telic rationale for some particular measure regarding an extraneous activity, comparable findings in support of amendatory provisions added later might simply be presumed. See, e.g., Maryland v. Wirtz, 392 U.S. 183, 190 n. 13 (1968). Moreover, Congress is not restricted to the knowledge it might gain in a particular legislative inquiry: "After Congress has legislated repeatedly in an area of national concern, its Members gain experience that may reduce the need for fresh hearings or prolonged debate when Congress again considers action in that area." Powell, J., concurring in Fullilove v.

Klutznick, 448 U.S. 448, 502–03 (1980). There might even be instances when the requisite telic relation is so obvious and commonly recognized as to seem appropriate for judicial notice. See, e.g., Wilson v. New, 243 U.S. 332 (1917); Southern Ry. Co. v. U.S., 222 U.S. 20 (1911). But cf. § 3.08, supra.

The difficulties typically inherent in ascertaining legislative "purpose," however, cannot diminish the importance of this inquiry under the necessary and proper clause. It cannot be sufficient for litigants or judges merely to speculate about what ends Congress *might* have had in view, or how an extraneous measure in question might *conceivably* conduce to such ends. If the classic approach illustrated by *McCulloch* is to be followed, there must be some sufficient indication that Congress *did* have a legitimate objective, *perceived* the telic connection, and acted upon that ground.

There are constitutional issues *other than* those under the necessary and proper clause as to which telic relations are dispositive. One pertains to Congress' taxing power, and is discussed in § 7.05. More illuminating, however, are issues arising under the fourteenth amendment—issues which for the most part are beyond the scope of this book. For example, state action which results in racially disparate treatment is held not to violate the equal protection clause unless discriminatory "purpose" is found. See, e.g., Washington v. Davis, 426 U.S. 229 (1976). The problems of "purpose" inquiries in

§ 3.10 NECESSARY & PROPER CLAUSE

that context have been explored elaborately and critically in scholarly literature. See, e.g., Colloquium on "Legislative Motivation," 15 San Diego L. Rev. 925–1183 (1978); many other excellent articles readily can be found. Yet the judiciary continues to judge "purpose" in equal protection cases, as it must. See, e.g., *Washington,* supra; Arlington Hts. v. Metropolitan Housing Development Corp., 429 U.S. 252 (1977); Rogers v. Lodge, 458 U.S. 613 (1982).

"Purpose" inquiries also are important in many freedom of expression cases, as well as in some "substantive due process" cases. Such inquiries sometimes are facilitated by judicially devised presumptions, or special allocations of burdens of proof; but the Court is not always so indulgent. For example, for *due process* purposes it has been said to be "constitutionally irrelevant whether [a judicially posited line of] reasoning in fact underlay the legislative decision * * *," Flemming v. Nestor, 363 U.S. 603, 612 (1960); but when that proposition was recited in a recent "equal protection" case, Justice Brennan pointed out that "we are not powerless to probe beneath claims by Government attorneys concerning the means and ends of Congress. Otherwise, we would defer not to the considered judgment of Congress, but to the arguments of litigators." U.S. Railroad Retirement Bd. v. Fritz, 449 U.S. 166, 197–98 (1980) (dissent, joined by Marshall).

Here, where the very foundation of federal power is a telic relation which Congress is responsible to find, it seems that the fundamentality of enumerated powers doctrine should counsel particular caution. The necessary and proper clause, like the commerce clause, "is, after all, a grant of authority to Congress, not to the courts." Rehnquist, joined by Burger and Stewart, dissenting in Kassel v. Consolidated Frtwys. Corp., 450 U.S. 662, 690 (1981). And, to borrow an apt comment from a different context, "[a] rule requiring a clear expression * * * by Congress ensures that there is, in fact, * * * a collective decision * * *." South-Central Timber Devel. Co. v. Wunnicke, 467 U.S. 82, 92 (1984).

§ 3.11 Change of Circumstances

Henry Clay urged Congress to charter the second United States Bank in 1817 although he had opposed the first Bank on constitutional grounds in 1811; he explained that circumstances had so changed by the latter date that a bank had become necessary and proper to effectuate federal powers. Conversely, circumstances might so change as to make no longer rational a finding of telic relation made at an earlier time. Cf. Leary v. U.S., 395 U.S. 6, 38 n. 68 (1969); see also Chastelton Corp. v. Sinclair, 264 U.S. 543, 547–48 (1924). There may be few practical applications for this, however; for as to matters given any subsequent attention, Congress' failure to change the law might reflect a rational conclusion that a sufficient telic relation still is present despite the change in circumstances. Cf. Brotherhood of Firemen & Enginemen v. Chicago, R.I. & P. Ry., 393 U.S. 129, 136 (1968) (rational relation requisite of due process); Rome v. U.S., 446 U.S. 156, 180–82 (1980) (enforcement of 15th amendment).

§ 3.12 The Dangers of Imprecise Expression

It is common for judges to speak elliptically, describing a law applied to extraneous matters but serving an end legitimate by virtue of some particular clause as sustainable under that clause itself, rather than under the necessary and proper clause. This convenient habit of imprecise expression has three unhappy consequences: First, it obscures the crucial "particularity" feature, explained in § 3.04. Second, it encourages segregation of these cases as "commerce" cases, "taxing" cases, "postal" cases, "war" cases, etc., impeding recognition that they all illustrate the same, generic necessary and proper clause principle at work in various contexts. Thus the help which each set of cases can provide for analyzing the others is frequently lost. Third, and most unfortunately, it makes it very easy to overlook distinctions that are crucial to correct application of the concept of preemptive capability, examined in Chapter Five.

This habit of imprecise expression, therefore, should be resisted. It is noteworthy that, notwithstanding its frequent imprecision, the Supreme Court often has emphasized the distinction between questions under the necessary and proper clause and those under other clauses whose ends might be served. E.g., *McClung,* 379 U.S. at 301–02; *Wickard,* 317 U.S. at 121; Oklahoma ex rel. Phillips v. Guy F. Atkinson Co., 313 U.S. 508, 526 (1941); *Darby,* 312 U.S. at 118–19, 123–24; *Jones & Laughlin,* 301 U.S. at 36–37; McDermott v. Wisconsin, 228 U.S. 115, 135–37 (1913); Houston, E. & W. Tex. Ry. v. U.S., 234 U.S. 342, 353–55 (1914).

Unfortunately, there are other cases in which terribly imprecise talk of some "tie-in" between local activity and interstate commerce, Perez v. U.S., 402 U.S. 146 (1971), or some "nexus" between the two, *Scarborough,* supra, has been allowed to carry the day. The job of the Justices is to decide cases, not to write systematic treatises on constitutional law; but it seems fair to expect of them much greater care in expression than this.

§ 3.13 Congress Alone Has This Power

The necessary and proper clause is among those conferring power upon *Congress;* no other branch has a similar power. This is critical to the "separation of powers" among the three federal branches. Although adequate treatment of that topic is beyond the scope of this book, it deserves at least this much notice here.

By virtue of this power, for example, Congress *can* prescribe liability standards for interstate carriers if it finds that to be a means to its policy ends for interstate commerce. Even though this refutes

§ 3.13 *NECESSARY & PROPER CLAUSE* 51

an element of the reasoning articulated in Erie R.R. Co. v. Tompkins, 304 U.S. 64 (1938), however, that opinion's conclusion and its stark reaffirmation of the doctrine of enumerated powers remain sound: *Congress* may do so (contrary to the Erie Court's assumption) because the enumeration of *its* powers includes the necessary and proper clause; but federal *courts* by themselves are not free to do so, because *they* have no "necessary and proper" power.

Similarly, in domestic matters the executive cannot act as it wills, without statutory authorization, even to protect or promote national policy or interests. The reason is more straightforward than those separately tendered by the several majority Justices in Youngstown Sheet & Tube Co. v. Sawyer, 343 U.S. 579 (1952): Only the Congress, and not the President, is entrusted by the Constitution with the latitude of discretion contemplated by the necessary and proper clause. (As to foreign affairs, however, where the doctrine of enumerated powers is inapplicable—see § 9.01—the room for executive initiative without statutory direction may be greater.)

CHAPTER FOUR

ENUMERATED POWERS AND EXTRANEOUS ENDS

§ 4.01 The Mischievous *McCulloch* Dictum

After articulating in *McCulloch v. Maryland* the classic principle of the necessary and proper clause, Chief Justice Marshall added in dictum that Congress could *not,* "under the pretext of executing its powers, pass laws for the accomplishment of objects not intrusted to the government." 4 Wheat. (17 U.S.) at 423. What this 1819 "pretext" dictum deemed forbidden is illustrated in Figure 5. As in the earlier diagrams, the arrow here represents a telic (means to end) relation; but

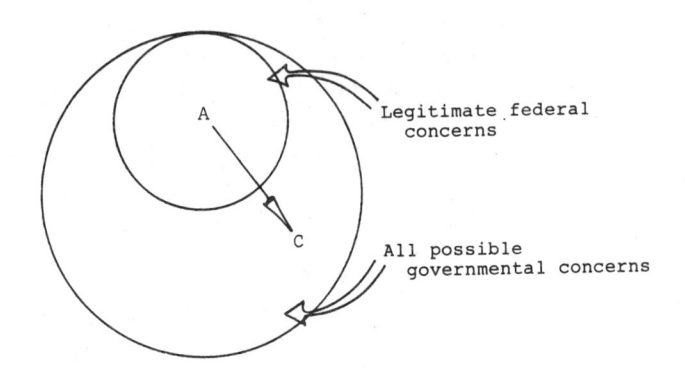

FIGURE 5

here the telic relation runs *from* the circle of legitimate federal concerns *to* an extraneous matter. This represents laws applied to matters within the scope of some enumerated power, but having as their object the accomplishment of some extraneous end.

Had Marshall given this *McCulloch* dictum the critical thought he ordinarily gave to points actually material to decision, he might have noted its error himself: It is incompatible with the point he emphasized five years later, that each power vested in Congress is "plenary" in the sense that it "acknowledges no limitations, other than are prescribed in the constitution." Gibbons v. Ogden, 9 Wheat. (22 U.S.) 1, 196 (1824). The Constitution places no limit whatever on the ends Congress may use its enumerated powers as means to attain. The unfounded *McCulloch* dictum anticipated the pie-slice error of "dual federalism" thought; and for generations it confounded constitutional jurisprudence.

§ 4.02 Progress Through Confusion: Emergence of the So-Called "Federal Police Power" (a Misnomer)

The error of Marshall's *McCulloch* dictum was not clearly recognized until 1941. Before that, for a century and a half the principle which it denies was repeatedly applied in practice, but generally was repudiated in theory. This contradiction, resulting in puzzling inconsistency among decisions, was due to conceptual confusion and resulting faulty analysis.

Toward the end of the nineteenth century, Congress increasingly concerned itself with matters traditionally considered within the "police power" of the states: E.g., matters of public health, safety, and morals. Because such matters generally are not within the circle of legitimate federal concerns, straightforward congressional attempts to govern them were held unconstitutional. E.g., U.S. v. Dewitt, 9 Wall. (76 U.S.) 41 (1870) (voiding a federal law prohibiting sales of dangerously flammable illuminating oils); Trade-Mark Cases, 100 U.S. 82 (1879) (voiding a federal law punishing counterfeiting of trademarks and sales of counterfeit trademarked goods).

At the same time, Congress enacted other laws which—while concerned with "police" matters—had as their objectives promotion or protection of matters within the circle of legitimate federal concerns. Some of these were applications of the necessary and proper clause principle examined in Chapter Three: E.g., a law punishing circulation of counterfeit coins, effectuating Congress' power to coin money and regulate the value thereof, see U.S. v. Marigold, 9 How. (50 U.S.) 560 (1850). Others were health or safety controls placed upon matters themselves within the circle of legitimate federal concerns, effectuating federal policy with regard to those matters themselves or other matters likewise of legitimate federal concern. For

§ 4.02 *EXTRANEOUS ENDS* 55

example, federal laws prescribed safety appliances for interstate steam vessels, regulated interstate transport of explosives, and governed the care of animals during the interstate transit—all for the protection of interstate commerce itself.

A different kind of measure, however, which became increasingly common, is illustrated by a provision in the Customs Act of 1842 which forbade importation of obscene materials. Importation is international commerce and thus within the circle of legitimate federal concerns; the objective of this regulation, however, was not any policy for that commerce itself but rather the promotion of conventional morals—a matter extraneous to federal concerns. The obvious inconsistency of this measure with the *McCulloch* dictum was never litigated; and near the end of the century Congress passed more legislation on this model.

The Animal Industry Act of 1884 prohibited interstate shipment of diseased livestock—not to protect interstate commerce, but to help states control disease. See Thornton v. U.S., 271 U.S. 414 (1926). An 1886 statute, amended in 1902, taxed oleomargarine in amounts and under conditions designed to combat consumer deception. See McCray v. U.S., 195 U.S. 27 (1904). An 1895 act prohibited mailing or interstate shipment of lottery tickets, not to protect commodities in transit but to combat the "moral pestilence" of lotteries. See Champion v. Ames, 188 U.S. 321 (1903). An 1897 act prohibited interstate distribution of obscene literature and contraceptives. See U.S. v. Popper, 98 Fed. 423 (N.D.Cal. 1899).

These were followed by others on the same pattern. One imposed severe taxes under conditions designed to deter undesirable transactions in narcotic drugs. Others prohibited interstate shipment of women induced into prostitution; of impure and misbranded foods and drugs; of prize fight films; and of spiritous liquors into states which prohibited their manufacture and sale. All of these were examples of Congress promoting "objects not entrusted to the [federal] government," under the "pretext" of exerting enumerated powers; and that is precisely what had been condemned in the *McCulloch* dictum.

These measures, nonetheless, were all upheld. E.g., *Champion,* supra; Hipolite Egg Co. v. U.S., 220 U.S. 45 (1911); Weeks v. U.S., 245 U.S. 618 (1918); Hoke v. U.S., 227 U.S. 308 (1913); Caminetti v. U.S., 242 U.S. 470 (1917); Weber v. Freed, 239 U.S. 325 (1915); U.S. v. Hill, 248 U.S. 420 (1919); U.S. v. Doremus, 249 U.S. 86, 93–4 (1919). (Certain features of the act upheld in *Doremus,* 249 U.S. at 94–5, turn on a different issue to be considered in connection with Figure 6 in § 4.05.)

What is most striking is the utter confusion of rationale in most of the foregoing cases. Instead of recognizing these measures as inconsistent with the venerated *McCulloch* dictum, the Justices fumbled with language befitting the necessary and proper clause. In *Champion,* for example, the

Court called prohibiting interstate shipment of lottery tickets "a means of executing the power to regulate interstate commerce," 188 U.S. at 345; "a fit or appropriate mode for the regulation of that particular kind of commerce," id. at 355; and a means "appropriate and necessary to protect the country at large against a species of interstate commerce," id. at 358. The necessary and proper clause, however, was actually irrelevant—for the *means* rather than the *end* was within the circle of legitimate federal concerns. Despite their confusion, the Justices were correct in upholding these laws; but they did not understand what they actually were doing, and mistakenly believed themselves faithful to the *McCulloch* dictum.

§ 4.03 The *Dagenhart* Error: Taking the *McCulloch* Dictum Seriously

In a 1918 case (now recognized as one of it's classic errors) the Supreme Court paid more than lip service to the *McCulloch* dictum. Hammer v. Dagenhart, 247 U.S. 251 (1918), held unconstitutional a law prohibiting interstate shipment of goods produced with child labor. This, again, was a use of the power over interstate commerce as a means to an extraneous end—identical in principle to the statutes concerning lottery tickets, prostitutes, and adulterated foods; but the *Dagenhart* majority grasped at meaningless distinctions to contrive an imagined constitutional difference.

Dissenting with three others, Justice Holmes recalled that Marshall himself had described the enumerated powers as conferred "in unqualified terms:" and from this Holmes concluded that Congress could promote its own policy ends on any matter whatever (i.e., *within or without* the circle of legitimate federal concerns) *by means of* any enumerated power. Id. at 281. The lottery, pure food, and similar cases, these dissenters realized, had approved Congress' "using the power to regulate [interstate] commerce as a foothold, but not proceeding because that commerce was the end actually in mind." Id. at 279.

The majority, however, still confusing this principle with the distinct and irrelevant necessary and proper clause, insisted: "The grant of power to Congress over the subject of interstate commerce was to enable it to regulate such commerce, and not to give it authority to control the States in their exercise of the police power * * *." Id. at 273–74.

The two clauses in the statement just quoted from the *Dagenhart* majority deserve separate comment. The first may be historically accurate, but is constitutionally irrelevant: Regardless *why* power over such commerce was given, the fact is that it *was*. The second clause is not a converse of the first, nor does federal "control" necessarily follow from the dissenters' view: Although Congress may use its powers as means to *influence* extraneous matters, those matters remain under state *control*. As will be fully explained in Chapter Five, federal plans for extraneous matters, promoted only by using enumerated powers as tools, can be frustrated without offense to the supremacy clause.

§ 4.04 Demise of the *McCulloch* Dictum and Affirmation of Sound Principle

The *McCulloch* dictum continued to be recited long after *Dagenhart*. See, e.g., Linder v. U.S., 268 U.S. 5, 17 (1925). Most often, however, the actual holdings belied the lip service paid. For example, the plurality in Ashwander v. TVA, 297 U.S. 288 (1936), declared Marshall's dictum an "essential limitation," id. at 326, yet *upheld* the exercise of an enumerated federal power for plainly extraneous ends; only one Justice apparently noticed the inconsistency, and dissented. The dictum was given lip service again in Electric Bond & Share Co. v. SEC, 303 U.S. 419, 442 (1938). Simultaneously, however, more and more uses of federal power toward extraneous ends were being approved: E.g, Helvering v. Davis, 301 U.S. 619 (1937); U.S. v. San Francisco, 310 U.S. 16 (1940); U.S. v. Appalachian Electric Power Co., 311 U.S. 377 (1940).

The error of the *McCulloch* dictum and the *Dagenhart* majority opinion was not clearly perceived and discarded until 1941, in U.S. v. Darby, 312 U.S. 100, 114–17. (A *different* passage in *Darby,* id. at 119 et seq., dealt with the necessary and proper clause, and was discussed in Chapter Three.) Thus, while uses of enumerated powers to promote extraneous objectives had been upheld for generations, accurate perception of the constitutional principle involved (and candid admission of its validity) dates only from 1941.

Exclusions from interstate commerce and impositions of burdensome taxes are the simplest illustrations of this principle at work. Other illustrations include conditioning federal grants, contracts, or permits, or exemptions from federal taxes, upon the recipients' compliance with stipulations which Congress otherwise lacks power to enforce. The requirements thus attached as conditions *need not* bear a telic relation to any matter of legitimate federal concern. *San Francisco,* supra; *Appalachian Power,* supra. They may be—and most commonly are—designed to promote federal policy with regard to matters wholly extraneous to the circle of legitimate federal concerns.

In this way, federal policies for extraneous matters often are very effectively accomplished. Farmers are induced to reduce productive acreage to qualify for financial assistance; states are induced to observe federal rules for welfare assistance and school desegregation guidelines to qualify for grants-in-aid; and contractors agree to specified employment practices or business operations to qualify for government contracts. It is no offense to the Constitution that under the "pretext" (to use Marshall's term) of its enumerated powers Congress thus influences (and often as a *practical* matter controls) matters beyond its "legitimate" concerns and in the states' traditional domain. See King. v. Smith, 392 U.S. 309 (1968);

Oklahoma v. U.S. Civil Service Comm'n, 330 U.S. 127, 143 (1947); *Darby,* 312 U.S. at 112–17.

In other words, the diagram in Figure 5 represents a perfectly valid use of federal power; the *McCulloch* dictum to the contrary is not and never was sound.

Of course this does not mean that Congress may promote ends which are constitutionally *forbidden.* Matters *forbidden* must be distinguished from those merely outside the circle of "legitimate" federal concerns. It should be evident by now why the reader was cautioned in § 2.02 against concluding that it must be "*il* legitimate" for Congress to deal with matters outside the circle of "legitimate" federal concerns; for two separate ways now have been discovered in which Congress quite constitutionally may do so. When we speak of the circle of "legitimate" federal concerns, we use the term "legitimate" in a narrow and specialized sense, just as Chief Justice Marshall did in his classic statement quoted at the end of § 3.01: We use it to mean those concerns which are designated by the enumerating clauses themselves. Matters *outside* the circle of concerns "legitimate" in this sense may nonetheless be impacted by the federal government, either via the necessary and proper clause (as examined in Chapter Three) or as extraneous ends promoted by the exercise of enumerated powers (as discussed in this Chapter). In either event, the impact on the extraneous matter could be called legitimate in the *broader* sense of being constitutional, even though the matter thus impacted is not "legitimate" for the federal government in the *narrow, more specialized* sense indicated here.

This book is concerned with conceptual bases of power which give constitutional support to federal actions; any action having no valid conceptual power basis is unconstitutional. Actions which *do have* such a power basis, however, nonetheless are unconstitutional if they violate some constitutional prohibition. Among such prohibitions are those in Art. I, § 9, cls. 3 & 5 against bills of attainder, ex post facto laws, and taxes on exports, as well as several provisions contained in the Bill of Rights. The fact that this book for the most part ignores such prohibitions certainly does not mean that they are unimportant; it simply means that they are beyond the scope of this book.

§ 4.05 Extraneous Ends of Necessary and Proper Clause Measures

The diagram in Figure 5 is not sufficient by itself to illustrate the full significance of the principle that enumerated powers may be used to promote extraneous ends; for while most enumerated powers authorize the federal government to deal with designated matters *within* the circle of legitimate federal concerns, the power conferred by *the necessary and proper clause* authorizes Congress to deal with matters which, considered by themselves, are *extraneous,* see Chapter Three.

§ 4.05 *EXTRANEOUS ENDS* 63

Of course it would be possible to conceive of a matter reached under that clause as pro tanto within the circle of legitimate federal concerns; but to conceive it that way would obscure the essential character of this peculiar power: I.e., that it enables Congress to govern *extraneous* matters as a means to some legitimate federal end. That is why the diagram in Figure 2 in § 3.01 is more useful for illustrating the necessary and proper clause power.

As a consequence, however, the fact that *any* federal power may be used to promote extraneous ends means that legislation on the model of Figure 6 is just as valid—and for just the same reasons— as legislation on the model of Figure 5 in § 4.01. In order to be valid under the necessary and proper clause, any regulation of an extraneous matter (B in Figure 6) *must* bear a telic relation to some

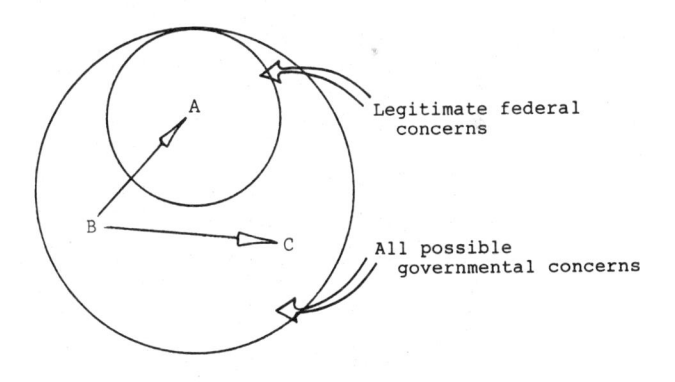

FIGURE 6

end within the circle of legitimate federal concerns; but any given regulation might have more than a single objective, and so long as *one* of them passes muster under the necessary and proper clause the fact that the same regulation also promotes other, extraneous ends, is constitutionally immaterial. It would be inconsistent with the latitude afforded Congress by that clause to prohibit selecting as the means to any legitimate objective a measure which simultaneously serves to promote an extraneous end.

Thus, for example, because the detailed record-keeping requirements of the Harrison Narcotic Drug Act were sustainable as means to enforce the collection of the tax (an end within the circle of legitimate federal concerns), it was constitutionally immaterial that those same requirements served as deterrents to unwanted transactions in drugs. U.S. v. Doremus, 249 U.S. 86, 94–95 (1919). For another example, see Currin v. Wallace, 306 U.S. 1 (1939). It makes no difference even if the extraneous objective is the principal or dominant objective of the federal measure—so long as a legitimate (i.e., enumerated) objective is sufficiently served. Oklahoma ex rel. Phillips v. Guy F. Atkinson Co., 313 U.S. 508, 533–34 (1941).

It therefore is quite unremarkable that the public accommodations provisions of the Civil Rights Act of 1964 were upheld: They were means sustainable under the necessary and proper clause to facilitate interstate travel, an end "legitimate" by virtue of the commerce clause; and therefore it was simply immaterial that those same regulations also were designed (and were *predominately* designed) to promote racial equality in private interpersonal relations—an end extraneous to the circle of enumerated federal concerns. Heart of Atlanta Motel, Inc. v. U.S., 379 U.S. 241 (1964); Katzenbach v. McClung, 379 U.S. 294 (1964).

§ 4.06 Avoiding the "Bootstrap" Error

Since Congress' power under the necessary and proper clause may be used to promote extraneous ends, even a slight lapse of attentive analysis could lead one into what is here called the "bootstrap" error. (There is no magic in this label; and it might even be confusing, because some other authors have used the same term with reference to one or another perfectly valid concept already discussed. The student must look beyond labels and distinguish the concepts referred to. The diagrams employed in this book can be a valuable aid in so doing.)

What is here called the "bootstrap" rationale is illustrated in Figure 7. Our concern is with the validity of a federal measure applied to the matter represented by B in this diagram.

Consider a concrete example: Congress forbids interstate shipment of certain handguns (A in the diagram). This is an exercise of power over a matter within the circle of legitimate federal concerns, a part of interstate commerce (see Chapter

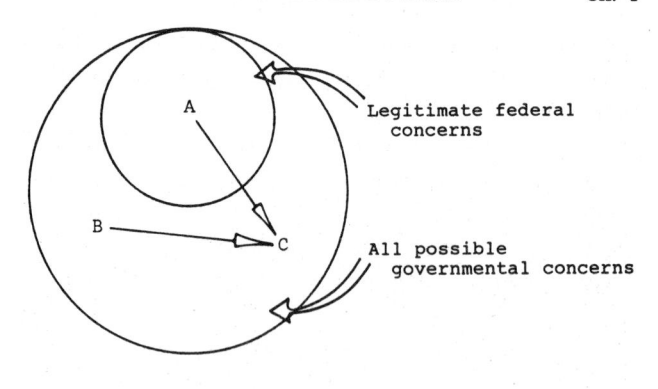

FIGURE 7

Six). Congress does this as a means toward deterring local handgun crimes (C in the diagram). Such crimes are a matter extraneous to legitimate federal concerns; but of course it is permissible for Congress to use its commerce power to this extraneous end, by virtue of the principle elucidated in this Chapter. Prohibiting interstate shipment of handguns, however, is not fully effective by itself to accomplish that extraneous objective; it would further promote that end for Congress to prohibit local sale of those weapons, or their manufacture. (Those activities are represented by B in the diagram).

Consider another example: Congress imposes a very high tax (A) on certain local transaction in various drugs. This is an exercise of its nearly unlimited taxing power (see Chapter Seven). Congress designs this tax for the extraneous end (C) of

§ 4.06 *EXTRANEOUS ENDS* 67

discouraging persons from engaging in such transactions, and this is permissible by virtue of the principle discussed in this Chapter. It would further promote that extraneous objective, however, for Congress to prescribe criminal penalities for engaging in those transactions, or even to punish actual or constructive possession of the drugs (since such possession is necessary for any transactions to occur). Again, the activity thus prohibited (e.g., drug possession) is represented by B in Figure 7.

However, there is *no way constitutionally to justify* federal regulation of B on the pattern of this diagram! B is extraneous to the circle of legitimate federal concerns (and is not even an end toward which some exercise of an enumerated power is aimed). Its regulation by Congress thus would require application of the necessary and proper clause; *but that is impossible on the pattern of Figure 7.* That clause only supports regulations targeting objectives *within* the circle of legitimate federal concerns, and here the targeted objective is *extraneous.*

Put more abstractly, the necessary and proper clause cannot justify federal regulation of an extraneous matter solely as a means to effectuate an *extraneous* end, even though that same extraneous end is promoted in part by regulation of some matter within the circle of legitimate federal concerns. To sustain the federal regulation of B on the pattern of Figure 7 would be to countenance Congress' "lifting itself by its own bootstraps" into a position of general legislative competence regarding an extraneous matter (C), merely by impacting that matter to some extent by means of its control over something within the circle of legitimate federal concerns.

Yet hundreds of cases have been decided by various courts on reasoning which reduces to nothing more than is represented by Figure 7. The reasons why this error, so flagrant, is so frequently made, has to do with the seductive capacity of words to obscure analysis of concepts.

Since before *McCulloch* the necessary and proper clause has been regarded as applicable whenever the end is "legitimate;" and the principle elucidated in this Chapter recognizes that it is "legitimate" to use enumerated powers toward extraneous ends or—what seems the same thing—that an extraneous end (such as C in Figure 7) is "legitimate" for Congress to promote with whatever power it has. The root of the "bootstrap" error is the equivocation evident here in the meaning of the word "legitimate."

Recall the discussion earlier in § 2.02: It is "legitimate" for Congress to promote extraneous ends with its enumerated powers *only in the broad sense* of being constitutionally unforbidden; but the necessary and proper clause applies only where the end is "legitimate" *in the narrower, specialized sense* of being within the circle of legitimate federal concerns. See § 3.01.

§ 4.06   *EXTRANEOUS ENDS*   69

Figure 7 should be compared with the very different diagram in Figure 8. B in Figure 8, unlike in Figure 7, has a telic link to an end which is "legitimate" *in the narrower, specialized sense* required to invoke the necessary and proper clause. That link is indispensable to the validity of Congress' regulation of B. To return to the handgun example: Congress may prohibit manufacture or local sale of the handguns involved as a means to effectuate its prohibition of their interstate shipment (A); curtailing either the supply or the market, or both, surely will help to promote that policy for interstate commerce, which is within the circle of legitimate federal concerns. That the prohibition of interstate shipment is itself targeted at reducing local handgun crimes (an extraneous end) of course is constitutionally immaterial.

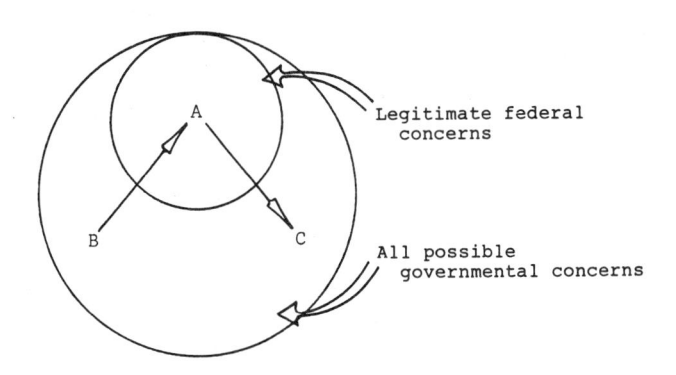

FIGURE 8

70   *ENUMERATED POWERS*   Ch. 4

But the process of sound constitutional reasoning does not stop with Figure 8; for as earlier illustrated with Figure 6 in § 4.05, Congress' necessary and proper power (no less than any of its others) may be used to promote extraneous ends. Consider, therefore, the diagram in Figure 9: While prohibiting the manufacture or sale of the handguns in question will help to effectuate the ban on their interstate shipment, the same prohibition manifestly will promote the extraneous end of deterring handgun crimes. In every respect *material to the validity of the federal regulation of B,* Figure 9 (like Figure 8 and also like Figure 6) is indistinguishable from Figure 2 in Chapter Three—and wholly *unlike* the diagram in Figure 7. The one respect in which Figure 9 resembles Figure 7—the telic relation of B to the extraneous end, C—is immaterial to the validity of the federal regulation

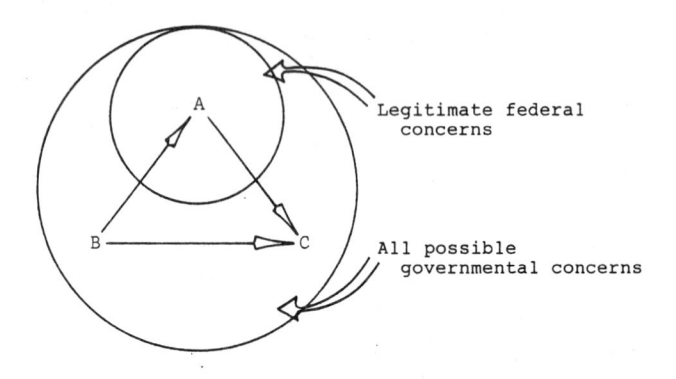

FIGURE 9

of B; it merely illustrates that Congress is not forbidden to employ its powers as means to extraneous ends.

A variation on the theme of Figure 9 is illustrated in Figure 10. The only difference here is that the extraneous end toward which one enumerated power is being employed is further promoted by a regulation of some other extraneous matter, that particular regulation of which is justified under the necessary and proper clause by its telic relation to a matter (E) within the scope of a *different* enumerated power.

So to repeat: The indispensable condition of power under the necessary and proper clause is a sufficient telic relation to some end *within* the circle of federal concerns "legitimate" in the narrower, specialized sense: and it is immaterial

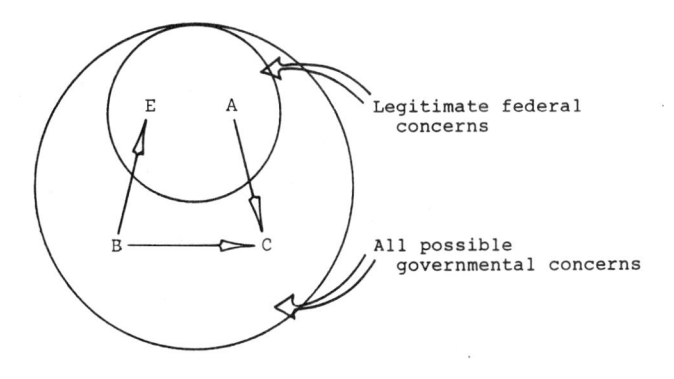

FIGURE 10

whether any *other* end is also served. That is why a federal regulation of B on the pattern of Figure 9 (or 10) would be constitutional, while a regulation of B merely on the pattern of Figure 7 would be void. This would hold true even though the substantive terms of the regulation imposed on B in each instance were identical! For what matters is only the presence or absence of a telic link to some matter of legitimate federal concern, sufficient to satisfy all the requisites of the necessary and proper clause (see Chapter Three).

As a practical matter, all of this has very important implications for the federal legislative process: It means that whether the matter to be regulated is or is not itself within the circle of legitimate federal concerns can make a crucial difference in political strategy, in shaping the course of legislative inquiry (frequently including hearings), and of course in statutory drafting. For what determines a federal measure's political or social desirability and what determines its constitutionality often are totally different; and as the handgun example should show, universal approbation of a sales ban as a means to deter crime cannot take the place of Congress' constitutionally requisite determination that the ban serves some policy goal it has chosen for a matter within its legitimate domain.

Successful utilization of the rationale represented in Figure 9 is illustrated by Congress' imposition of wage and hour standards on intrastate industries, as justified by that paragraph of U.S. v.

Darby, 312 U.S. 100 (1941), beginning on page 121. Having adopted as its policy for interstate commerce the exclusion from interstate shipment of all goods produced under less satisfactory conditions, Congress applied its wage and hour standards directly so that there would less likely be such goods to be shipped; and its *policy against their interstate shipment* was thus more effectively promoted. *That* was the requisite necessary and proper clause link. The fact that the policy for interstate shipments was itself aimed at an extraneous objective (better conditions for workers), and the fact that the wage and hour standards as directly applied obviously also promoted that same extraneous end, both were constitutionally immaterial.

For an illustration of the rationale represented by Figure 10, see the discussion in § 8.03 of how Alexander Hamilton probably would have analyzed the Cumberland Road Bill vetoed by President Monroe in 1822.

CHAPTER FIVE

PREEMPTIVE CAPABILITY

§ 5.01 The Concept of Preemptive Capability

The supremacy clause, Art. VI, cl. 2, declares the Constitution, such federal laws as are "made in Pursuance thereof," and treaties "made under the authority of the United States," to be "the supreme Law of the Land * * *." The clause goes on specifically to say that state judges "shall be bound thereby, any Thing in the Constitution or Laws of any State to the Contrary notwithstanding." The reason that *state* judges are singled out by the latter phrase is simply that the supremacy clause was adopted by the Convention from Paterson's "New Jersey" plan, which had provided for no federal courts; obviously the supremacy declared by the earlier phrase is enough by itself to require federal judges, as well, to disregard contrary state law.

Among the three categories to which it refers—federal Constitution, federal laws, and treaties—the supremacy clause on its face establishes no hierarchy of authority. The relationships of treaties to federal laws and the Constitution are complex, and will be explored briefly in Chapter Nine. As between the Constitution and other federal laws, the priority in authority of the former is a postulate of American constitutionalism which needed no textual affirmation.

"[T]he Laws of the United States which shall be made in Pursuance" of the Constitution, is a phrase which deserves some comment. Although the Confederation Congress had adopted a few measures which would prove to have enduring significance (e.g., the Northwest Ordinance), this clause did not give *them* supremacy status; the notion of a central lawmaker with power to bind the nation and its existing states in significant areas of domestic affairs was new with the Constitution. Moreover, when the Constitution was drafted and ratified it was far from clear whether the common law as adapted from England (which all of the original *states* had taken as the foundation of their respective systems of jurisprudence) was to be considered as the law of the *nation*. Into the early nineteenth century it would be debated, for example, whether the common law of crimes should be applied to federal defendants (and to the misfortune of some miscreants, in several cases it was). Since in pre-positivist theory the common law traced to immemorial custom and was "discovered" by judges, not "made," had they heeded the terms of this phrase in the supremacy clause the Justices might never have developed the habit of displacing state law with a "federal general common law" in diversity cases, which at last was broken in Erie R.R. Co. v. Tompkins, 304 U.S. 64 (1938). (The peculiar species of law described today as "federal common law," see, e.g., Hinderlider v. La Plata R. & C.C. Ditch Co., 304 U.S. 92 (1938); Clearfield Trust Co. v. U.S., 318 U.S. 363 (1943); Textile Workers Union v. Lincoln Mills, 353 U.S. 448 (1957), date from long after it came universally to be recognized that judges "make" law.)

"Laws * * * which shall be made * * *," therefore, most fundamentally meant legislation enacted by the new national Congress. But the additional phrase, "in Pursuance [of the Constitution]," was not idle. It had a meaning, perhaps only nascent at the time, which has come to have considerable significance even though it often has been overlooked. That will be examined especially in § 5.05.

By virtue of the supremacy clause, every federal law "made in Pursuance" of the Constitution has the capacity to supersede, or preempt, state law. At periods in the past it was maintained that preemption was automatic whenever Congress acted. The dominance and demise of that view is examined in Chapter Twelve; today it is recognized to be untrue, and what it takes to accomplish preemption in circumstances where that is possible is also examined in Chapter Twelve. In this Chapter we focus on the preliminary question whether, or when, or to what extent, Congress constitutionally has *legal competence* to supersede state law— what is here called "preemptive capability".

§ 5.02 Preemptive Capability and Matters Within the Circle of Legitimate Federal Concerns

Every exercise by Congress of a legislative power, *insofar as as it deals with a matter within the circle of legitimate federal concerns,* enjoys the capability of preempting state law dealing with the same matter. Each element of this statement is important: It says nothing about any power of Congress which properly should not be characterized as "legislative" in nature; see, e.g., § 9.07. It says nothing about federal measures insofar as they deal with what this book refers to as "extraneous" matters; as to that, see §§ 5.03, 5.04, and 5.05. It says nothing about state laws dealing with "matters" other than those dealt with by the federal law; as to that, see § 5.04. And notice particularly the limiting phrase, "insofar as."

This statement does not mark the outer bounds of preemptive capability; but it is essential to sound understanding that the boundary be explored in stages.

§ 5.03 Preemptive Capability and the Necessary and Proper Clause

In addition, every exercise by Congress of *its power under the necessary and proper clause,* to effectuate any of its *other legislative* powers (or any power of the executive or judicial branch), enjoys the capability of preempting state law conflicting with that exercise. This means that preemptive capability can extend beyond the circle of legitimate federal concerns; but it justifies that reach only where the necessary and proper clause applies. Moreover, it says nothing about the use of the necessary and proper clause in conjunction with any power of Congress which properly should not be characterized as "legislative" in nature; again, see § 9.07.

§ 5.04 Preemptive Capability as to "Matters" Not Touched by Congress

At the outer limit, preemptive capability exists even *as to particular matters not addressed by Congress, but state regulation of which might interfere with enforcement or effective implementation* of the rule established by Congress either for some matter within the circle of legitimate federal concerns, or by virtue of the necessary and proper clause. (Again, an exception must be reserved as to any power of Congress not "legislative" in character, see § 9.07.) This is abstract enough that some illustrations are in order.

For example, even if there were no federal requirement regarding labels to appear on products while held for resale, state labelling regulations could be preempted insofar as they encumbered *enforcement* of a federal law requiring certain labelling to appear on those products at the time they were in interstate commerce. (Checking items on retail shelves could be a convenient means of checking compliance with the interstate labelling requirement, but would be useless if the labelling had been changed in the interim.) See McDermott

v. Wisconsin, 228 U.S. 115 (1913). Similarly, even though Congress made no rule requiring that state courts deciding damage claims of employers against unions apply the same principles in construing labor contracts that federal courts would apply, separate principles of construction could be preempted because disuniformity or uncertainty in construction would interfere with Congress' design of stable and predictable labor-management relations as a means to prevent disruption of interstate commerce. See Local 174, Teamsters v. Lucas Flour Co., 369 U.S. 95, 103–04 (1962).

This outer fringe of preemptive capability is conceptually akin to (although different from) the principle of federal immunity discussed in §§ 14.02–14.05. The student, however, should not expect this kinship to become apparent until the second or third reading of this book.

§ 5.05 *No* Preemptive Capability With Respect to Extraneous Ends

Congress *lacks* preemptive capability, however, *as to its policies regarding extraneous matters, promoted only by the exercise of some enumerated power as a means.* This statement has reference to such situations as are contemplated by Figure 5 in § 4.01. A in that diagram is a matter within the circle of legitimate federal concerns, and whatever rule Congress makes for A therefore has preemptive capability; but its policy for C, an extraneous matter, which Congress seeks to effectuate by exercising its power over A, has no preemptive capability at all. (Likewise as to C in Figures 6, 8, 9 and 10 in §§ 4.05 & 4.06.) Constitutionally there is nothing to prevent a state, if it chooses, from interfering with or completely frustrating Congress' wishes for C.

Take a simple example: Congress even today might wish to rid the nation of the "moral pestilence" of lotteries, and to that end ban the interstate shipment of lottery tickets; cf. Champion v. Ames, 188 U.S. 321 (1903). Certainly no state could countermand that prohibition of interstate shipment; but any state nonetheless could carry on its own lotteries, or permit private ones, using locally printed tickets, to the helpless dismay of the upright in Congress.

In other words, the matter legitimately regulated as a means (A in Figure 5) and the extraneous end (C in Figure 5) must be distinguished for purposes of preemptive capability in much the same way that the Supreme Court distinguished between the "giving" aspect and the "receiving" aspect of a testamentary transfer in U.S. v. Burnison, 339 U.S. 87, 91 (1950), where it was held that a state may prohibit testators from willing property to the United States even though it could not preclude the United States from accepting a bequest or devise.

Recall that the supremacy clause gives overriding effect only to "the Laws of the United States which shall be made in Pursuance" of the Constitution. The pursuit by Congress of extraneous ends—while it is permissible as explained in Chapter Four—cannot be regarded as a pursuit of ends contemplated for the federal government by the Constitution; therefore *insofar as* extraneous ends are pursued, such laws are *not* "made in Pursuance" of the Constitution for purposes of the supremacy clause.

Because this limit to preemptive capability is confronted only with respect to extraneous matters which Congress seeks to influence by virtue of the concept examined in Chapter Four, it deserves emphasis that (although it often had operated earlier in practice) that Chapter Four concept was not frankly acknowledged as valid and incorporated into constitutional jurisprudence until *1941*. See § 4.04. Consequently, this limit to preemptive capability was *still indiscernible* when most of the judges and professors of the generation now passing were in school. Indeed, only five years before 1941 the Supreme Court in bold terms had denounced the suggestion of such a limit on preemptive capability as "plainly fallacious." U.S. v. Butler, 297 U.S. 1, 74 (1936). (What is sound and what unsound in the *Butler* opinion will be discussed further in Chapter Eight.) While now it is clear that this denunciation itself was plainly fallacious, see § 8.06, no subsequent case has enunciated the limit to preemptive capability in terms quite so blunt and forceful as the denunciation of it in *Butler*.

It thus is not surprising that the limit to preemptive capability has been widely disregarded in judicial and extrajudicial discussions of federal supremacy questions. There nonetheless are cases which demonstrate its application.

§ 5.06 Cases Illustrating the Lack of Preemptive Capability

The case best illustrating this limit to preemptive capability is mentioned in no constitutional law casebook published today. In Regents v. Carroll, 338 U.S. 586 (1950), the Federal Communications Commission had refused to renew the Regents' broadcasting license on the ground that the Regents' contract with Southern Broadcasting Stations, Inc., jeopardized their financial ability to operate their station in the public interest, but had invited a renewed application on condition that the Regents show no further effect would be given to that contract. Thereupon the Regents disaffirmed the contract, reapplied, and were licensed. Southern thereafter sued for an accounting on the contract, and prevailed against the Regents' defense that because their disaffirmance was in fulfillment of a condition prerequisite to broadcast licensure (a delegated exercise of Congress' commerce power), and was accomplished to FCC's satisfaction, enforcing the contract would frustrate the manifest federal will.

The Supreme Court construed the statute as authorizing FCC to grant or deny licenses on conditions; and for purposes of constitutional *validity,* of course, it was immaterial whether the license conditions were aimed at legitimate federal ends or extraneous ones. See Chapter Four. The crucial constitutional question, therefore, concerned the *effect* of that condition (and the Regents' satisfaction of it) *upon the state law* otherwise determining contract rights; that state law disallowed unilateral disaffirmance.

Reserving broadcast licenses for financially sound applicants of course would promote Congress' policy of efficient use of the limited radio frequency band (a policy for interstate commerce), and thus would be supportable under the necessary and proper clause; but licensing any one particular applicant rather than another, or inducing the fiscal soundness of a *particular* applicant to render it eligible for licensure, probably could not (and at least in the circumstances did not) rest on that clause. The federal will regarding this contract, therefore, was only a policy for an extraneous matter promoted by an exercise of the commerce power; and the Court held that it could not supersede the state law which bound the Regents to their contract. 338 U.S. at 600. (For a more complete discussion of the *Regents* case, see Engdahl, "Preemptive Capability of Federal Power," 45 U.Colo.L.Rev. 51, 70–72 (1973).)

Even more interesting, because of their obvious irreconcilability with the bold denunciation in *Butler,* are numerous cases applying this limit to preemptive capability in the context of Congress' spending power. The spending of federal funds (see Chapter Eight) is of course within the circle of legitimate federal concerns; and since its spending power is plenary, Congress may make its expenditures contingent upon any conditions it might choose, even conditions designed to effect policies for extraneous matters. Again, see Chapter Four. For example, grants for highway construction may be offered to states conditioned upon the states' restricting partisan political activities of their own employees (a matter extraneous to legitimate federal concerns). See Oklahoma v. U.S. Civil Service Comm'n, 330 U.S. 127 (1947). No state can modify the conditions of the federal offer; but neither can Congress compel acceptance of the grant. See id. at 143–44; Chas. C. Steward Machine Co. v. Davis, 301 U.S. 548, 589–90 (1937); Massachusetts v. Mellon, 262 U.S. 447, 482 (1923). Thus the federal policy for the extraneous matter can be frustrated by any state willing to forgo the federal funds.

If the grant were accepted, its conditioning terms certainly would be enforcible; but as more fully discussed in § 8.07, this is simply a function of contract law. One can find many opinions, even at the Supreme Court level, discussing the effectiveness of state statutes or rules inconsistent with accepted grant conditions in terms of "preemption;" but this is plainly mistaken. As Chief Justice Burger wrote, Congress has used the "power of the purse" to force the States to adhere to its wishes to a certain extent; but adherence to the provisions * * * is in no way mandatory upon the States under the Supremacy Clause. Townsend v. Swank, 404 U.S. 282, 292 (1971) (concurring opinion).

The same principle applies when conditioned federal grants are offered, not to states themselves, but to state subdivisions or to private persons. While the states are powerless to eliminate the federally prescribed conditions (even if aimed toward extraneous ends), they certainly may prevent or forbid satisfaction of the requisite conditions. If it comes to a contest between federal policy for some extraneous matter promoted through conditions to a grant, and a state's contrary will for that matter, it is the state's policy and not Congress' which must prevail: The United States and a state subdivision or private person cannot by their agreement supersede state control over a matter extraneous to the circle of legitimate federal concerns.

A Supreme Court majority recently held otherwise, in a radically wrong decision discussed in § 12.07. The only way a different result could be justified is if the necessary and proper clause were involved, in the manner discussed next in § 5.07.

§ 5.07 Circuitous Means to Legitimate Ends

The limit to preemptive capability is confronted only when an extraneous matter is influenced by Congress *solely* by virtue of the principle discussed in Chapter Four. It is entirely possible that a measure which appears on its face to be merely an exercise of an enumerated power as a means to promote some extraneous end might on closer examination prove to be a circuitous means of accomplishing an end within the circle of legitimate federal concerns; and in that event, preemptive capability would be present.

For example, in order to increase the quantity of certain farm products in interstate commerce it might rationally be found appropriate ("necessary and proper") to increase the acreage in production of those crops. Federal tax benefits might then be offered to farmers to induce them to increase their acreage in those crops. On its face this might appear to be an exercise of the taxing power toward the extraneous end of increasing agricultural production; in the full picture, however, a telic relation to Congress' policy for interstate commerce, sufficient to invoke the necessary and proper clause, would emerge.

Abstractly this is illustrated by the diagram in Figure 11. If all that were present were the federal tax incentive program, A, designed to influence production, C, state laws (if there were any) restricting agricultural acreage or acreage in those particular crops would retain binding effect (and that state's farmers would lose out on the tax break), because the federal policy as to C would lack preemptive capability. But if the production policy being advanced by the tax incentive pro-

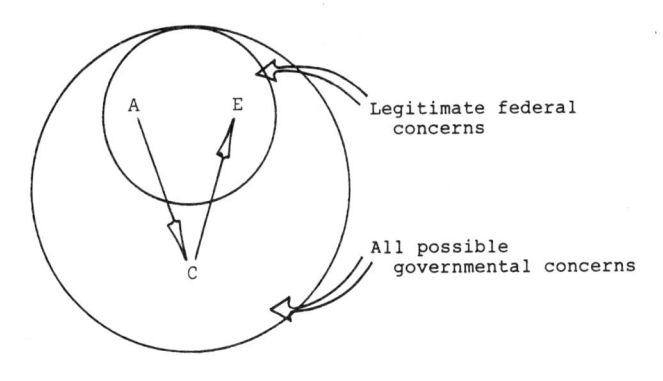

FIGURE 11

gram were in turn a means of effectuating Congress' will for interstate commerce in those products, E, then the federal policy as to production, C, would be supported by the necessary and proper clause, and consequently the federal policy would enjoy preemptive capability as much as to C as to A and E.

Occasionally the courts, conditioned to casual disregard of the limits of preemptive capability, and without sensitized lawyers to guide them, have overlooked this distinction. An excellent example in the context of Congress' spending power is Alabama NAACP v. Wallace, 269 F. Supp. 346 (M.D. Ala.1967). Under Title VI of the Civil Rights Act of 1964 it was required that school boards give assurance of compliance with desegregation guidelines as a condition to receiving federal financial assistance for their schools. Alabama's legislature prohibited that state's school boards from giving such assurance, and promised state financial aid to boards which might lose federal assistance for failure to fulfill this condition. The District Court in a perfunctory per curam opinion declared the Alabama Act invalid under the supremacy clause, and the decision was not appealed. The constitutional issue, however, merited much more serious thought.

The operation of public schools is plainly a matter outside the circle of legitimate federal concerns. Thus if Title VI were nothing more than an effort by Congress to influence public school practices through manipulation of its spending power, the decision in *Wallace* was plainly wrong. If, on the other hand, the decision was correct, it can only be for reasons which appear nowhere on the face of the impatient per curam opinion.

What probably underlay the decision was an awareness that among Congress' enumerated powers is that conferred by section five of the fourteenth amendment to enforce by appropriate legislation the restrictions on state action imposed by that amendment. (See Chapter Ten.) One of those restrictions is the requirement of "equal protection," which has come to be understood as prohibiting racial segregation in public schools. Section five traditionally has been applied in close analogy to the necessary and proper clause: Thus Title VI arguably might be viewed, in terms of Figure 11, as a spending condition (A) affecting school practices

(C) as a means to effectuate state equal protection (E), a matter of legitimate federal concern by virtue of the fourteenth amendment.

The problem with this argument is that while Congress *could* have done so, it *did* not proceed in this way. Indeed, by virtue of its section five enforcement power Congress could have required compliance, and assurance of compliance, with school desegregation guidelines *regardless* whether any federal aid were accepted; and in other Titles of the same statute Congress in fact did do exactly that with regard to various activities *other than* schools. In Title VI, however, all Congress did was to attach the material condition to funds which the schools were legally free to take or leave—and which the state, whose creatures they were, was competent to tell them to take or leave.

In the 1960's, and in the 1980's, perhaps it puts little strain on a tolerant legal mind to impute, as if by judicial notice, a circuitous telic linkage like that illustrated in Figure 11 when curtailment of racial discrimination is involved; but recall the discussion in § 3.09. It seems fair to observe that the decision in *Wallace* was more certainly morally righteous than constitutionally sound.

Imagine a situation similar to that presented in *Wallace,* but involving funds conditioned on certifying compliance with federal guidelines regarding age discrimination. State action discriminating on that basis, unlike on the basis of race, has not yet been held to violate the fourteenth amendment.

Whatever the merits of *Wallace* on its racial facts, therefore, a similar decision regarding assurance of compliance with federally prescribed age discrimination guidelines certainly could not be justified.

§ 5.08 Particularized Analysis for Preemptive Capability

Any particular federal contract, license, grant, etc., may be subject to several different conditions regarding extraneous matters; and the preemptive capability of each of these conditions must be separately assessed. Suppose, for example, that Congress sought to increase the quantity of some commodity in interstate commerce, and to that end sought to increase the quantity of that commodity produced. Congress might offer grants (or loans, or tax breaks) to farmers, one condition of eligibility being that the farmer use a certain experimental hybrid seed expected to increase per-acre yield. Because of the evident telic relation to the interstate commerce policy objective (fitting the pattern of Figure 11), *this* condition would be capable of preempting a state law forbidding the use of seed not approved by the state's department of agriculture. Another condition of eligibility, however, might be that the farmer meet federal standards of sanitation and comfort in on-farm housing for agricultural workers—a matter represented by H in the diagram in Figure 12. Unless *these* standards could be shown to have been rationally found by Congress to bear a sufficient telic relation to increasing the quantity of the commodity in inter-

FIGURE 12

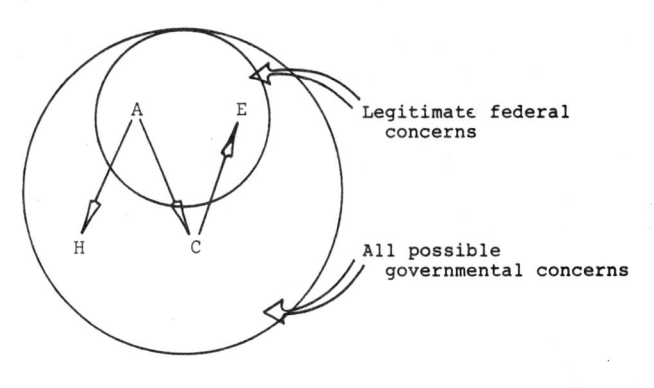

state commerce (or, of course, to some other legitimate federal end), *this* condition would have no preemptive capability. It certainly would be *valid* as a condition to the grant, and a non-complying farmer would be ineligible for the program: but if state law imposed conflicting or more stringent standards for farm worker housing, a participating farmer could not excuse his non-compliance with the state standards by claiming that he had to conform to the federal standards instead, in order to qualify for the grant. The relation of A to H in Figure 12 is the same as the relation of A to C in Figure 5 in § 4.01; and the fact that A also is a means to E (via C) does not give H any telic relation to E at all. H being strictly extraneous, without the telic relation needed to invoke the necessary and proper clause, Congress' will for it can have no preemptive capability.

This has an interesting consequence, which at first might seem surprising. If the federal government were to insist on the strictly extraneous condition (H in the diagram), then for any state to prevent satisfaction of that condition would be to render its farmers ineligible to participate in the productivity enhancement program at all—and to that extent, progress toward Congress' *legitimate* goal, E, would be impaired. This would be true, however, only insofar as (and because) Congress by incorporating the strictly extraneous condition had attempted to shoehorn its way into a position of control over an extraneous matter (H) for its own sake, *control of H* not being a means to any legitimate end. Remember the discussion in § 3.04 of the "particularity" feature of the necessary and proper clause.

CHAPTER SIX

CONGRESS' POWER OVER INTERSTATE COMMERCE

§ 6.01 The Terms of the Commerce Clause

The commerce clause (Art. 1, § 8, cl. 3) gives Congress power "To regulate," "Commerce," "among the several States" (as well as with foreign nations and the Indian tribes. Foreign commerce is discussed briefly at the end of this Chapter; Indian commerce is left out of account.) It is appropriate to reflect upon each of these terms.

Etymologically, and in most frequent usage, "commerce" denotes mercantile interaction. But the word also has secondary and metaphorical meanings, so that it sometimes is used to connote social interaction, the exchange of sentiments and ideas, and even sexual intercourse. The mercantile denotation is clearly the core constitutional meaning. The word was used repeatedly in this sense (and never in any other) by all three authors of The Federalist Papers: E.g., Nos. 5, 6, 7, 11, 12, 17, 22, 23, 42, 44, 60, 64. This power was essential to the central government, Hamilton wrote, "if we mean to be a commercial people", id., Nos. 24, 34. Madison took care to make verbal distinction between "commerce," in this mercantile sense, and other forms of "intercourse among those of different states," id., No. 53. As Chief Justice Marshall wrote in 1824 (curiously using the word to define itself), it means "commercial intercourse * * * in all its branches * * *." Gibbons v. Ogden, 9 Wheat. (22 U.S.) 1, 189–90.

It will be discovered, however, that some cases have attributed to "commerce" a somewhat broader meaning, see § 6.02. (Indeed, in the special context of Amercian Indian tribes—where other constitutional provisions also are involved—the Court sometimes has carelessly equated "commerce" with all "relations" of any kind; see, e.g., Montana v. Blackfeet Tribe, 471 U.S. 759, 764 (1985).) Obviously the scope of Congress' power is affected by the latitude given this word.

One commentator suggested a generation ago that "among the several States" should be understood as if it were written, "among the people of the several states," so that Congress' power would reach all commerce in the entire country. W. Crosskey, 1 Politics And The Constitution, ch. 3 (1953). It takes little imagination to perceive what this would portend if the word "commerce" were given more than its mercantile meaning. Crosskey's thesis never has enjoyed wide acceptance.

The orthodox view has been that Congress' power under this clause is "restricted to that commerce which concerns more States than one." *Gibbons,* supra, at 194. But this explication is not free of difficulty. Marshall distinguished "that commerce which is completely internal, which is

§ 6.01 *INTERSTATE COMMERCE* 95

carried on between man and man in a State, or between different parts of the same State, and which does not extend to or affect other States." Id. at 194. Had he omitted the last phrase, the potential for confusion might have been somewhat less. Without doubt, that "Commerce" which is "among the several States" always consists of acts taking place within the various states—just as the transit involved in *Gibbons* itself involved movement within New York and New Jersey, not merely the momentary crossing of the mathematical line between them, id., at 195–96. But phrases like "concerns more States than one" and "affect other States" are pregnant with greater potential meaning.

The verbal dichotomy employed from a very early date (although these words do not appear in the Constitution) is between "in*ter* state" and "in*tra* state" commerce. Practical affairs often are difficult to characterize in terms of this dichotomy; and they have become more so as business practices and technology have changed. Judicial efforts at characterization frequently have been unsatisfactory, and developing a feel for the distinction necessitates much reading between the lines (not to say rewriting the lines).

Yet whatever the difficulty, the effort at characterization cannot be abandoned in despair, for reasons which should become clearer as this discussion proceeds. The cavalier conclusion of some that "everything is interstate commerce" (e.g.,

Tushnet, "Rethinking the Dormant Commerce Clause," 1979 Wis.L.Rev. 125, 148) is a sophomoric flippancy no more consistent with the cases than with the constitutional language or common sense. Like it or not, the Constitution does contemplate the drawing of lines between that "Commerce" which is, and that which is not, "among the several States;" and even if the lines can be drawn only by judgment (which might differ from case to case), profoundly significant consequences sometimes depend upon where the lines are drawn.

Congress' power is "To regulate" commerce among the several states. Chief Justice Marshall ventured that such commerce "is regulated by prescribing rules for carrying on that intercourse," *Gibbons,* supra, at 190; but that was an inadequate explication. Occasionally it has been argued that the power to "regulate" imports no power to "prohibit" any part of interstate commerce, but only power to fix the terms and conditions under which it may be carried on. E.g., Hammer v. Dagenhart, 247 U.S. 251 (1918). Every prescription of terms and conditions, however, is a prohibition of conduct that does not conform; the distinction between "regulation" and "prohibition" is illusory, and has absolutely no significance under the commerce clause. See, e.g., U.S. v. Carolene Prod. Co., 304 U.S. 144, 147–48 (1938); U.S. v. Darby, 312 U.S. 100, 113–14 (1941). As Marshall himself recognized, Congress' power over whatever it is that constitutes "Commerce * * * among the several

States" is "plenary" in the sense that it "may be exercised to its utmost extent, and acknowledges no limitations, other than are prescribed in the constitution." *Gibbons,* supra, 9 Wheat. (22 U.S.) at 196–97. "Congress may keep the way open, confine it broadly or closely, or close it entirely, subject only to the restrictions placed upon its authority by other constitutional provisions * * *." Prudential Ins. Co. v. Benjamin, 328 U.S. 408, 434 (1946); see also id. at 423.

The power to "regulate" interstate commerce is best understood as authority to establish any policy Congress might choose as the will of the nation for any matter deemed to be "commerce * * * among the several States * * *." Understanding it this way helps make evident the soundness of the principle to be discussed below in § 6.06, as well as the absurdity of the prevalent error to be discussed in § 6.07. Furthermore, with the power understood this way the profound significance of characterizing a particular matter as in*ter* state or in*tra* state commerce can be perceived.

Since the commerce power is "plenary," it is of no constitutional significance why Congress chooses one policy rather than another for interstate commerce itself. If a matter is "in" interstate commerce, the objective at which a regulation of it aims is entirely immaterial to that regulation's validity; the objective may be some goal for interstate commerce itself, or a goal with regard to defense or some other legitimate federal concern, or a policy end regarding public health or morals or another *extraneous* concern. This is merely to recognize in the commerce clause context the generic concept discussed in Chapter Four. (Of course, if the objective *is* to effectuate policy for some *extraneous* concern, Congress' will for that extraneous matter—unlike the policy for interstate commerce which is employed as a means—has no preemptive capability; see Chapter Five.)

On the other hand, if the matter being regulated is *not* "in" interstate commerce the validity of Congress' regulation is entirely contingent upon the finding of a telic relation between that particular regulation, as a means, and the end of effectuating some federal policy with respect to interstate commerce itself (or some matter otherwise within the circle of legitimate federal concerns); see Chapter Three. In the latter circumstance, to declare (as judical opinions often imprecisely do) that the regulation is valid "under the commerce clause" obscures the critical point that it actually is the *necessary and proper clause* at work, and that therefore the requisites for validity under *that* clause must be met.

In other words, both the applicable requisites for validity and the possession of preemptive capability may depend upon whether the matter which Congress undertakes to govern (or the policy which it undertakes to promote) is an activity *in* (or a policy *for*) "interstate commerce" itself.

§ 6.02 Non-Commercial Interstate "Commerce"

Fundamentally, as already noted, the term "commerce" in the Constitution denotes mercantile affairs. During the last quarter of the nineteenth century, however, the Supreme Court's perception of what is included in "commerce" among the states began to expand.

Since mid-century telegraph companies had stretched wires thoughout the land, carrying messages encoded in electrical impulses hither and yon across state lines. Such transmission of intelligence had become indispensable to business (as well as to the operation of government); and denominating telegraphy an "agency of [interstate] commerce" the Supreme Court held the telegraph business to be within Congress' commerce power. Pensacola Tel. Co. v. Western Union Tel. Co., 96 U.S. 1 (1878).

The reasoning employed in *that* case was *not* that the transmitted impulses constituted commerce crossing state lines; but that *was* the effect four years later when the court analogized between telegraph companies as carriers of messages and railroads as carriers of goods, Western Union Tel. Co. v. Texas, 105 U.S. 460 (1882). Telegraphy was done for a financial consideration, but it soon became clear that this was not the controlling factor; for no less than paid carriage of persons and goods by ferry, Gloucester Ferry Co. v. Pennsylvania, 114 U.S. 196 (1885), the Court held (without elaboration or explanation) that persons walking across an interstate bridge constituted interstate commerce, Covington & Cincinnati Bridge Co. v. Kentucky, 154 U.S. 204 (1894).

Within a few years interstate "commerce" was held to include interstate movement not only of prostitutes for commercialized vice, Hoke v. U.S., 227 U.S. 308 (1913), but also of one's own mistress, Caminetti v. U.S., 242 U.S. 470 (1917); not only the driving of live stock from range to market, Kelley v. Rhoads, 188 U.S. 1 (1903), but also the meandering of cattle within a pasture which straddled a state line, Thornton v. U.S., 271 U.S. 414 (1926); the carrying across state lines of liquor for *personal* use, not only on a common carrier, U.S. v. Hill, 248 U.S. 420 (1919), but even in one's private vehicle, U.S. v. Simpson, 252 U.S. 465 (1920); and the movement of one's own petroleum through one's own pipelines across state lines, Pipe Line Cases, 234 U.S. 548 (1914).

After all of this, it should come as no surprise that radio communication, see Federal Radio Comm'n v. Nelson Bros. Bond & Mtge. Co., 289 U.S. 266 (1933), electrical power transmission, see FPC v. Florida Power & Light Co., 404 U.S. 453 (1972), and the interstate movement of pollutants in ambient air, see U.S. v. Bishop Processing Co., 287 F.Supp. 624 (D.Md.1968), and water, see Illinois v. Milwaukee, 406 U.S. 91, 103 (1972), have been considered interstate "commerce."

§ 6.02   *INTERSTATE COMMERCE*   101

For a time while this judicial expansion of "commerce" beyond anything remotely mercantile was taking place, dissenters objected to the reaching of things which were not even "articles of commerce." See, e.g, Champion v. Ames, 188 U.S. 321, 371 (1903) (Fuller, with Brewer, Shiras & Peckham, dissenting). The *Champion* dissenters were hopelessly mired in "dual federalism" thinking; but the view that the "commerce" power reaches only to mercantile matters (and thus chiefly to vendible items or "articles of commerce") is not inextricably bound to that error.

The "articles of commerce" notion is a very old one, dating at least to 1837 when the majority distinguished state regulations regarding entering *passengers* from those regarding entering *cargoes* in part on the ground that "the goods are the subject of commerce, the persons are not * * *. [Persons] * * * are not the subject of commerce; and * * * cannot fall within a train of reasoning founded upon the construction of a power given to Congress to regulate commerce * * *." New York v. Miln, 11 Pet. (36 U.S.) 102, 136–37 (1837); see also id. at 142.

By its absence from the Reports for some three quarters of a century, however, one might have judged the "articles of commerce" notion a relic of history had it not become the main point of discussion and disagreement in a 1982 case, Sporhase v. Nebraska ex rel. Douglas, 458 U.S. 941 (1982). There Justice Rehnquist (with O'Connor), dissenting, argued that ground water in which state law recognized only usufructory rights, so that it could not be reduced to possession, owned, sold, rented, traded, or transferred, could not be considered an "article of commerce," id. at 963. The majority used the same phrase repeatedly, and expressly concluded that the water involved "is an article of commerce." Id. at 954. What (if anything) this curious revival of old terminology portends for the future of commerce power doctrine, it is impossible yet to say.

It seems now, however, that the prospect of again confining the commerce clause entirely to its basic mercantile meaning is rather remote. Therefore it merits particular emphasis that all of the cases treating *non*-mercantile activities as "commerce" at least have involved actual, discernible crossing of state lines. This is important; for in *mercantile* contexts activities which involve no such discernible line-crossing sometimes nonetheless have been held to be "interstate commerce."

§ 6.03 Interstate Commerce Without Discernible Line-Crossing

It is possible to identify three different factors responsible for the hundreds of cases characterizing as "interstate commerce" various mercantile (investment, merchandising, industrial, and other business) activities which by themselves involve no discernible crossing of state lines. Two of these factors emerged at stages of constitutional jurisprudence when the integrated operation of sound generic principles was in one degree or another obscured; and the cases influenced by these factors should be regarded as of dubious significance today. The third is rooted in the basic nature of the Constitution, but always will be difficult to apply.

The first identifiable factor is the premise of "dual federalism" which dominated constitutional jurisprudence during the period when extensive discussion of the boundary between interstate and intrastate commerce began. Litigation turning on this distinction was relatively uncommon until after the Civil War, when state needs for revenue and popular demands for greater public control of increasingly concentrated economic power caused taxation and regulation of business activities to become more extensive than before. Even then, it was *state* impositions on business which were most substantial; significant use by Congress of its powers regarding commerce began only with the Interstate Commerce Act (1887) and the Sherman Anti-Trust Act (1890). The pattern of inquiry into the interstate-intrastate commerce distinction, therefore, was set in cases testing *state* legislation under the supposed "negative implication" of Congress' dormant commerce power.

The "negative implication" doctrine will be examined more fully in Chapter Eleven. According to that doctrine, if in*ter* state commerce were involved state action was at least impaired if not foreclosed—even though Congress had not exercised its power. Underlying this doctrine is the dual federalism thesis that, by virtue of the distribution of governing power under the Constitution, any given matter must be subject to governance only by either the states or the United States, and not by both: Each slice of the pie must be on one plate or the other. Thus, in all of the older cases what drove the effort to distinguish between interstate and intrastate commerce was a conviction that the one characterization ordinarily would foreclose state, while the other always would foreclose federal, regulation.

Often this was made explicit on the face of the opinions—something being declared interstate commerce for the reason that otherwise a matter seeming to warrant national attention would be placed beyond Congress' reach (see, e.g., The Daniel Ball, 10 Wall. (77 U.S.) 557 (1871)), or a state law being upheld with the gratuitous observation that Congress (which had not tried) could not reach the matter (e.g., Kidd v. Pearson, 128 U.S. 1, 20–22 (1888)).

In consequence, many of the cases between Reconstruction and the New Deal which characterize activities as "interstate commerce" as a reason for invalidating state regulation or taxation are less illustrative of meaningful elements of definition for that phrase than of the pervasive laissez faire attitude prevalent among the business-oriented Justices of that time. On the other hand, during the same era many activities as to which federal regulation was deemed warranted were characterized as "interstate commerce" because, on the dual federalist thesis with its imperfect recognition of the force of the necessary and proper clause, that seemed the only way to sustain federal power.

The second identifiable factor accounting for characterization of many seemingly local activities as "interstate commerce" is the notion of "agents," or "agencies," or "instruments," or "instrumentalities," and "incidents" of interstate commerce. Reference already has been made to the 1878 ruling that telegraphy was an "agency of commerce," an indispensable instrument by which interstate business was carried on. *Pensacola Tel. Co.,* supra. In like fashion, a sales agent drumming up orders for an out-of-state seller, Robbins v. Shelby County, 120 U.S. 489 (1887), an agent locally soliciting persons to travel his principal's rail line interstate, McCall v. California, 136 U.S. 104 (1890), and an agent delivering goods ordered from his out-of-state principal, Rearick v. Pennsylvania, 203 U.S. 507 (1906), were held to be agencies of interstate commerce and their activities to be interstate commerce itself. Similarly an employee cooking food for a crew of carpenters then located for weeks at one place but from time to time moved to different places as needed to repair the bridges of an interstate railroad, was held to be engaged in interstate commerce as he cooked, Philadelphia, B. & W. R.R. Co. v. Smith, 250 U.S. 101 (1919): He, they, and the bridges they repaired were said to be "instrumentalities of interstate commerce * * * so closely related to such commerce as to be, in practice and in legal contemplation, a part of it * * *," id. at 103. Likewise it was held that the posting of advertising posters on billboards could not be regarded as a "purely local service" where it was part of a business involving solicitation, preparation, design, and out-of-state manufacture of such posters. Ramsay Co. v. Associated Billposters, 260 U.S. 501 (1923).

Insofar as such cases foreclosed state action, they also rested on the "dual federalism" error; and insofar as they upheld federal action, they could have been based—with far less strain on credibility—on the necessary and proper clause had its operation then been more clearly understood. (On occasion, in fact, an "instrumentality" holding *was* buttressed by reference to the *McCulloch* case; see, e.g., Mondou v. New York, N.H. & Hartford R.R. Co., 223 U.S. 1, 53–4 (1912), applying the second Employers Liability Act.)

To take at face value the old cases explicable by either of the two foregoing factors is unnecessarily to import into modern commerce clause doctrine distortions of reality which the careful analysis of concepts ought to dispel.

The third factor which leads to characterizing as "interstate commerce" some business activities regardless of any discernible crossing of state lines, however, cannot be disposed of so easily. There are business activities, superficially intrastate, which yet may be characterized as interstate commerce because (to use the terminology of the old *Gibbons* case) they "affect other States" or "concern[ ] more States than one."

The business of insurance provides an example. The foundation of this business consists of the issuance, for a consideration, of indemnity contracts and the payment of claims in the event of a covered loss. Execution of the contracts, and payment of premiums and claims, are events which all occur within single states. Moreover, the contracts themselves are not objects of tangible value; they merely represent obligations undertaken by the parties, and "are not articles of commerce in any proper meaning of the word." Paul v. Virginia, 8 Wall. (75 U.S.) 168, 183 (1869). Therefore in *Paul* the Court held that the business of insurance (even though involving insurors and insureds in different states) was *not* interstate commerce.

Seventy-five years later, however, the Court announced the opposite conclusion that insurance *is* interstate commerce: U.S. v. South-Eastern Underwriters Ass'n, 322 U.S. 533 (1944). What was decisive was not whether the contracts were "articles of commerce," or that there were countless movements of agents, instructions, documents, and payments across state boundaries, but rather that the insurance business as conducted by modern insurors (and as reached by the federal statute there in question) plainly constitutes an integrated and interdependent series of activities which "concerns more States than one." Quoting that phrase from *Gibbons,* Justice Black wrote for the majority: "The precise boundary between national and state power over commerce has never yet been, and doubtless never can be, delineated by a single abstract definition." 322 U.S. at 550–51.

§ 6.04 The Importance of Caution in Characterization

The *South-Eastern* holding that the business of insurance is interstate commerce would not have surprised Alexander Hamilton, who had articulated a comparable view of the then fledgling insurance business in 1791 (see 322 U.S. at 539 n. 9). There is reason to exercise considerable caution, however, before characterizing apparently local activities as "in" interstate commerce. The reason should be apparent from the last two paragraphs of § 6.01: The characterization affects *both* the applicable requisites for *validity* of federal measures concerning the matter, *and* the issue of *preemptive capability.*

It is easy to exaggerate the element of truth contained in Justice Holmes' observation that "commerce among the States is not a technical legal conception, but a practical one, drawn from the course of business," Swift & Co. v. U.S., 196 U.S. 375, 398 (1905): Although its meaning is, indeed, to be drawn from the course of practical business dealings, the term as used in the Constitution *is* a "legal conception" which, like other concepts in the coherent whole of organic constitution-

§ 6.04 INTERSTATE COMMERCE 109

al theory, has connections and implications which, if disregarded, can produce unintended results.

Where nothing is in issue but the validity of a federal law or its application in particular circumstances, and the requisites of the necessary and proper clause are satisfied, characterization of the regulated activity as interstate or intrastate can be immaterial to the outcome in a particular case. It might have been material to validity on the facts in *South-Eastern,* because at least a part of the Association's *goal* there was to control premium rates and monopolize policy sales; but it certainly was not material to validity on the facts in *Swift,* where the arrangements involving stockyard operatives were designed and adapted to constrain not merely the local stockyard activities themselves, but interstate meat product commerce. (The Sherman Act reaches not only monopolistic practices *in* interstate commerce, but also—by virtue of the necessary and proper clause—practices, however local, which operate "in restraint of trade or commerce among the several states;" see Addyston Pipe & Steel Co. v. U.S., 175 U.S. 211 (1899).) But inaccurate or unclear characterization in a case where the characterization is not immediately material can wreak havoc as precedent.

That is why the obfuscating "stream of commerce" metaphor coined by Justice Holmes in the *Swift* case is so mischievous. If that were taken to mean that the stockyards were themselves "in" interstate commerce, it would follow from the plenary nature of Congress' power over interstate commerce that Congress could, for example, ban the vending of contraceptive condoms in stockyard latrines, regardless whether its purpose were to prevent disease, or to combat loose morals, or any other; for *why* Congress does what it does with interstate commerce itself is constitutionally immaterial.

Obviously the Court in *Swift* contemplated no such thing; and in 1937 the Court made it clear that "[t]he instances in which that metaphor has been used are but particular * * * illustrations of" the power Congress has *under the necessary and proper clause;* NLRB v. Jones & Laughlin Steel Corp., 301 U.S. 1, 36–37 (1937). In the interim, however, the metaphor had been used in legislation and in court opinions as if it broadened the horizons of the *commerce clause* itself. Unfortunately, the metaphor is so attractive and its author so respected that it still tends to deflect analysis exactly the same way today.

§ 6.05 Putting the Old Cases in Their Place

Most substantial business enterprises involve a host of activities, some of which plainly constitute interstate commerce but others of which very well may not. It was recognized in the first Employers Liability Cases, 207 U.S. 463, 502–03 (1908), that one does not, by engaging in interstate commerce, ipso facto subject all of his intrastate business activities to federal control. That proposition still

§ 6.05 *INTERSTATE COMMERCE* 111

is good law; its only shortcoming is its failure to point out that those intrastate activities might be reachable by Congress in numerous respects *by virtue of the necessary and proper clause,* to effectuate interstate commerce policy goals. Cf. Mondou v. New York, N.H. & Hartford R.R. Co., 223 U.S. 1 (1912), upholding on the reasoning of the *McCulloch* case a liberal application of the more narrowly drawn *second* Employers Liability Act of 1909.

It must be remembered that as late as 1937 the Supreme Court still was hesitant to admit the true scope of Congress' power under the necessary and proper clause, and had not yet fully cut loose from the unsound "dual federalism" premise of mutual exclusivity underlying its earlier efforts to distinguish interstate from intrastate commerce. Even in *Jones & Laughlin* the *majority* deemed it necessary to truncate the NLRA—in defiance of its explicit language—for the articulated reason that to allow it so broad a reach as it claimed necessarily would negate the competence of states; see 301 U.S. at 29–30, endorsing passages cited from A.L.A. Schechter Poultry Corp v. U.S., 295 U.S. 495 (1935). See the discussion in § 3.03. (The *Jones & Laughlin* dissenters were even more explicit in exclaiming that to admit power in Congress necessarily was to exclude the states; see 301 U.S. at 94–5.)

It now is clear, in retrospect, that straining to characterize local activities as parts of interstate commerce really was not necessary to render them subject to many of the federal laws being challenged in the old cases. For example, federal inspection and licensing of vessels using the Grand River in Michigan, see *The Daniel Ball*, supra, and federal prohibition of an interstate carrier's discrimination in allowing use of its local wharves, see Southern Pacific Terminal Co. v. ICC, 219 U.S. 498 (1911), are justifiable under the necessary and proper clause insofar as they effectuate policies chosen by Congress for interstate commerce. By the same token, to acknowledge that manufacturing, see, e.g., U.S. v. E.C. Knight Co., 156 U.S. 1 (1895), or agricultural production, see, e.g., McCready v. Virginia, 94 U.S. 391 (1876), or mineral extraction, see, e.g., Carter v. Carter Coal Co., 298 U.S. 238 (1936), are not themselves interstate commerce, ought never to have been thought to foreclose regulation thereof by Congress within the latitude properly afforded by classic necessary and proper clause doctrine. *That* clause, and not the commerce clause itself, had supported, for example, the statute upheld in Stafford v. Wallace, 258 U.S. 495 (1922) (notwithstanding Congress' distraction by Holmes' "stream of commerce" metaphor), the statute upheld in Wilson v. New, 243 U.S. 332 (1917), and the federal control of intrastate railroad rates and equipment in such cases as Railroad Comm'n of Wisconsin v. Chicago B. & Q. R.R. Co., 257 U.S. 563 (1922); The Shreveport Case, 234 U.S. 342 (1914); and Southern Ry. Co. v. U.S., 222 U.S. 20 (1911).

With the dual federalism error behind us, there is likewise the same reason (whether or not there is any other) no longer to credit old decisions characterizing as "in" interstate commerce that part of the commingled gas in an interstate pipeline which is drawn off before leaving the state of origin, United Fuel Gas Co. v. Hallanan, 257 U.S. 277 (1921), or a local transaction in grain involving its delivery on board railroad cars with the understanding that the purchaser intends to transport it later across a state line, Dahnke-Walker Milling Co. v. Bondurant, 257 U.S. 282 (1921). The same may be said as to railroad maintenance crew cooks, sales drummers, and billboard posters.

If any such activities are to be considered today as "in" interstate commerce, it should not be on the basis of precedents conditioned by the misconceptions of a bygone day, but only on the basis of a deliberate determination—made with full awareness of the consequences for requisites to validity and for preemptive capability—that they are integral parts of a course of business that "concerns more States than one." And it will be discovered that, if one has a firm grasp of the function of the necessary and proper clause, more often than not that difficult determination is one that need not be made.

Unfortunately, however, constitutional litigation often is conducted with shallow understanding of the historical and conceptual setting of old precedents, and with little reckoning with the erroneous premises upon which they rest; and consequently old cases like *Dahnke-Walker* sometimes still rule from their graves. See, e.g., Allenberg Cotton Co. v. Pittman, 419 U.S. 20 (1974).

§ 6.06 Congress and Competition in Interstate Commerce

Understanding the power "To regulate" interstate commerce as meaning that Congress may establish policy regarding any facet of that commerce, it seems clear that Congress may oversee competition in interstate business—and by virtue of the necessary and proper clause, take measures designed to work its will regarding that competition, even if those measures regulate local activities. The federal anti-trust laws are built on this premise.

The premise has not always been fully acknowledged, however. One of the arguments tendered in support of the Child Labor Law in Hammer v. Dagenhart, 247 U.S. 251 (1918), was that lax child labor standards in several states placed manufacturers in more stringently regulating states at a competitive disadvantage in interstate commerce because of consequent higher labor costs, and the federal law would eliminate this factor of overhead differential. The Court's response was to observe (quite correctly) that "[m]any causes may cooperate to give one State, by reason of local laws or conditions, an economic advantage over others," and (quite superfluously) that "[t]he Commerce Clause was not intended to give Congress a general authority to equalize such conditions." 247 U.S. at 273. (What the clause was "intended" for is quite

§ 6.06 *INTERSTATE COMMERCE* 115

irrelevant if in fact the authority it gives is capable of being used to police competition.) The *Dagenhart* Court compounded its error by adding that:

> The grant of power to Congress over the subject of interstate commerce was to enable it to regulate such commerce, and not to give it authority to control the States in their exercise of the police power over local trade and manufacture.

Id. at 273–74. Of course the Child Labor Act did not try to control the States at all; it simply forbade interstate shipment of child-made goods whether child labor was legal in the manufacturer's state or not.

Dagenhart was overruled in U.S. v. Darby, 312 U.S. 100 (1941), on reasoning that included a somewhat muddled discussion of the "competition" rationale. Upholding the exclusion from interstate commerce of goods produced under wage and hour standards less favorable to workers than Congress desired, the Court said that the Fair Labor Standards Act was designed

> to make effective the Congressional conception of public policy that interstate commerce should not be made the instrument of competition in the distribution of goods produced under substandard labor conditions, which competition is injurious to the commerce and to the states from and to which the commerce flows.

312 U.S. at 115. That the competition injured the states was irrelevant to Congress' power, and that it injured interstate commerce was problematic and unnecessary to be shown; the key was not whether interstate commerce should be an "instrument of competition," but whether Congress wished differentials in overhead resulting from disparate wage and hour standards to be among the factors affecting competition in interstate commerce itself. Congress' judgment was that it should not; and that policy for interstate commerce itself was the objective that supported direct imposition of national wage and hour standards upon manufacturers as a means passing muster under the necessary and proper clause.

The operative rationale was more cleanly stated in Maryland v. Wirtz, 392 U.S. 183 (1968), where upholding an amendment broadening the coverage of the FLSA the Court observed that Congress originally had "decided as a matter of policy" that the low-wage and long-hours employers' "advantage in interstate competition was an 'unfair' one" which it wished to eliminate. (The Court also observed that this advantage had other undesirable effects; but those were constitutionally immaterial.) 392 U.S. at 189. The amendment expanding coverage to additional employees was justified because "[w]hen a company does an interstate business, its competition with companies elsewhere is affected by all its significant labor costs * * *." Id. at 190. The *Wirtz* Court made quite explicit its understanding that the FLSA was justified (among other grounds) as a means under the necessary and proper clause to promote Congress' will regarding competition in interstate commerce.

§ 6.07 The "Scarlet Letter" Error

Although, as we have seen, interstate commerce might sometimes be found to be present without it, a discernible crossing of state lines can be counted on to support a conclusion that interstate commerce is involved. In addition, certainly at least since *Gibbons* (the 1824 steamboat monopoly case), it has been recognized that "the [commerce] power of Congress does not stop at the jurisdictional lines * * *. [It] * * * must be exercised within the territorial jurisdiction of the several States." 9 Wheat. (22 U.S.) at 195–96. This leaves unanswered, however, the question of just where or when in the course of events following a crossing of state lines the power given to Congress by the commerce clause itself might end.

The same question arises as to international commerce, and it was in that context that the first attempt at an answer was made. Brown v. Maryland, 12 Wheat. (25 U.S.) 419 (1827) involved not the commerce clause, but the prohibition in Art. I, § 10, cl. 2, against state taxes on "imports." The question was when, after being imported, goods introduced from abroad might lose that tax immunity. The Court held that the prohibition applied so long as the goods remained "the property of the importer, in his warehouse, in the original form or package" in which imported, and had not "become incorporated and mixed up with the mass of property in the country" so as to lose their "distinctive character as an import." 12 Wheat. (25 U.S.) at 441–42. Lawyers in their quest for litmus paper criteria before long reduced this case-specific and multi-factored rationale to a rather mechanical "original package" test; and as such it came to be applied also to mark the terminus ad quem of inter*state* commerce. See, e.g., Leisy v. Hardin, 135 U.S. 100 (1890).

It has come to be recognized that *Brown's* "original package" statement "was an illustration, rather than a formula, and that its application is evidentiary, and not substantive * * *." Galveston v. Mexican Petrol. Corp., 15 F.2d 208 (S.D.Tex. 1926), quoted with approval in Michelin Tire Corp. v. Wages, 423 U.S. 276, 297 (1976). While there is no simple test, however, the broader considerations suggested in the *Brown* case retain some utility today as factors to guide judgment as to when interstate commerce ends. In any event, it is certain that interstate commerce, once begun, does not continue forever; and it must follow that—regardless what might be possible under the necessary and proper clause—Congress' power *under the commerce clause* does not endure eternal over items that once moved interstate.

Thus it is curious that Congress frequently recites among the asserted bases of its authority,

§ 6.07 *INTERSTATE COMMERCE* 119

either in legislative history or on the face of a statute, the fact that the item it undertakes to regulate once upon a time crossed a state line. Sometimes this is the *only* basis of authority claimed. And sometimes, as with § 201(b)(2) and (c) of the public accommodations provisions of the 1964 Civil Rights Act applicable to restaurants, see Katzenbach v. McClung, 379 U.S. 294 (1964), Congress quite needlessly *limits* the reach of legislation to the trail of goods which have previously crossed state lines.

All this suggests the prevalence of a radical misconception—that Congress' power *under the commerce clause* somehow extends to matters which once were, *because* they once were, "in" interstate commerce. Laid bare, this notion is patently absurd. It might be called the "herpes theory" of federal power: Once you've got it, you've got it. More delicately put, it is reminiscent of the colonial practice, memorialized by Nathaniel Hawthorne, of marking the perpetrators of a certain offense with a "scarlet letter," ever afterward a testament to their character.

There is absolutely no basis in text, logic, or precedent for the evidently widespread notion that once an article has passed through interstate commerce it continues to bear the mark of that commerce, as if indelibly stamped with a scarlet letter, so that Congress may exercise its plenary commerce power over it long after any actual interstate commerce is done. Few adult Americans in this mobile age still reside in the state where they were born, and few of those have never journeyed beyond their state's bounds; does Congress therefore enjoy plenary competence over us (it being of course immaterial to what end Congress exercises its commerce power)? To lay bare the thesis is to refute it; yet with astonishing frequency this "scarlet letter" theory is relied upon in congressional consideration and enactment of legislation today. One sees it recited, for example, among the purported foundations for some gun control and narcotics laws, and it was the avowed premise of several provisions of various drafts of the recent prolonged but ill-fated effort at comprehensive revision of the federal criminal code.

Prior movement in interstate commerce can be an element in constructing a viable necessary and proper clause argument. Prohibiting possession or sale of certain items after their interstate movement, for example, by destroying their market can be as effective as prohibiting their manufacture as a means to effectuate a ban on their shipment. But the mere fact of prior interstate movement does not by itself satisfy the requisites for invoking the necessary and proper clause; see Chapter Three.

While there is no precedent to support this preposterous error, there is at least one Supreme Court case lending it seeming support because the facts fit this pattern and the decision has no other leg to stand on. U.S v. Sullivan, 332 U.S. 689

(1948), upheld application of the misbranding provisions of the Food, Drug & Cosmetic Act to a box of pills filled locally on prescription out of a bulk package which had been properly labeled when it passed interstate. (The legislative history of an amendment to the Act pending when *Sullivan* was decided set forth adequate necessary and proper clause justifications for new statutory language clearly applying to such cases, H.Rep. 807, 80th Cong., 1st Sess. (1947); but that was irrelevant to the statute as it stood at the time material to the *Sullivan* decision.)

The Court claimed as precedent McDermott v. Wisconsin, 228 U.S. 115 (1913); but that case was not in point: In *McDermott,* removal of a federally prescribed label after interstate commerce had ended was precluded because Congress had provided for inspection on store shelves as a means to ensure that proper labels had been on the product when it was moving interstate; Congress' extraneous goal of consumer protection was immaterial to the validity (and preemptive capability) of that chosen enforcement means. See § 5.04. Labelling on the consumer's pill box in *Sullivan* could give no information about the labelling on the interstate package; and the goal of consumer protection, being extraneous, could not itself support application of the federal law. See Figure 7 in § 4.06. The Court in *Sullivan* did not articulate the "scarlet letter" thesis; but with *McDermott* irrelevant as precedent, the holding could stand on nothing else.

Justice Frankfurter once sagely observed that "[d]ecisions of this Court do not have equal intrinsic authority." Adamson v. California, 332 U.S. 46, 59 (1947) (concurring opinion). It would be difficult to find a decision with less "intrinsic authority" than *Sullivan*.

§ 6.08 Confusion From Imprecise Expression

Although the "dual federalism" error now is behind us, imprecise modes of expression still induce serious conceptual errors. Soon after the late New Deal Court rediscovered Congress' real power under the necessary and proper clause, its opinions began to apply the phrase "affecting interstate commerce" to the *activities* federally regulated, rather than to *particular regulations* thereof. This produced a line of cases seeming to indicate that Congress has *general* regulatory authority over everything that "affects interstate commerce."

There is absolutely no constitutional basis, however, for an "affecting commerce" doctrine so misunderstood: The commerce clause supports federal regulation only of interstate commerce itself; and the necessary and proper clause supports, not *any* desired regulation of matters because those matters affect interstate commerce, but only *such* regulations as, when applied to those matters, conduce to Congress' interstate commerce policy ends. This distinction was explored in § 3.04, which should be reviewed at this time.

Occasionally this distinction has been emphasized during congressional deliberations: For example, on its face the bill for the 1964 Civil Rights Act prohibiting racial discrimination in local public accommodations described *those facilities* as "affecting [interstate] commerce;" but in support of the measure Assistant Attorney General Burke Marshall explained: "Discrimination by the establishments covered in the bill should be prohibited because it is that discrimination itself which adversely affects interstate commerce." Hearings on S. 1732, Sen. Commerce Comm., 88th Cong., 1st Sess., ser. 26, pt. 1 at 206 (1963).

More often, however, the distinction is overlooked: Federal labor legislation, for example, once was carefully rationalized in terms of the impact particular provisions would have in diminishing the prospect of unrest potentially disruptive of interstate commerce; more recently, however, this field has been dealt with as if labor-management relations per se were within Congress' plenary control, by virtue of the commerce clause alone and without any need to show that particular provisions satisfy the requisites of the necessary and proper clause. Whether as a consequence some labor provisions have been enacted which really cannot pass muster under that clause, is a question which the student might wish to explore.

Imprecise expression (and failure to recognize that sound concepts were rediscovered after 1936 only in gradual stages) has contributed also to some other confusion in commerce clause doctrine, including some of the uncertainty over what constitutes interstate commerce itself. This can be illustrated with some cases involving different provisions of the Public Utility Holding Company Act of 1935, 49 Stat. 803.

Electric Bond & Share Co. v. SEC, 303 U.S. 419 (1938), sustained §§ 4(a) and 5 of the Act, which prohibited any such holding company from using any instrumentality of interstate commerce or the mails unless the holding company first registered with the SEC and satisfied certain other requirements—those requirements being extraneous to any legitimate federal concerns. To the reflective student today it is obvious that this was an application of the concept discussed in Chapter Four—the use of enumerated powers to promote extraneous ends. In 1938, however, the Supreme Court did not yet have a firm grasp on that concept, and still nominally maintained allegiance to the erroneous "pretext" dictum of *McCulloch* (not definitively laid to rest until 1941; see § 4.04, supra).

The opinion in *Electric Bond & Share* makes this very obvious, bluntly (and of course wrongly) declaring that "Congress may not exercise its control over the mails to enforce a requirement which lies outside its constitutional province * * *." 303 U.S. at 442. Having thus disavowed the concept which actually provides the constitutional support for the legislation being sustained, the opinion writer groped for some seeming explanation to justify the holding. The best he could articulate—"When Congress lays down a valid rule to govern those engaged in transactions in interstate commerce, Congress may deny to those who violate the rule the right to engage in such transactions" (id. at 442)—was no explanation at all. It begged the whole question of validity, and ignored the fact that the particular requirements at issue in that case pertained to the holding companies' intrastate activities, not to any of the admittedly interstate activities in which they also engaged. If taken at face value, this bit of addlepated doubletalk would mean that simply by engaging in some act in interstate commerce (or simply by using the mails) one opens *all* his activities to federal regulation! That baseless proposition had been repudiated earlier in the first *Employers Liability Cases,* and it manifestly is not the principle which actually justifies those sections of the Public Utilities Holding Company Act.

Two other parts of the same Act—§§ 11(b)(1) and 11(b)(2)—were quite different in principle: Instead of employing the concept discussed in Chapter Four, they regulated intrastate activities as a means to Congress' desired end of unburdening interstate commerce, and thus were simple applications of the necessary and proper clause. The opinions in North American Co. v. SEC, 327 U.S.

686 (1946), and American Power Co. v. SEC, 329 U.S. 90 (1946), upholding these two provisions do demonstrate the Court's awareness that the necessary and proper clause was their basis; but those opinions also contain some obfuscating statements.

North American, for example, was said to engage "in activities which bring it within the ambit of congressional authority"—with no explanation whether it was brought *wholly* within that ambit as to *all* of its activities or whether some of its activities were only subject to regulations (like those at stake in that case) which bore a telic relation to some end for what concededly was interstate commerce. There is reference to the "interstate character" of the companies, apparent from a "survey of their activities"—with no indication whether that meant that all their activities (and in particular, those activities the regulation of which was there at issue) should be considered as "in" interstate commerce. Some passages are worded as though these sections could be upheld under the commerce clause itself rather than under the necessary and proper clause (e.g., 327 U.S. at 706); and at one point the Court said, "the federal commerce power is as broad as the economic needs of the nation," 329 U.S. at 104.

Such grandiose generalities are the stuff of which conceptual confusion is made. If taken at face value, these examples of imprecise expression could be understood to mean that such matters as the ownership of securities and the organizational structure of corporations (both matters regulated by that legislation) are themselves "in" interstate commerce—and thus are within the plenary power of Congress to regulate however it wishes regardless at what end its regulation might be aimed. The legislation there in question, however, and the facts of those cases, called for no such sweeping new view of what constitutes interstate commerce itself; they called for simple application of the necessary and proper clause. The loose language is best understood as imprecision in expression, perhaps reflecting some confusion in conception, but nothing more. To take it as authority expanding the scope of power under the commerce clause itself is to make of these decisions something which the Justices who decided them surely did not understand them to be.

§ 6.09 Immaterial Predominant Ends

It is worth reemphasizing here a principle of generic application which has had particularly noteworthy application in connection with the commerce clause. When a particular federal regulation is justified under the necessary and proper clause by its telic relation to some interstate commerce policy end, it is constitutionally immaterial that the same regulation might promote one or more extraneous objectives as well. See Figure 6 and accompanying text in § 4.05. The purpose to effectuate some policy for interstate commerce is constitutionally indispensable; but it makes no constitutional difference at all if, politically, the desire to effectuate some extraneous end is the overriding impetus for the legislation.

§ 6.10 Navigable Waters: A Peculiar Case

One aspect of Congress' "commerce power"—its power over navigable waters—has undergone dramatic expansion since it was first held in *Gibbons* that "commerce" includes "navigation."

From the premise that interstate *navigation* is an aspect of interstate commerce it necessarily followed (by virtue of the necessary and proper clause) that Congress could enact regulations of navigable *waters* which had as their objective the effectuation of federal policy regarding interstate navigation. See Gilman v. Philadelphia, 3 Wall. (70 U.S.) 713, 724–25 (1866). This gave Congress a great deal of authority over navigable *waters*—although any measure regarding the *waters* would have to meet the requirements for validity under the necessary and proper clause, discussed in Chapter Three.

The expansion of federal power over navigable waters was the result of two changes: The attribution of Congress' power over those waters to the commerce clause itself rather than the necessary and proper clause; and enlargement of the concept of "navigability."

So long as *navigation,* but not the *waters* being navigated, was regarded as within the commerce power, Congress could regulate the waters for navigation objectives but could not validly regulate

§ 6.10 *INTERSTATE COMMERCE* 129

them in ways which bore no telic relation to navigation (or other legitimate federal) ends. Thus, for example, Congress would not have been able to regulate the discharge into those waters of wastes that could not interfere with navigation. (Of course a single regulation might serve both a navigation objective and some extraneous objective as well, on the pattern of Figure 6 in § 4.05; and in such circumstances, serving the extraneous objective could not detract from the validity of the regulation. See U.S. v. Chandler-Dunbar Water Power Co., 229 U.S. 53, 72–73 (1913). But if no telic relation to any *navigation* objective could be found for the particular regulation at stake, it would have to be regarded as void.) This explains the urgency of the search for some navigation objective that is apparent, for example, in Arizona v. California, 283 U.S. 423 (1931), where the Court seemed still to view Congress' power over navigable *waters* as a function of the necessary and proper clause.

In 1940, however, the Court decided U.S. v. Appalachian Electric Power Co., 311 U.S. 377 (1940). The Court's opinion in that case plainly proceeds on the premise that what is to be considered as "in" interstate commerce is not merely *navigation,* but navigable waters per se. The federal measures there were upheld without any showing that those particular measures were means to any navigation end.

This innovation in doctrine might be attributable simply to a lapse in precision of analysis or expression by the author of that particular opinion; for an opinion of the Court written the next year by a different Justice articulated carefully a means-to-*navigation*-end rationale in supporting a watershed-wide federal flood control program. Oklahoma ex rel. Phillips v. Guy F. Atkinson Co., 313 U.S. 508, 525–34 (1941). Nevertheless, the evident premise of the *Appalachian* opinion has predominated in subsequent discussions of Congress' power over navigable waters. On this view, as with any other matter that is itself "in" interstate commerce, the objective at which a particular regulation of navigable waters is aimed becomes immaterial to the question of constitutional validity.

The enlargement of the concept of "navigability" occurred roughly at the same time. The traditional American view had been that

> Those rivers must be regarded as public navigable rivers in law which are navigable in fact. And they are navigable in fact when they are used, or are susceptible of being used, in their ordinary condition, as highways for commerce, over which trade and travel are or may be conducted in the customary modes of trade and travel on water. And they constitute navigable waters of the United States * * * when they form in their ordinary condition by themselves, or by uniting with other waters, a continued highway over which commerce is or may be

carried on with other States or foreign countries * * *.

The Daniel Ball, 10 Wall. (77 U.S.) 557, 563 (1871).

In 1931 this was modified so as to sustain federal power over a river which at the time was not navigable in fact, but a part of which formerly had been navigable and parts of which could be rendered navigable by the federal measure then under consideration. "Commercial disuse resulting from changed geographical conditions and a Congressional failure to deal with them," said the Court, "does not amount to an abandonment of a navigable river or prohibit future exertion of federal control." Arizona v. California, supra, 283 U.S. at 453–54.

Nine years later the Court went still further, saying that: To appraise the evidence of navigability on the natural condition only of the waterway is erroneous. Its availability for navigation must also be considered. "natural and ordinary condition" refers to volume of water, the gradients and the regularity of the flow. A waterway, otherwise suitable for navigation, is not barred from that classification merely because artificial aids must make the highway suitable for use before commercial navigation may be undertaken. * * * Nor is it necessary that the improvements should be actually completed or even authorized. * * * Nor is it necessary for navigability that the use should be continuous. * * *

Appalachian Electric Power, supra, 311 U.S. at 407–10 (1940). On this reasoning, waters plainly non-navigable in their natural state could be regarded as navigable, even though no improvements were contemplated! Moreover, "[w]hen once found to be navigable, a waterway remains so." Id. at 408.

Finally, in Utah v. U.S., 403 U.S. 9 (1971), the Court affirmed that the concept of "navigability" applies to lakes as well as rivers, and applies even to the Great Salt Lake—which never had but a pittance of small boat traffic, and that over a century ago. That lake, moreover, is wholly within Utah and connects with no other waterway; but no matter: The Court held that "the fact that the Great Salt Lake is not part of a navigable interstate or international commercial highway in no way interferes with" its being considered a navigable waterway of the United States in the constitutional sense! 403 U.S. at 10.

Under this marvelous line of cases, it appears that the federal government now enjoys plenary power (in the sense explained in Chapter Four) over all of the significant streams and bodies of water in the United States, and probably over a number of quite insignificant ones as well, because they are conceived as themselves "in" interstate commerce per se. The remarkable development of doctrine regarding navigable waters thus is illustrative of the breadth of power that would gravitate to the federal government over all activity in

§ 6.10   *INTERSTATE COMMERCE*   133

the country, whether "commerce" in the mercantile sense or otherwise, if discriminating constitutional analysis were abandoned—or merely neglected.

Today the exercise of federal authority under the peculiar line of "navigable waters" cases, for purposes having nothing whatever to do with navigation, is approved as extending even to "wetlands"—or at least to wetlands adjacent to waters. U.S. v. Riverside Bayview Homes, Inc., 106 S.Ct. 455 (1985). Whether the constitutional justification for the statutory construction there sustained is that the wetlands, too, are "in" interstate commerce, or rather (as would seem a bit less extravagant) that their regulation is sustainable under the necessary and proper clause to promote Congress' goal for the waters, the Court was not called upon to say.

Because of the substantial investments that have been made in reliance upon this enhanced federal authority over waters—investments both in money and in legislative effort (e.g., pollution control legislation)—it surely is unrealistic to expect any curtailment of federal authority over waters in the future; and this is so, even though the scope of authority now exercised evolved through patent failures of analysis and misapplication of concepts. The navigable waters cases, however, constitute an isolated and peculiar body of precedent. One might either criticize or applaud the resulting plenary federal control over waters; but these cases should not be taken as a pattern, or as an excuse for departures from careful analysis in other "commerce" cases.

§ 6.11 Navigable Waters and Preemptive Capability

As noted repeatedly in the foregoing sections, the generic principles discussed in Chapters Two through Five apply as fully in the context of the commerce power as in the context of any other legislative power. This includes the principle of preemptive capability. Indeed, one of the cases most forcefully illustrating this principle, discussed in § 5.06, was a commerce power case, *Regents v. Carroll*. The student is encouraged to re-read that discussion at this point.

As just explained, the cases of approximately the past fifty years have treated navigable waters as "in" interstate commerce per se. On this view, of course, *any* federal policy regarding navigable waters (whether or not that policy has to do with navigation) is within the circle of legitimate federal concerns, and enjoys preemptive capability. This distinguishes conditions unrelated to navigation, contained in permits or licenses regarding navigable waters, from extraneous conditions in *other* interstate commerce permits or licenses (such as that involved in *Regents*); for the former need not have any navigation (or other commercial) objective so long as the waters themselves are regarded as "in" interstate commerce, since Congress' power over that commerce itself is plenary.

See, e.g., First Iowa Hydro-Electric Coop. v. FPC, 328 U.S. 152 (1946); Chapman v. Public Utilities Dist., 367 F.2d 163 (9th Cir.1966); Public Utilities Dist. v. FPC, 308 F.2d 318 (D.C.Cir.1962), cert. denied, 372 U.S. 908 (1963).

Not even these cases, however, suggest any preemptive capability as to *extraneous objectives* at which the (navigation or non-navigation) utilization of navigable waters might be aimed. For example, Congress might authorize the building of a dam in a river, not to enhance navigation but strictly for power generation, Congress' objective being the extraneous one of providing electricity for consumers. Assuming the modern view that any federal policy regarding the river is an exercise of Congress' power over interstate commerce itself, a state certainly could be preempted from prohibiting (or from regulating the design or construction of) the dam; but it does not at all follow that a state rate structure for intrastate sale of the electricity generated could be preempted. Whether such a state rate structure could be preempted or not must depend upon a separate analysis; and unless a necessary and proper clause basis could be found for superseding the state's intrastate rate controls (as conceivably it might be, on the pattern of Figure 11 in § 5.07), the principle illustrated in the *Regents* case should control.

§ 6.12 International Commerce

The Constitution contains some special limitations on Congress' regulation of "Commerce with

Foreign Nations." Congress was forbidden to prohibit immigration or importation of persons (particularly contemplating the slave trade) before 1808, Art. I, § 9, cl. 1; and it was was forbidden to tax exports or to establish preferences among the ports of different states, id., cls. 5, 6. But for these limitations, however, Congress' power over international commerce clearly is plenary. There is no doubt that it may be exercised in the form of prohibition (embargo), quota, or specially favored treatment, regardless whether the objective of any particular regulation is commercial or otherwise.

> Foreign commerce is preeminently a matter of national concern. * * * Although the Constitution * * * grants Congress power to regulate commerce "with foreign Nations" and "among the several States" in parallel phrases, there is evidence that the Founders intended the scope of the foreign commerce power to be the greater.

Japan Line, Ltd. v. Los Angeles, 441 U.S. 434, 448 (1979).

Even if power to regulate commerce with foreign nations had not been conferred specifically by the commerce clause, the national government certainly would have enjoyed complete discretion over international commerce by virtue of its power over foreign affairs, examined more fully in § 9.01. That the power is conferred expressly, however, removes any possible doubt that the necessary and proper clause is applicable to enable Congress to deal with matters which are not themselves international commerce, insofar as it does so to effectuate its international commerce goals. Among the easiest of measures to justify on this ground are laws against receiving, concealing, or even possessing forbidden imports, or facilitating their importation. See, e.g., Brolan v. U.S., 236 U.S. 216, 219–21 (1915).

CHAPTER SEVEN

CONGRESS' POWER TO TAX

§ 7.01 "Direct" Taxes and "Apportionment"

Article I, § 8, cl. 1 provides that "[t]he Congress shall have Power To lay and collect Taxes, Duties, Imposts and Excises * * *." Together these terms comprehend all possible forms of taxation. Most technical distinctions which might be drawn among "excises," "imposts," "duties," and other "taxes," see Pacific Insurance Co. v. Soule, 7 Wall. (74 U.S.) 433, 445 (1869), have no constitutional significance.

A significant distinction, however, is drawn between so-called "direct" taxes and all others. Art. I, § 9, cl. 4 provides that "[n]o Capitation, or other direct, Tax shall be laid, unless in Proportion to the Census * * *;" and Art. I, § 2, cl. 3 provides that "direct Taxes shall be apportioned among the several States * * * according to their respective Numbers." (For apportionment purposes, slaves were to be counted as fractions, and untaxed Indians not at all.)

The apportionment requirement was a compromise chiefly to prevent certain possible taxes from bearing too heavily upon the relatively poor plantation states. It meant that those taxes must be calculated to generate from each state a *share of*

§ 7.01 CONGRESS' POWER TO TAX 139

the total revenue (from that tax) equivalent to that state's share of the total population, adjusted for slaves and Indians. To accomplish this, however, the *rate* of those taxes would have to vary widely from state to state.

Simple arithmetic will show that apportionment of a per capita tax would ameliorate the relative burden otherwise falling on slaveowners, and that apportionment of a property tax would ameliorate the relative burden on landowners where large agricultural holdings were common but acreage did not necessarily translate into ability to pay. Apportionment of virtually any other kind of tax, however, would produce considerable inequity through differing rates: It generally would make the tax rate on any article higher where that article was more rare—and was more rare precisely because the people there were poorer and thus less able to pay.

The verbal distinction between "direct" and other taxes can be traced to such early economists as Adam Smith; but from an early date, for constitutional purposes the distinction was dealt with less in theoretical than in practical terms. In Hylton v. U.S., 3 Dall. (3 U.S.) 171 (1796), the Justices agreed that any tax, the apportionment of which would aggravate rather than ameliorate the disparity between tax obligations and the ability to pay, should *not* be considered "direct." In effect this meant that none but head taxes and property taxes could be considered "direct" (and thus apportionable). See *Soule,* supra.

As wealth became increasingly unrelated to land ownership, even real estate taxes on the apportionment formula became more inequitable. The gradual changes in the economy did not change the classification of property taxes for constitutional purposes, but it did cause enactment of federal taxes on real property to become politically impracticable: No federal tax on real property has been enacted since the Civil War.

Consistently with the "ability to pay" approach of the earliest cases, federal taxes on *income* were held *not* to be "direct" taxes in *Soule,* supra, and again in Springer v. U.S., 102 U.S. 586 (1881). Several years later, however, a Court consisting of different Justices by bare majority held that a tax on income *from property,* real or personal (i.e., a tax on income from capital), *is* "direct" and therefore must be apportioned. The federal income tax law enacted in 1894 did tax income from capital (just like other income) *without* apportionment; and because they considered the provisions taxing income from capital to be non-severable from the provisions validly taxing other income, the majority held the entire law unconstitutional. Pollock v. Farmers' Loan & Trust Co., 157 U.S. 429 (1895), and 158 U.S. 601 (1895).

This turnabout in judicial opinion was quite dramatic. In 1869 the practical fact that apportioning an income tax would require different rates in each state—very low in some and so high as to amount to annihilation in others—had been taken by the court as reason to hold income taxes *not* to be "direct." See *Soule,* supra. But in 1895, the fact that such inequity would make a tax on income from capital politically unacceptable was applauded by the majority as "prevent[ing] an attack upon accumulated property by mere force of numbers," and as a "rule of protection" constituting "one of the bulwarks of private rights and private property." 157 U.S. at 582–83.

The public's rather rapid response to this judicial departure from the tradition of correlating taxes at least roughly with ability to pay was the sixteenth amendment: It authorizes federal taxation of incomes from *whatever* source derived, without apportionment.

§ 7.02 "Indirect" Taxes and "Uniformity"

Those taxes which are not regarded as "direct" may not be apportioned, but instead must be "uniform throughout the United States." Art. I, § 8, cl. 1. This is literally required only as to "Duties, Imposts and Excises;" and therefore it could be argued that *some* taxes (such as the income tax) fall outside those three categories so that neither the apportionment nor the uniformity requirement applies. This argument, however, has not been pursued. In fact, precisely to avoid that result the Court has construed the sixteenth amendment as transforming such taxes as were held "direct" in

Pollock into "excises" instead. Brushaber v. Union Pac. R.R. Co., 240 U.S. 1 (1916). In practice, the "uniformity" requirement is regarded as applying to all federal taxes except those to which the "apportionment" requirement applies; and since those for which apportionment is required no longer are utilized in fact, as a practical matter all federal taxes must be "uniform throughout the United States."

The "uniformity" requirement, however, means only that "what Congress has properly selected for taxation must be identically taxed in every state where it is found." Fernandez v. Wiener, 326 U.S. 340 (1945). It does not require that similar things be similarly taxed; it does not preclude graduated rates; it makes no difference that the thing or activity taxed might not occur in every state, or equally in every state; and it does not matter that the tax is contingent upon circumstances controlled by state law and for that reason might vary from state to state. It sometimes is said that what is required is "geographic," not "intrinsic" uniformity. However, Congress may take account of "geographically isolated problems" in taxing, and even "where Congress does choose to frame a tax in geographical terms," it will be upheld if that determination is "based on neutral factors" not inconsistent with the "purpose" of the uniformity requirement, to prevent "actual geographic discrimination." U.S. v. Ptasynski, 462 U.S. 74 (1983). On the uniformity requirement generally, see *Ptasynski,* supra; *Fernandez,* supra; Chas. C. Steward Machine Co. v. Davis, 301 U.S. 548 (1937); and Knowlton v. Moore, 178 U.S. 41 (1900).

§ 7.03 Other Limits On Federal Taxes

Two other limitations on federal taxing deserve passing notice. Article I, § 9, cl. 6 reinforces the uniformity requirement for certain taxes by providing that "[n]o Preference shall be given by any Regulation of * * * Revenue to the Ports of one State over those of another * * *." And Art. I, § 9, cl. 5 provides that "No Tax or Duty shall be laid on Articles exported from any State."

The latter clause applies only to articles exported to a foreign country, not to a sister state or a territory. Dooley v. U.S., 183 U.S. 151 (1901). It protects goods which are in the channels of exportation, but does not protect goods from undifferentiated taxation merely because the particular goods are destined ultimately for exportation. For example, a federal sales tax could not be applied to a sale for export, the sale taxed being the very act which places the goods in export channels, A.G. Spalding & Bros. v. Edwards, 262 U.S. 66 (1923); but a tax on cheese, levied against manufacturers, could be applied even as to cheese manufactured under contract expressly for export, Cornell v. Coyne, 192 U.S. 418 (1904). A federal tax imposed on the income derived from engaging in the business of exporting is not a tax on exports. Peck v. Lowe, 247 U.S. 165 (1918).

Subject only to these few limitations, the federal power to tax "is exhaustive and embraces every conceivable power of taxation * * *." *Brushaber,* supra, 240 U.S. at 12. "Thus limited, and thus only, it reaches every subject, and may be exercised at discretion." License Tax Cases, 5 Wall. (72 U.S.) 462, 471 (1867). Congress may tax any item, article, act, transaction, activity, event, occurrence, enterprise, or other tangible or intangible thing it might choose. It may tax the exercise of any right or duty as freely as it may tax any privilege. See *Steward Machine,* supra, 301 U.S. at 590–91. And it may tax as heavily as it might choose, at least unless some "due process" limit on confiscation is conceived.

Moreover, Congress may impose taxes the revenue from which is earmarked to be expended for a particular purpose, Cincinnati Soap Co. v. U.S., 301 U.S. 308, 313 (1937), provided the expenditure purpose is permissible (see Chapter Eight).

§ 7.04 Taxes and Non-revenue Objectives

There never has been reason to doubt that Congress may use taxes to promote non-revenue objectives *within* the circle of legitimate federal concerns. For example, the imposition or rate of a tax imposed upon owners of vessels bringing aliens from foreign ports might serve to further Congress' policy concerning that species of commerce with foreign nations. Head Money Cases, 112 U.S. 580 (1884). Likewise, taxes may be imposed or adjusted to promote protectionist or other mercantile policy objectives. Hampton, Jr. & Co. v. U.S., 276 U.S. 394 (1928). As illustrated in Figure 13, this is the imposition of a tax, A, as a means to effectuate federal policy with regard to some non-revenue matter of legitimate federal concern, E. (Despite the telic relation, resort to the necessary and proper clause in this circumstance is superfluous so long as the "tax" is really a tax; for revenue raising by taxation is itself a matter within the circle of legitimate federal concerns.)

More confusion has attended the use of federal taxes to promote non-revenue objectives *outside* the circle of legitimate federal concerns. For well over a century now, taxes have been used on the pattern of Figure 5 in § 4.01. For example, the tax on state bank notes upheld in Veazie Bank v. Fenno, 8 Wall. (75 U.S.) 533 (1869), could be forced

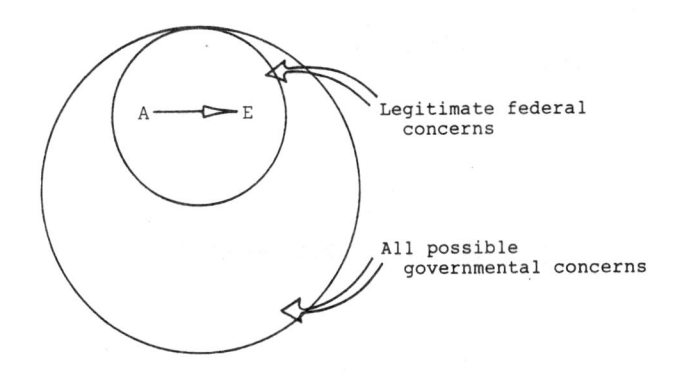

FIGURE 13

into the pattern of Figure 13 only by substantially distorting Congress' enumerated power to regulate the value of coined money; but it easily fits the pattern of Figure 5. For another example, the tax upheld in McCray v. U.S., 195 U.S. 27 (1904), was set at a much higher rate on colored than on white oleomargarine, with the extraneous objectives of assisting dairy farmers and deterring consumer deception—matters extraneous to the circle of legitimate federal concerns.

Figure 5, of course, illustrates the use of an enumerated power toward extraneous objectives. It is interesting that the use of the *taxing* power on this pattern was approved judicially, and was widespread in practice, for decades before the generic principle which this reflects was openly admitted—and while the old *McCulloch* dictum to the contrary (see §§ 4.01–4.03) still was regarded as sound.

Because the use of the taxing power, in particular, on this pattern was so early and so well established, it is remarkable and rather amusing that as late as a generation ago, even while reaffirming that Congress may use taxes to promote extraneous ends, a Supreme Court majority opinion asserted that "the court has never questioned" the *McCulloch* pretext dictum! U.S. v. Kahriger, 345 U.S. 22, 29 (1953). Nothing could better illustrate the conceptual confusion which frequently permeates the judicial opinions from which students are expected to learn Constitutional Law!

With respect to the taxing power and the *Kahriger* statement, this confusion can be dispelled by taking care to distinguish between two different questions, which tend easily to become confused in discussions. One is the question whether a financial exaction which Congress has called a "tax" *really is* a tax in constitutional terms; the other is the question of how a *real* tax may be *used*. The latter is the only question addressed in this section; the former is considered in the section which follows.

Non-revenue objectives may be promoted either by the imposition of a tax, or by affording tax credits, exemptions, or rebates under specified conditions. All of these represent applications, in the taxing power context, of the generic principle examined in Chapter Four.

§ 7.05 "Taxes" That Are Not Taxes, and Taxes That Really Are

Just like Humpty Dumpty (L. Carroll, THROUGH THE LOOKING GLASS ch. 6), Congress can call *anything* a tax. Such labelling by Congress, however, cannot determine whether a financial exaction is truly a tax as contemplated by the Constitution.

Congress' power is to tax "to pay the Debts and provide for the common Defence and general Welfare of the United States"—i.e., to raise funds to be expended in so doing. It therefore seems clear that a tax in its essence is a revenue device. Of course there are other transactions which also produce revenue for the United States: For example, the collection of civil and criminal sanctions and the sale of surplus government property. Revenue production, however, is the sole essential or characteristic function of a tax.

Sometimes it makes no practical difference whether a so-called "tax" *is* a tax, or instead is a penal exaction, a regulatory device. "Where the sovereign enacting the law has power to impose both tax and penalty the difference between revenue production and mere regulation may be immaterial * * *." Bailey v. Drexel Furniture Co., 259 U.S. 20, 38 (1922). In such cases, even if a measure denominated a "tax" were held to be really a regulatory penalty, the outcome would be the same so long as a legitimate federal end were served. See Sunshine Anthracite Coal Co. v. Adkins, 310 U.S. 381, 393–94 (1940); see also *Kahriger,* supra, 345 U.S. at 37 (Frankfurter, concurring). In other words, if A in Figure 12 were deemed *not* really a tax, it might nevertheless be valid on the pattern illustrated by Figure 2 in § 3.01. In fact, a so-called "tax" promoting some non-revenue but *legitimate* federal objective might actually confront fewer constitutional obstacles if it were held *not* to be a tax; for the uniformity and apportionment requirements discussed in §§ 7.01 and 7.02 apply only to true taxes, not to regulations. See Alaska v. Troy, 258 U.S. 101, 110–11 (1922); see also Rogers v. U.S., 138 F.2d 992, 995 (6th Cir.1943).

§ 7.05   CONGRESS' POWER TO TAX   149

But the difference between a true tax, and a regulation or penalty masquerading as a tax, is crucial when the non-revenue end is extraneous to the circle of legitimate federal concerns. In such cases, (unless the exaction is also simultaneously supported by a telic relation to some *legitimate* federal end) it must stand or fall on the determination whether it really *is* a tax as contemplated by the Constitution and thus is itself within the circle of legitimate federal concerns.

Not since *Bailey* in 1922 and U.S. v. Constantine, 296 U.S. 287, in 1935, has the Supreme Court held a measure which Congress has labelled a tax to be not truly a tax in the constitutional sense. Dissenting in *Constantine* Justice Cardozo protested against probing congressional "purpose" to ascertain whether the revenue-raising function characteristic of true taxes was the purpose of the particular "taxing" measure. Of course inquiries into legislative "purpose" always are difficult; see § 3.10. But Cardozo's objection was singularly out of place in *Constantine,* which involved an exorbitant "tax" on dealings in liquor contrary to state law; for that "tax" was enacted in 1926 when, by virtue of the eighteenth amendment, Congress enjoyed *regulatory* power over int*ra*state liquor transactions. When enacted, in other words, that "tax" was equally valid whether or not it was a true tax; whether it was a true tax became crucial only when the twenty-first amendment repealed the eleventh, eliminating Congress' relevant *regulatory* power, seven years after Congress had enacted the statute deliberately as a liquor control rather than as a revenue measure.

Nonetheless, beginning with Sonzinsky v. U.S., 300 U.S. 506 (1937), Supreme Court majorities repeatedly have shared Cardozo's disinclination to look into congressional "purpose" or "motive" to determine whether a so-called "tax" really is a tax. "Taxes" productive of negligible revenue, and plainly designed less as revenue devices than to suppress or discourage (or provide prosecutorial bases regarding) the activities concerned, repeatedly have been upheld. E.g., U.S. v. Sanchez, 340 U.S. 42 (1950); *Kahriger,* supra.

There is a fundamental flaw in these modern decisions, which has troubled some Justices but has not yet been laid starkly bare. The inclination evident in decisions for the past fifty years uncritically to accept as a tax in the constitutional sense any so-called "tax" which is "productive of some revenue," *Sonzinsky,* supra, 300 U.S. at 514, confounds two very different questions.

If a measure *is* a tax, it certainly is improper for the judiciary to ask *why* Congress has imposed it where or when it has, or what extraneous policy objectives might have led Congress to design it as it did; for (ignoring Bill of Rights-type restrictions) purpose is constitutionally immaterial *if* in fact Congress is employing a power given to it by the Constitution.

But there are instances when "purpose" is *the measure* of Congress' power. One example is when Congress acts under the necessary and proper clause: Telic purpose to promote some objective within the circle of legitimate federal concerns is the sine qua non of Congress' power under that clause. It would seem that another example must be the taxing power: If a tax in its essence is a revenue device, nothing which happens to produce a bit of revenue (including penal fines) can be distinguished from taxes except by reference to the "purpose" of the particular exaction. Without a bona fide revenue purpose, it is transparent subterfuge to call the measure a tax at all. "[T]he Court cannot shut its eyes to what is obviously, because designedly, an attempt to control conduct * * * merely because Congress wrapped the legislation in the verbal cellophane of a revenue measure." Frankfurter, dissenting in *Kahriger,* supra, 345 U.S. at 38. It must be "a rational or good-faith revenue measure * * *." Jackson, concurring, id. at 35.

Other constitutional questions to which legislative "purpose" is material were mentioned in § 3.10. No accusation is heard in such instances that judicial inquiry into "purpose" spreads "the process of psychoanalysis * * * to unaccustomed fields" (Cardozo, dissenting in *Constantine,* supra, 296 U.S. at 229). Certainly when legislative "intent" or "purpose" is material in *any* context there are possibilities of disagreement; often there are grounds for conflicting inferences, and sometimes there is a need to look beyond legislative history to circumstantial indications of intent. Yet the judiciary surmounts these difficulties, and proceeds to judge "purpose" in other contexts despite them. See § 3.10.

Thus there is neither principle nor reason prohibiting judicial inquiry into "purpose" in order to determine whether what purports to be a "tax" really is. The judicial disinclination to embark on such inquiries is attributable in large part to the unwillingness of many modern Justices and scholars to think seriously and critically about federalism as posing legal, rather than merely political, issues. It seems attributable also, in part, to unwarranted confidence that candor and restraint can be expected to prevail in Congress itself. In his notably unenthusiastic concurring opinion in *Kahriger,* for example, Justice Jackson expressed hope that the evil of "efforts to accomplish by [dubious so-called] taxation moral reforms that cannot be accomplished by direct [federal] legislation * * * will probably soon make itself manifest to Congress * * *." 345 U.S. at 36. After more than thirty years, however, it now seems quite evident that such hope for candor on the part of Congress is misplaced.

The four particular features identified by the Court in the *Bailey* case, supra, the two others identified in *Constantine,* or any one or combination of them, are neither necessary nor exclusive

§ 7.05   *CONGRESS' POWER TO TAX*   153

as factors to distinguish real from sham taxes. While Frankfurter, dissenting in *Kahriger,* remarked that the *Bailey* discussion was helpful, he took care to add that "[i]ssues of such gravity affecting the balance of powers within our federal system are not susceptible of comprehensive statement by smooth formulas * * *." 345 U.S. at 38. What is called for, Frankfurter maintained, is *judgment,* based not only on "the history of [the] legislation as it went through Congress" but also on "the context of the circumstances which brought forth [the] enactment * * *." Id. at 38–9. Cases where "purpose" is material to other constitutional issues can offer valuable guidance to intelligent lawyers who are not too smug to take seriously the challenge of ascertaining "purpose." See § 3.10. Of course any single factor identified as crucial in a particular case might be avoided by deft maneuvers in drafting the next sham-tax legislation; but the necessity for *judgment* whether any so-called "tax" really is a tax will remain open to such argument as resourceful lawyers might make.

Sham taxes most commonly have been used to accomplish national control of traffic in items justly deemed worthy of strict regulation, such as certain weapons (e.g., grenades, machine guns, and sawed-off shotguns) having no significant utility among law-abiding citizens, and mind-altering drugs deemed subject to serious abuse. The practice of resorting to pretended taxation to accomplish this became established early in this century, when distortions of commerce clause and necessary and proper clause doctrine made *those* bases for federal action seem foreclosed. That excuse for tolerating perfidious horseplay with taxation no longer exists today. Given a competent understanding of the generic concepts examined in Chapters Two, Three, and Four, there are ample *sound* bases upon which Congress can act against such evils—although new legislation might be required.

Consequently, the appropriate response no longer is indulgence, but rather is angry, impatient, and resolute assault on the judicial bad habit of sustaining sham taxes. The dissenting protest of Justice Douglas, joined by Justice Black, in Minor v. U.S., 396 U.S. 87, 98 et seq. (1969), deserves sober reflection, elaboration, and courageous repetition.

§ 7.06 Necessary and Proper Means to Revenue Ends

The necessary and proper clause applies as fully to help effectuate the taxing power as to help effectuate any other federal power. Thus Congress may authorize distraint and sale of real or personal property to collect delinquent taxes, Springer v. U.S., 102 U.S. 586 (1880); may create tax liens independent of state law, U.S. v. Smith, 209 Va. 5, 161 S.E.2d 709 (1968); and may prescribe penalties for failure to pay a tax which is due, U.S. v. Smith, 62 F.Supp. 594 (W.D.Mich.1945). Likewise, Congress may require a person to provide information from which that person's liability for a federal tax

§ 7.06 *CONGRESS' POWER TO TAX* 155

can be determined, U.S. v. Acker, 415 F.2d 328 (6th Cir.1969), cert. denied, 396 U.S. 1003 (1970). Forcing self-disclosure of facts showing liability for a tax is no more a violation of the constitutional privilege against self incrimination than is forced testimony or discovery in civil proceedings. (However, if the same disclosures might also expose one to criminal prosecution, that privilege might be a bar. See Marchetti v. U.S., 390 U.S. 39 (1968); Grosso v. U.S., 390 U.S. 62 (1968); Haynes v. U.S., 390 U.S. 85 (1968).)

Such provisions sometimes have been characterized as assertions of the taxing power itself. Stated more precisely, however, they are applications of Congress' necessary and proper clause power in conjunction with the taxing power. Appropriately, therefore, a great deal of latitude is allowed to Congress in selecting means it deems useful to accomplish its revenue end. The Court has said that the provisions "must be naturally and reasonably adapted to the collection of the tax * * *," *Bailey,* supra, 259 U.S. at 43, and must not be "plainly inappropriate and unnecessary to reasonable enforcement of a revenue measure." Linder v. U.S., 268 U.S. 5, 18 (1925). More useful guides than such phrases snatched out of opinions, however, are the generic principles of the necessary and proper clause, discussed in Chapter Three: Thus, any regulation attending a genuine revenue measure will be valid if Congress has found, on a rational basis, that the particular regulation bears a substantial telic relation to the raising of revenue, the end within the circle of legitimate federal concerns by virtue of the taxing power.

Since we deal here simply with another application of this generic principle, it should be apparent without further explanation that tax enforcement measures may be chosen which *also* have *extraneous* aims—indeed, may be chosen in preference to other possible enforcement measures precisely *because* they simultaneously serve extraneous ends. See § 4.05. Detailed requirements in the Harrison Narcotics Act (which taxes transactions in narcotic drugs), for example, call for elaborate recordkeeping and the use of prescribed written order forms for narcotics transactions. The sufficient constitutional justification for those requirements is that they are rationally adapted to facilitate collection of the taxes due. See U.S. v. Doremus, 249 U.S. 86 (1919). It is no secret, however, that these same requirements make socially undesirable traffic in those drugs more difficult—or at least punishable insofar as it occurs without satisfaction of these requirements, see Nigro v. U.S., 276 U.S. 332 (1928); and it would defy candor to deny that these enforcement means were chosen precisely because they would simultaneously serve that other end.

§ 7.07 "Provisions Extraneous to Any Tax Need"

Admitting the applicability here of the generic principle discussed in § 4.05, however, does not mean that every regulatory provision tacked on to

§ 7.07 CONGRESS' POWER TO TAX 157

a bona fide revenue measure necessarily is valid. To reach that conclusion would be to disregard the "particularity" feature of the necessary and proper clause, as surely as to conclude that any activity "affecting interstate commerce" is subject to comprehensive regulation by Congress; see §§ 3.04 & 6.08. This was made plain enough in *Linder,* supra, 268 U.S. at 22, even though the opinion in that 1925 case unsurprisingly was encumbered by recitation of the erroneous old *McCulloch* dictum, see id. at 17. It is confirmed by the care taken in other cases to point out that various requirements sustained were "supportable as in aid of a revenue purpose," e.g. *Sonzinsky,* supra, 300 U.S. at 513. The contrary suggestion in one curious old forgotten case, Felsenheld v. U.S., 186 U.S. 126 (1902), deserves the obscurity it has attained.

An example will serve to illustrate the point. The National Firearms Act, as amended after *Haynes,* supra, to eliminate self incrimination objections, was upheld in U.S. v. Freed, 401 U.S. 601 (1971). That Act imposes a tax on transfers and other acts involving certain kinds of firearms; and it contains several regulatory provisions requiring disclosure of information about such taxable acts and the persons engaged in them. Insofar as any of those provisions serve the revenue purpose of the Act, they are supportable of course under the necessary and proper clause—and the fact that such disclosure might also assist local efforts against violent crime is constitutionally immaterial, see § 7.06. Among that Act's requirements, however, are some which received no particular attention in *Freed,* and which it seems difficult if not impossible to sustain.

There is, for example, a requirement that the photograph and fingerprints of the transferee of any such firearm be submitted to the government; and it is also required as a precondition to transfer that a certificate be submitted by which some local or federal law enforcement official attests that he is satisfied that the weapon to be transferred is intended for lawful uses. These particular provisions manifestly promote the objective of deterring violent crime; but that is merely an extraneous objective. There is no indication in the Act or its history, and indeed it is difficult to imagine, that these particular provisions serve any *revenue* objective. That being the case, the fact that they are included amongst valid "necessary and proper" provisions in a valid revenue measure can do nothing to render them constitutional.

Unfortunately, the fact that particular provisions contained in taxing measures might appear, when carefully considered, to be wholly without constitutional support, does not guarantee that they will not be judicially enforced. It takes perspicacious lawyers to recognize the fallacies and persuasively point them out. What can happen when lawyers (and thus judges) fail to notice them, is well illustrated by Minor v. U.S., 396 U.S. 87 (1969).

Minor had sold heroin, and was convicted under the provision of the Harrison Act prohibiting sales of narcotics except pursuant to the written order form prescribed by that Act. (The order form requirement, of course, is valid only as a means of enforcing the tax which the Harrison Act imposes on such transactions; see *Doremus* and *Nigro,* supra.) Minor objected that because other laws, both federal and state, make virtually all dealing (and certainly his dealing) in heroin criminal, the Harrison Act's requirement that he use a prescribed order form to be procured by the buyer, identifying the seller (as well as the buyer) and on which the seller was required to indicate the quantity sold and the date, violated the seller's privilege against self incrimination. The Supreme Court majority replied that the risk of self incrimination was only "imaginary and insubstantial" because no prospective heroin buyer could lawfully procure an order form for that drug, none would volunteer for prison by trying, and therefore no occasion for the seller to execute the form (with its incriminating disclosures) could ever actually arise.

But wait a minute! If it is certain that no heroin buyer would ever seek to procure such a form or present it to the seller for execution, what possible telic relation could a rational mind perceive between requiring the seller to utilize that form and collecting the tax on heroin sales? It's a very nice scheme for putting the lid on heroin sales, but it has nothing to do with enforcing the tax; and the

Harrison Act on its face, and as declared repeatedly by the Court, is nothing more than a taxing act! Thus the very same reasoning used to dispose of the self incrimination objection simultaneously destroyed the only possible constitutional basis supporting the order form requirement, for the violation of which Minor was convicted and packed off to jail! If Minor had no self incrimination defense, the Act's prohibition of heroin sales other than pursuant to the prescribed order form was utterly without constitutional basis!

The foregoing paragraphs have focused on the validity of "provisions extraneous to any tax need" on the assumption that the "tax" imposed by the law in which they appear is itself valid as a tax. The quoted phrase, however, is taken from a passage in the *Kahriger* majority opinion suggesting that the presence of such provisions might cast doubt on the validity of the entire measure—might support a conclusion that the so-called "tax" is not really a true tax at all. 345 U.S. at 31.

The significance of this suggestion should not be exaggerated; but neither should it be disregarded. As discussed in § 7.05, the distinction between true and sham taxes deserves more serious attention than it has received for some time; and the presence at least of several provisions which have no apparent revenue purpose—perhaps even the presence of several provisions whose arguable revenue purpose seems distinctly secondary to other, extraneous objectives—might be developed into a persuasive argument that Humpty Dumpty and the purveyors of verbal cellophane have been at work.

§ 7.08 Preemptive Capability and the Taxing Power

That Congress may promote extraneous ends with its taxing power, and even with means necessary and proper to revenue ends, does not mean that Congress' will for such extraneous matters necessarily must prevail. The limit of preemptive capability examined in Chapter Five applies here as well.

That a federal tax has been paid by no means precludes the imposition of a state tax on the very same activity. Moreover, the payment of the federal tax imposed on a given activity confers no authority to conduct that activity in the face of an otherwise valid prohibitory or regulatory state law. See License Tax Cases, 5 Wall. (72 U.S.) 462, 470–71 (1867). For the same reason, a federal tax designed to deter some extraneous activity could not supersede state policy encouraging or requiring that same activity. Of course the federal tax would have to be paid, however onerous it might be; but the duty of obedience to the applicable state law could not be escaped on the plea that the manifest federal will was to the contrary, so long as the matter involved was extraneous to the circle of legitimate federal concerns. The taxing power gives Congress power to tax almost anything; but the power to tax does not by itself make the matter taxed one of legitimate federal concern.

CHAPTER EIGHT

CONGRESS' SPENDING AND BORROWING POWERS

§ 8.01 Source of the Power to Spend

Expenses necessarily are incurred in the normal operations of any government. The Constitution expressly requires that "a Compensation" be paid to the President, federal judges, and members of Congress. It contemplates also the creation of subordinate government offices, which necessarily involve expenses for supplies and operating costs as well as salaries. Expenses must be incurred in connection with defense: Materiel procurements, personnel pay, and training and operations costs. Buildings and furnishings for government office and meeting facilities must be purchased, built, or rented. These are only a few of the most obvious examples.

The need to provide for these inevitable expenses of government and defense without depending on requisitions from the States (as had been done during the Confederation period) is of course the principal reason Congress was given the power to tax: Art. I, § 8, cl. 1 confers the taxing power "to pay the Debts and provide for the common Defence and general Welfare of the United States." The impossibility of anticipating with precision what

§ 8.01   *CONGRESS' BORROWING POWERS*   163

the scale of these expenses might be was given by the eminently practical Hamilton as the chief reason why Congress' taxing power should not be confined to particular revenue sources or otherwise restricted by the Constitution, but should be left to be controlled instead by the political process. See The Federalist, e.g. Nos. 30–32, 34–36.

Two other clauses affecting the spending power should be noted. Article I, § 9, cl. 7 provides that "[n]o Money shall be drawn from the Treasury, but in Consequence of Appropriations made by Law * * *." And because money (or Fiscal assets, tangible or intangible) are a form of property, it is relevant that Art. IV, § 3, cl. 2 provides, "Congress shall have Power to dispose of * * * the * * * property belonging to the United States * * *." Spending measures (unlike revenue measures, see Art. I, § 7, cl. 1) need not originate in the House of Representatives, but may originate in either the House or the Senate.

While the spending power always has been significant, its significance has increased dramatically in the twentieth century. The principal reason is that the income tax, which saw only occasional and temporary use before, has become a permanent and predominant federal revenue device. With increasing use of this highly efficient tax, readily adjusted in rate, it became possible for the first time for the government to generate revenue far in excess of what was needed to support the traditional operations of national governance and defense.

With excess revenue at its disposal, Congress soon discovered that it had a powerful instrument for expanding its influence in domestic affairs.

Today probably no power of Congress has more diverse and pervasive impacts than the spending power. Nonetheless, a clear understanding of some of the principles involved in the use of this power is emerging only now, in the 1980's.

§ 8.02 The "General Welfare" Limitation

Because the clause authorizing federal taxation and spending contains the phrase "general welfare," it sometimes induces reference to a so-called "general welfare power." But Congress has no "general welfare power." This "general welfare" phrase always has been construed (as grammar requires) in conjunction with the rest of the clause in which it appears: Congress may *tax and spend* "to * * * provide for the * * * general Welfare * * *," and to pay the nation's debts and provide for its defense. The clause certainly confers no general power to legislate in promotion of the general welfare. In *this* respect the holding in U.S. v. Butler, 297 U.S. 1, 64 (1936), is absolutely sound and reliable authority.

As a limitation on spending, however, the "general welfare" requirement is really quite insubstantial. It forbids spending federal funds for the peculiar benefit of a privileged few; spending must be for the *general,* not some *particular* welfare. But general benefit might derive from payments to

§ 8.02   *CONGRESS' BORROWING POWERS*   165

particular groups; good examples are the unemployed, local disaster victims, economically distressed farmers, and even hard-pressed corporations. Federal assistance, either as grants or as loans, to Chrysler Corp. or New York City, for example, might have beneficial consequences far beyond the immediate recipient, reaching substantial segments of the work force and the economy of the nation as a whole. Grants for airport improvement benefit not merely the recipient airport operators, but airline companies and their passengers, the thousands of businesses which depend on air travel for communication and transport, the aircraft industry and related construction trades, scores of thousands of affected workers, and so on. See H. Rep. 91–601, p. 6 (1969), quoted in DOT v. Paralyzed Veterans of America, 106 S.Ct. 2705 (1986).

The judiciary avoids second-guessing Congress' judgments as to what expenditures are for the "general welfare." "The discretion * * * is not confided to the courts. The discretion belongs to Congress, unless the choice is clearly wrong, a display of arbitrary power, not an exercise of judgment." Helvering v. Davis, 301 U.S. 619, 640 (1937). So long as the political process remains vigorous, it is hard to imagine that any appropriation sufficiently parochial to be invalidated under this standard ever could be enacted. Thus the "general welfare" limitation is not analogous at all to the "public purpose" limitation (or any other limitation) imposed by many *state* constitutions upon *state* expenditures. (For a recent discussion of some such state limitations, see Levy, "Constitutional Limitations on Appropriations," 11 UCLA–Alaska L. Rev. 189 (1982).)

While the phrase "general welfare" is a limitation on the spending power, at the same time it suggests very substantial breadth. Its companion phrase—"to pay the Debts and provide for the common Defence"—by contrast indicates some finite scope of spending objectives; but the phrase "to * * * provide for the * * * general Welfare of the United States" is distinctly open-ended.

One consequently may forgive the technical inaccuracy of the per curiam assertion in Buckley v. Valeo, 424 U.S. 1, 90 (1976), that it is "erroneous" to "treat[ ] the General Welfare Clause as a limitation upon congressional power. It is rather a grant of power, the scope of which is quite expansive." The truth is that the general welfare *phrase,* in what *ought not* to be called the "General Welfare Clause," is *both* an (insubstantial) limitation *and* an expansive enhancement of Congress' spending power.

Unsurprisingly, there has been some disagreement over the variety of objectives which Congress may use its spending power to promote.

§ 8.03 The Classic Dispute Over the Spending Power: Madison, Hamilton, and Monroe

James Madison, as President from 1809 to 1817, maintained that Congress could spend only to effectuate the various other enumerated federal powers. In effect, on this view there really is no *independent* spending power; instead, the authorization to spend is reduced to no more than a fiscal "necessary and proper clause"—and Madison adopted Jefferson's miserly view of the latter, discussed in § 3.02. Therefore he vetoed the so-called "Bonus Bill" of 1817, which proposed to use federal receipts from the second Bank of the United States to construct roads and canals and other internal improvements. Such projects, he believed, were not within the scope of any enumerated power, nor justifiable under his narrow view of the necessary and proper clause; federal spending for such ends he thought therefore unconstitutional.

A contrary view had been maintained by Alexander Hamilton. In his 1791 Report on Manufactures, prepared when he was Secretary of the Treasury, Hamilton had urged government subsidization of fledgling industries. He argued that the power to spend was independent of the other enumerated powers, and that the phrase "general welfare" was deliberately chosen

> because this necessarily embraces a vast variety of particulars which are susceptible neither of specification nor of definition. It is, therefore, of necessity left to the discretion of the national legislature to pronounce upon the objects which concern the general welfare, and for which, under that description, an appropriation of money is requisite and proper. And there seems no room for a doubt that, whatever concerns the general interests of learning, of agriculture, or

manufactures, and of commerce, are within the sphere of the national councils, *so far as regards an application of money.*

(Emphasis in original.) Joseph Story, in his 1833 Commentaries on the Constitution, pointed out that Congress had acted repeatedly on the Hamiltonian premise during the Washington administration, and even (despite some ideological misgivings) under President Jefferson—spending money for humanitarian relief, to subsidize fisheries, to promote education, manufacturing, agriculture, commerce, and navigation, and even to fund the commencement of construction on the Cumberland Road in 1806.

James Monroe, who succeeded Madison as President, confessed that he earlier had shared Madison's view, but that "on further reflection and observation my mind has undergone a change * * *." Although still Jeffersonian in other respects, Monroe had become a convert to Hamilton's view of the spending power. It therefore is particularly enlightening to study the reasons he gave for vetoing the ambitious Cumberland Road bill of 1822: Richardson, Messages and Papers of the Presidents 144–83 (1896).

As Monroe viewed it, that bill contemplated more than the expenditure of money to pay costs of building the road. It would necessarily entail selection and survey of a route, condemnation of the needed land when owners refused to sell, permanent crews for toll collection, maintenance, and repair, enforcement of sanctions to deter and punish vandals, and other measures beyond the mere spending of money. Monroe's position was that the power to spend entails no such "incidental power * * *. All that Congress could do under [the spending power] in the case of internal improvements would be to appropriate the money necessary to make them."

That was exactly Hamilton's view: In his Report on Manufactures Hamilton had said only that Congress could promote learning, agriculture, and all manner of other things

> *so far as regards an application of money.* * * * No objection ought to arise to this construction from a supposition that it would imply a power to do whatever else should appear to Congress conducive to the general welfare. A power to *appropriate money* with this latitude, which is granted in express terms, would not carry a power to do any other thing not authorized in the Constitution * * *.

(Emphasis in original.)

Hamilton probably would have approved the *non*-spending features of the Cumberland Road Bill on necessary and proper clause grounds, as facilitating movement of troops and war materiel, the mails, and articles of interstate commerce; Monroe could not do so because of his narrow, Jeffersonian view of the necessary and proper clause. So far as the *spending power alone* was concerned, however, Monroe's and Hamilton's views were the same;

and it is very important to recognize this, lest the Hamiltonian view be misunderstood.

The reader should have perceived from the foregoing discussion that (in contrast to Madison) Monroe and Hamilton agreed that Congress' spending power may be employed on the pattern of Figure 5 in § 4.01, supra. Monroe's veto, like Hamilton's caveat, was based on a recognition that reasoning on the pattern of Figure 7 in § 4.06 supra, is fallacious. Only his attachment to the miserly, Jeffersonian view of the necessary and proper clause (which disallowed such "filliations of necessities" as are illustrated by Figure 3 in § 3.02) prevented Monroe from seeing the Cumberland Road Bill (as Hamilton probably would have) as valid on the pattern of Figure 10 in § 4.06.

§ 8.04 The Dim Dawning of Awareness: *Butler* and the Social Security Act Cases

As the foregoing discussion suggests, the spending power was probably the first of Congress' powers routinely and regularly to be used as a means to extraneous ends, illustrating the generic concept examined in Chapter Four. So long as the validity and generic nature of that concept remained obscured, however, there were not only instances of its repudiation (as illustrated by Madison's veto of the Bonus Bill), but also curious instances of conceptual confusion in judicial decision.

The classic case of judicial confusion regarding the spending power is *Butler,* supra, decided in

1936. There in unequivocal terms the court verbally repudiated the Madisonian view and endorsed the view of Hamilton (and of Story). Anomalously, however, the view thus verbally endorsed did not actually control the *Butler* decision. Instead, while purporting to reject Madison's view that spending may only effectuate the other enumerated powers, the *Butler* Court held that the spending power is limited by the reserved powers of the states. 297 U.S. at 68.

But the doctrines of enumerated federal powers and reserved state powers are merely two sides of the same coin: All that can be said to be reserved to the states is what has not been delegated to the nation. And in 1936 the Court still was mired in "dual federalism;" thus it took this proposition to mean that the state and federal governments occupy mutually exclusive spheres. Consequently, in a curious feat of intellectual onanism (see Gen. 38:9), the *Butler* Court endorsed the Hamiltonian view until it came to the climax of decision, then suddenly backed off and applied the Madisonian view.

This fault was corrected the next year; and since then the Court has applied the Hamiltonian view consistently, even though its full implications often have been obscured. Anyone who credulously follows the rationalizations offered by Justice Cardozo to reconcile the 1937 Social Security Act decisions with *Butler,* however, must certainly finish bewildered. Cardozo's majority opinions in Chas. C. Steward Machine Co. v. Davis, 301 U.S. 548 (1937), and Helvering v. Davis, 301 U.S. 619 (1937), do contain several memorable passages important both because they are concise expressions of certain valid principles and because they are frequently quoted. These opinions, however, also contain some totally inappropriate and unsupportable language suggesting restrictions on the spending power which simply do not exist; and the distinctions which Cardozo offered as supposedly reconciling *Steward* with the outcome in *Butler,* 301 U.S. at 592–93, have absolutely no validity at all. Those distinctions, and the unsupportable restricting caveats, might have seemed cogent enough to one or two of the Justices to persuade them to join the *Butler* dissenters and so constitute the new majority emerging in the 1937 decisions; but in fact *none* of the Justices in 1937 clearly understood (or at least correctly articulated) the concept to which they really were giving effect.

The concept which Hamilton had applied to the spending power, and for which the holdings (not the opinions) in *Steward* and *Helvering* really stand, is simply that enumerated powers may be used to promote extraneous ends; see Chapter Four. In 1937, of course, that proposition still was vehemently denounced whenever it was openly stated—even though it was being applied in the context not only of the spending power, but of others; see, e.g., U.S. v. San Francisco, 310 U.S. 16 (1940); U.S. v. Appalachian Electric Power Co., 311 U.S. 377 (1940). It was finally openly acknowl-

§ 8.04   CONGRESS' BORROWING POWERS   173

edged as a sound and fundamental generic principle only in 1941, in U.S. v. Darby, 312 U.S. 100, 114–17, as discussed in § 4.04 supra.

Consequently when *Steward, Helvering,* and even *Butler* are used today as authority on Congress' spending power, it must not be assumed that the real meaning of those decisions can be discovered by reading the opinions themselves. The principle which justifies federal spending toward extraneous ends is the generic concept much more clearly articulated in the particular passage in *Darby* here cited—312 U.S. at 114–17. *Darby* is thus the most fitting authority to cite—even though citing that so-called "commerce power" case in a spending power context, absent the foregoing explanation, might seem anomalous to lawyers poorly schooled in organic constitutional theory.

The Hamiltonian view of the spending power is just one more application of the generic concept examined in Chapter Four, which tardily received its judicial imprimatur in *Darby.* The caveats and suggestions of possible limitations contained in certain passages of the *Steward* and *Helvering* opinions must therefore be dismissed as misconceived dicta, attributable to the fact that, when they were written, even the most perceptive of the Justices still were wrestling for a grip on that elusive generic concept, which they did not firmly secure until *Darby* in 1941.

§ 8.05 Modern Use of the Spending Power to Promote Extraneous Ends

With the populace now (grudgingly) accustomed to heavy federal utilization of that very efficient revenue device, the income tax, state and local efforts to raise revenue have borne the brunt of popular resistance to the onerous accumulation of tax burdens. Thus disabled as a practical matter to raise locally enough revenue to fund services which the public demands, state and local governments have become increasingly dependent on federal financial aid. Decades of government financing on this pattern have contributed to a troubling federal deficit, since demands (and political incentives for their generous satisfaction) have outstripped even the federal revenue supply; and it is possible that during the next decade or two political reaction will produce significant change. As of this date, however, the practice of federal funding—begun on a large scale during the New Deal and multiplied in magnitude particularly during the 1960's, remains a very prominent feature of American government.

This practical dependence upon federal funding has put Congress in the position of being able to influence, and often practically to control, the policies of recipient state and local governments and institutions, as well as private recipients of federal funds, with respect to all manner of activities extraneous to legitimate federal concerns; for having absolute discretion over the expenditure of federal

§ 8.05 *CONGRESS' BORROWING POWERS* 177

ria to be satisfied before spending conditions can be held valid, e.g., South Dakota v. Adams, 506 F.Supp. 50 (D.S.D. 1980), only show that the principle still is not universally understood.

Occasionally even the Supreme Court has stated the rule with unwarranted reservations, as for example that "the Federal Government may * * * impose reasonable conditions relevant to federal interest * * *." Ivanhoe Irrig. Dist. v. McCracken, 357 U.S. 275, 295 (1958). In reality there is no requirement of "reasonableness" (unless some *due process* objection could be raised against extreme arbitrariness), and there is no requirement of relevance to "federal interest" at all. See, e.g., Oklahoma v. U.S. Civil Service Comm'n, 330 U.S. 127 (1947), which upheld the conditioning of highway funds upon compliance by state employees with federal rules restricting partisan political activities. (Political partisanship of state employees is no legitimate concern whatever of the federal government.) See also U.S. v. Appalachian Elec. Power Co., 311 U.S. 377 (1940).

Examples of extraneous conditions attached to federal procurement or grant funds are legion. Desegregation conditions are attached to school aid and other grants; minority hire or other affirmative action requirements are attached to procurement and other government contracts; a myriad of conditions, some concerning administrative details and others with social objectives, are attached to federal funds supporting state welfare and unemployment compensation programs; conditions regarding privacy and disclosure of student records are attached to financial aid to public and private educational institutions; wage and price guidelines, small business participation requirements, and age anti-discrimination requirements condition eligibility for procurement contracts; sex and handicap anti-discrimination conditions accompany all manner of grants and procurement contracts. Scores of additional examples easily could be listed.

Overzealous executive branch elaboration of such conditions might exceed statutory authority; see, e.g., Grove City College v. Bell, 465 U.S. 555 (1984); U.S. Dept. of Transp. v. Paralyzed Veterans of America, 106 S.Ct. 2705 (1986). Questions regarding delegation and delegability of legislative power in this regard might be raised; see, e.g., AFL & CIO v. Kahn, 618 F.2d 784 (D.C.Cir.1979), cert. denied, 443 U.S. 915 (1979). The practical burdens and even dysfunctions entailed by elaborate conditions might be decried; see, e.g., former Yale President Brewster, "Does the Constitution Care About Coercive Federal Funding?" 34 Case W. Res. L. Rev. 1 (1983); Congressman Gribbs, "The New Federalism Is Here To Stay," 552 J. Urban L. 55, 56–57 (1974). But the fact is that, when Congress does indeed impose or authorize extraneous conditions to the disbursement of federal funds, the Constitution does *not* care—unless delegability limits or Bill of Rights-type limitations (both beyond the scope of this book) are offended, or unless the concept of "state immunity" (see §§ 14.05–14.06) is applied. It would be just as permissible for Congress to condition federal highway grants on states' enactment of statutory or state constitutional provisions equivalent to the long debated Equal Rights Amendment as it is to condition such grants on states' enforcement of a 55 mph speed limit or highway beautification standards. In sum, the merits of any conditions which might be attached to disbursement of federal funds are matters for debate and decision in the political forum, with no material constitutional restraint.

§ 8.06 Preemptive Capability and the Spending Power

The spending power is an enumerated power; thus by virtue of the supremacy clause no state may interfere with Congress' exercise of that power itself. This means that federal funds may be tendered for whatever purpose and on whatever terms Congress might choose, without regard to state law, no state being competent to change the conditions or to force a funds transfer if, in federal eyes, those conditions are not met.

In addition, that small class of measures viewable as "necessary and proper" to effectuate the spending power itself, see § 8.09—as distinguished from effectuating ends at which the spending might be aimed—also certainly have preemptive capability. This is one reason why "[t]he rights and duties of the United States on commercial paper which it issues are governed by federal rather than local law." Clearfield Trust Co. v. U.S., 318 U.S. 363, 366 (1943).

Moreover, insofar as spending is utilized to effectuate some objective within the circle of legitimate federal concerns (cf. Figure 13 in § 7.04, supra), Congress obviously is capable of preempting any state law interfering with accomplishment of that legitimate objective.

However, insofar as Congress tries to promote an *extraneous* objective by means of its spending power, states retain their own power over that extraneous matter unencumbered, and may exercise their power even if in doing so they frustrate or interfere with the federal government's will for that matter. This is merely the application in the spending power context of the generic concept discussed in Chapter Five.

While Congress has complete power over the terms on which federal money will be offered, it is powerless to compel acceptance. (There is one exception to this powerlessness, which may be illustrated with an example: Congress surely could compel a reluctant manufacturer to accept a procurement contract for war materiel, *by virtue of its necessary and proper power* in conjunction with its powers to support and maintain the armed forces.)

Consequently, where a state (or state subdivision or institution) is the prospective grantee the extraneous federal purpose "may be effectively frustrated by the simple expedient of not yielding." Massachusetts v. Mellon, 262 U.S. 447, 482 (1923). See

§ 8.06 *CONGRESS' BORROWING POWERS* 181

also King v. Smith, 392 U.S. 309, 316 (1968); Oklahoma v. U.S. Civil Service Comm'n, 330 U.S. 127 (1947). See generally § 5.06. The fact that economic realities—such as the fiscal incapacity of the states to fund needed programs on their own— might make the temptation to accept federal aid practically irresistible is irrelevant constitutionally; legally, the state is quite free to forego the federal funds and flout the extraneous federal objectives at which the funding conditions are aimed.

The same principle holds where a private person or entity, rather than a state, is the prospective grantee. While a state may not alter the terms of the federal offer, it may regulate any entity over which it has jurisdiction in ways that will render it ineligible, or prevent its fulfillment of the federally prescribed conditions. This is because, so long as the matter in question is extraneous to the circle of legitimate federal concerns (and so long as a situation like that illustrated by Figure 11 in § 5.07 is not involved), the federal policy with which it is trying to "buy compliance" simply lacks preemptive capability, as discussed in Chapter Five. A recipient could not excuse his violation of state law on the ground that he acted in fulfillment of a requirement imposed as a condition to the federal grant, even though it was lawful thus to condition the grant; unless he could secure federal waiver of that condition, his only lawful alternative would be to forego the grant. See § 5.06.

This of course is the very proposition the Supreme Court denounced as "plainly fallacious" in its 1936 *Butler* opinion. See § 5.05. Its reasoning there was that

> The United States can make the [grant] contract [with a farmer under the AAA] only if the federal power * * * to appropriate reaches the subject matter of the contract. If this does reach the subject matter, its exertion cannot be displaced by state action. To say otherwise is to deny the supremacy of the laws of the United States * * *.

297 U.S. at 74. But this reasoning reflects the erroneous view that some "subject matters" *cannot* be "reached" by the spending power for the reason that they are within the states' reserved powers; and that, of course, is the erroneous "dual federalism" pie-slice view.

Now, after the Social Security Act cases and the recognition in *Darby* of the generic concept which they illustrate (see § 8.04), it is clear that the spending power can "reach" *every* conceivable subject matter, *in the sense* that federal spending may be used to promote even extraneous ends. The supremacy clause cannot apply to everything the spending power might "reach" *in this sense.* See § 5.05, supra. Thus, once one escapes the quagmire of erroneous "dual federalism" thought, it becomes apparent that it was the *Butler* Court's rejection of this argument, and not the argument rejected, which was "plainly fallacious."

Bearing in mind the limit of preemptive capability, it is easy to recognize as an uncritical overstatement the Court's suggestion in U.S. v. Gerlach Live Stock Co., 339 U.S. 725, 738 (1950), that since *Butler* and the 1937 Social Security Act cases "the power of Congress to promote the general welfare through large-scale projects for reclamation, irrigation, or other internal improvement, is now as clear *and ample* as its power to accomplish the same results indirectly through resort to strained interpretation of the power over navigation." (Emphasis added.) The facts of *Gerlach* did not really test whether the spending power could be *as ample* for such ends as the power Congress has come to have over navigable waters. If they had, the overstatement should have become apparent: Given the peculiarities of doctrine regarding navigable waters, according to which any measure concerning them is regarded as an exercise of the commerce power itself (see §§ 6.10 & 6.11, supra), Congress' action under *that* guise enjoys preemptive capability, and therefore certainly is *more ample* to accomplish the federal government's will.

There is nothing novel in the proposition that if *only* the spending power is employed and the objective is extraneous to the circle of legitimate federal concerns, actual accomplishment of that objective is dependent upon state acquiescence or cooperation. This is the proposition which underlay President Madison's veto of the Cumberland Road Bill, and was implicit in Hamilton's 1791 observation that Congress could promote extraneous ends with the spending power only "*so far as regards an application of money*." See § 8.03, supra. Over the years, Supreme Court recognition of this principle has come and gone; but the sound constitutional principle never has changed.

Indeed, the principle seemed still lost to the Justices well into the 1970's; and some confusion about it lingers still. Cardozo had seriously clouded the principle with a passage in *Helvering* citing the supremacy clause as support for his statement that when federal "money is spent to promote the general welfare, the concept of welfare or the opposite is shaped by Congress, not the States." 301 U.S. at 645. If it could be understood merely as affirming that no state may second-guess Congress as to whether the "general welfare" limitation of the spending power (see § 8.02) has been satisfied, Cardozo's statement would be unobjectionable. The problem is that, in its full context, the statement virtually begs to be taken as an assertion that Congress' policy, to promote which it exercises the spending power, ipso facto prevails even though it pertain to a matter (like old age benefits) which itself is wholly outside the circle of legitimate federal concerns. Cardozo's hypothetical analogy to a state's laissez faire policy clashing with a federal scheme of protective tariffs (301 U.S. at 645) was wholly inapt; for assessment and collection of tariffs is the raising of revenue by taxation—a matter of legitimate federal concern—and moreover (as if any further basis for preemptive capability were needed) has as its non-revenue objective the regulation of international commerce, also a matter of legitimate federal concern.

Following the lead of so lustrous a predecessor, modern Justices until very recently tended to discuss differences between federal grant conditions and recipient states' laws in terms of preemption, a function of the supremacy clause. See, e.g., New York Dept. of Soc. Services v. Dublino, 413 U.S. 405 (1973); Philpott v. Essex Co. Welfare Bd., 409 U.S. 413 (1973); Carleson v. Remillard, 406 U.S. 598 (1972). Some still do: See, e.g., Brennan (with Marshall, Blackmun, and Stevens), dissenting in Green v. Mansour, 106 S.Ct. 423, 430 (1985). Only within the past decade or less has the correct manner of framing such issues become evident in Supreme Court majority opinions—as cases discussed in the following section will show.

§ 8.07 Congress' Power Over Recipients: The Contractual Character of Spending Conditions

The power to subsidize entails, of its own force, no power whatever to regulate that which is subsidized. There is an often repeated statement in Wickard v. Filburn, 317 U.S. 111, 131 (1942), that "[i]t is hardly lack of due process for the Government to regulate that which it subsidizes." That may be true; but the statement is addressed only to the due process issue and says nothing at all about the legal *basis* of the federal government's power. (The regulations in *Wickard* were supported by the necessary and proper clause in conjunction with the commerce power, see §§ 3.04 & 3.11, supra.) To take such a statement as authority for federal regulation of a matter grounded *only* on the fact of federal financial support would be to fall victim to the bootstrap error illustrated by Figure 7 in § 4.06, supra.

The control which Congress acquires over recipients of federal funds is not a function of constitutional law; it is rather a function of contract law. Whether identifiable contract documents are involved or not (and they usually are), by accepting federal funds which are offered on specified conditions a recipient binds itself contractually to comply with those conditions. Concepts of contract law having nothing to do with the supremacy clause are therefore the basis for—and fix the limits of—such power as the federal government might have over federal funds recipients not founded on any basis other than the spending power.

It is only in the 1980's, however, that the Supreme Court has begun clearly to realize this. " * * * Congress enters into an arrangement in the nature of a contract with the recipients of the funds: the recipient's acceptance of the funds triggers coverage under" the attendant conditions. U.S. Dept. of Transp. v. Paralyzed Veterans of America, 106 S.Ct. 2705, 2711 (1986). A handicap anti-discrimination condition attending grants to airport operators therefore could not be enforced against airlines using the improved airport facilities, because although substantially benefitted they were not the recipients contractually bound. A college which avoided all other participation but did certify applicant students to the Department of Education in order to qualify them for federal assistance which would enable them to pay the costs of attending that school had done enough to bind it contractually to comply with the conditions accompanying that indirect financial aid. Grove City College v. Bell, 465 U.S. 555 (1984).

Because of the contractual character of the obligation, however, purported conditions will not be enforced against a recipient unless "Congress spoke so clearly that we can fairly say that the [recipient] State could make an informed choice" and "knowingly decide whether or not to accept those funds" with their attendant conditions. Pennhurst State School & Hosp. v. Halderman, 451 U.S. 1, 24–5 (1981). Congress may attach "unambiguous conditions to federal financial assistance that [recipient] educational institutions are not obliged to accept;" but conditioning language sufficient only to forewarn that a relatively *limited* obligation might be incurred by acceptance will not be construed to entail more *sweeping* obligations—however noble the cause—which the recipient reasonably should not have been expected to anticipate. *Grove City College,* supra.

"Congress' power to legislate under the spending power * * * does not include surprising participating States [or other recipients] with postacceptance or 'retroactive' conditions." *Pennhurst,* supra, 451 U.S. at 25. Compliance with specified conditions is demanded of federal contractors and grantees "as a quid pro quo for the receipt of federal funds." Consolidated Rail Corp. v. Darrone, 465 U.S. 624, 633 n. 13 (1984). Congress can impose such requirements, otherwise beyond its power to enforce, only "upon those who are in a position to accept or reject those obligations as a part of the decision whether or not to 'receive' federal funds." *U.S. Dept. of Transp.,* supra, 106 S.Ct. at 2711.

No doubt additional implications of this newly rediscovered fact that the obligation of extraneous funding conditions is contractual rather than constitutional in character will emerge as intelligent and enlightened lawyers pursue their work. What might be made of arguable inequalities of bargaining power? Is there room for application of some "adhesion" contract principles? Where the potential or actual costs of compliance with obligations incurred are out of all proportion to the recipient's gain, is there room for some form of unconscionability argument? What more might be required in terms of clarity and cost delimitation to ensure that the recipient's obligations are knowingly incurred? Are there prerogatives which, even in dealing with the federal government, states or their subordinate entities might be held incompetent to "bargain away?" The answers to these and other questions affecting future use of the spending power will be developed through the imagination and industry of lawyers participating to influence judicial decision in cases yet to come.

§ 8.08 Enforcement of Spending Conditions

If a prospective contractor or grantee fails to satisfy the conditions prerequisite to a contract, loan, or grant, obviously it may be witheld. In the event of a breach after conferral, the government should be able to terminate the arrangement, or if it were otherwise renewable, decline to renew it. Depending upon the terms of the bargain, it might even be possible to enforce repayment, or some stipulated penalty.

Given the fact that many years of multi-billion dollar federal funding programs now have induced state and local government agencies and public and private educational institutions, for example, to render themselves heavily dependent upon federal financial aid, funding cut-offs and demands for repayment ordinarily are too Draconian to appear acceptable even to federal agencies intent on enforcing compliance. Much more common, therefore, have been comparatively modest administrative sanctions provided for under particular aid programs, and declaratory or injunctive judicial proceedings initiated against recipients by an appropriate federal agency.

The most interesting conditions accompanying federal spending programs, however, impose on recipients obligations designed for the benefit of third parties. Some of these are obligations which Congress has adequate power under the Constitution to enforce *independently* of funding sanctions, such as elimination of racial discrimination where state action is involved; but that by no means is true of them all.

Examples of obligations for the benefit of third parties which Congress might not otherwise be able to impose include elaborate beneficiary eligibility requirements accompanying federal funding of state welfare aid programs; minority contractor and affirmative action requirements accompanying procurement contracts and construction grants; student record privacy restrictions accompanying grants to educational institutions; and blanket provisions—accompanying much or all federal funding—prohibiting discrimination on the basis of age, marital status, sex, handicap, religion, or nationality. Unless, and except to the extent that, such bases of discrimination as sex, handicap, and nationality might be (or might come to be) regarded as violations of "equal protection" when state action is involved, all of these obligations rest only on contract.

That being the case, questions naturally arise as to what, if any, rights to enforce those conditions against funds recipients might be reposed in the third-party beneficiaries themselves.

Where the recipient of federal funds is a *private* entity, material questions of statutory construction might be involved but there certainly is no *constitutional* barrier to third-party enforcement, even by suits for damages. See, e.g., Consolidated Rail Corp. v. Darrone, 465 U.S. 624 (1984); Cannon v. University of Chicago, 441 U.S. 677 (1979).

Where the recipient is a state or state agency, however, constitutional problems are involved as a result of several facets of the tradition of state immunity from suit. (This must not be confused with the concept of "state immunity" to be discussed in §§ 14.05 & 14.06.)

Although it is anomalous in a republican polity, most states have claimed for themselves (with or without certain exceptions) the "sovereign immunity" from suit in *their own* courts which has its origin in feudal England. In the nation's earliest years, when the impecunious states were unable to afford payment of their debts, that doctrine served to protect them from collection suits; for out of comity toward one another, states normally would not entertain suits against their sister states. The new Constitution, however, gave *federal* courts jurisdiction over states as parties, and thus gave to creditors qualifying under the diversity terms of Article III (although not to a state's own citizens) a forum where they could sue for collection of such debts. To undo this, the narrowly crafted eleventh amendment was rapidly adopted. Its specific purpose was to preclude suits based upon state law brought by out-of-state creditors. No rights based on *federal* law and assertable against states as defendants existed at that time.

A century later, however, after the Reconstruction Amendments had provided significant grounds for *federal question* claims against states, the Supreme Court extrapolated far beyond the careful words of the eleventh amendment and denied jurisdiction over *any* suit brought against a state (unless the state had consented to suit in a federal forum)—even though brought by the state's own citizens, and even though based upon federal law. Hans v. Louisiana, 134 U.S. 1 (1890).

Several years later, by a fiction pretending that suits brought against state officials for their official actions are materially distinguishable from suits against a state itself, some possibility for federal court redress of state wrongs was restored in Ex parte Young, 209 U.S. 123 (1908). Under the *Young* doctrine, federal courts entertain suits seeking prospective declaratory or injunctive relief against state government officials for acts done illegally in their official capacity. The prospective relief given in such cases has no effect on the official personally; it governs only his acts as an official of the state, and thus has the same effect as if the state or state agency were named as defendant.

Using this silly fiction, made necessary only because of the Supreme Court's distortion of the eleventh amendment, third party beneficiary suits seeking prospective enforcement of federal funding conditions have been allowed for many years. See, e.g., Townsend v. Swank, 404 U.S. 282 (1971); California Dept. of Human Res. v. Java, 402 U.S. 121 (1971); Rosado v. Wyman, 397 U.S. 397 (1970); King v. Smith, 392 U.S. 309 (1968). However, the Supreme Court has refused to apply the *Young* fiction to allow third-party beneficiary suits for *retrospective* or *dollar* relief, whether in the nature of law or equity, because the obvious fact that any money judgment in such a case would be paid out of the state treasury has seemed too inconsistent with *Hans.* See, e.g., Edelman v. Jordan, 415 U.S. 651 (1974). As of the retirement of Chief Justice Burger, a bare majority still adhered to this view. See Green v. Mansour, 106 S.Ct. 423 (1985); Atascadero State Hosp. v. Scanlon, 105 S.Ct. 3142 (1985); see also Papasan v. Allain, 106 S.Ct. 2932 (1986).

Of course the immunity of the states against suit in federal courts may be waived; but merely participating in a federal funding program will not be regarded as a waiver. *Edelman,* supra, 415 U.S. at 673; *Atascadero,* supra, 105 S.Ct. at 3149. Congress could demand such waiver as a condition of eligibility for states; but the majority held in *Atascadero,* supra, that such a waiver would not be recognized unless the statute authorizing the federal assistance "manifest[s] a clear intent to condition participation * * * on a State's consent to waive its constitutional immunity."

This stringent requirement of explicit specificity applies, according to *Atascadero,* even when the funding condition is used as a device for enforcing the substantive guarantees of the fourteenth amendment, essentially on the pattern of Figure 10 in § 4.06, supra. (This is quite ironic, for the Court has allowed Congress much more freely to authorize federal courts to entertain suits and grant monetary relief against states as a means of enforcing that amendment where *no* financial assistance is involved, see Fitzpatrick v. Bitzer, 427 U.S. 445 (1976).) Assuming for the sake of argument (without holding) that the handicap anti-discrimination conditions attached to federal funding by the 1973 Rehabilitation Act might be viewed as enforcing the equal protection clause, the *Atascadero* majority insisted that Congress' intent to make state amenability to suit in federal courts a condition to federal assistance must be declared "specifically" and "unequivocally" in "unmistakable language in the statute itself." 105 S.Ct. at 3148.

The four dissenting Justices in *Atascadero,* however, mounted a frontal assault against the whole hundred year tradition of exaggerated state immunity from suit originated in *Hans*—an assault supported by a substantial body of critical scholarship. See 105 S.Ct. at 3151 n. 11. They reiterated their resolute dedication to this assault in *Green,* supra, and again in *Papasan,* supra (Brennan, joined by Marshall, Blackmun, & Stevens in each case). With one member of the *Atascadero* majority now

§ 8.08 *CONGRESS' BORROWING POWERS* 195

retired, a marked change facilitating third-party beneficiary suits against recipient states and state agencies themselves seems a real possibility for the near future.

Another avenue for third-party beneficiary enforcement of funding conditions has been suggested; but it cannot survive critical reflection. Relief for certain wrongful acts done under color of state law is available under 42 U.S.C. § 1983. Liability under § 1983 is *personal,* even where the person acts as a state official. Moreover, the "persons" potentially liable under § 1983 include municipalities and many local and state government agencies (even though technically not the states themselves). Monell v. Department of Soc. Services, 436 U.S. 658 (1978); Owen v. Independence, 445 U.S. 622 (1980). Because the liability is deemed "personal" (even where the "person" is a municipality or a local or state agency), § 1983 suits do not confront the *Hans* barrier even when compensatory or other dollar relief is sought. (However, exemplary damages against a municipality are not allowed; see Newport v. Facts Concerts, Inc., 453 U.S. 247 (1981).)

Traditionally § 1983 had been invoked only for alleged *constitutional* violations; but in 1980 a divided Court held that it is available for alleged violations of federal *statutes* as well. Maine v. Thiboutot, 448 U.S. 1 (1980). Even if this construction of § 1983 endures, however, there is reason to doubt that it will support claims by third-party beneficiaries of federally funded municipal or state agency programs.

This reason for doubt persists even though *Thiboutot* itself was a case of exactly that kind, the plaintiffs seeking dollar recovery for a state agency's non-compliance with requirements it had accepted as conditions of federal funding. For while such funding conditions are set forth in the *form* of law (statutes and administrative regulations), they are obligatory on recipient entities not as "law" at all, but only by virtue of contract. Given that the Court *since* 1980 has begun more clearly to recognize the merely *contractual* nature of funding conditions, *Thiboutot* on its facts now is likely to be recognized as a case falling outside the scope of its own declaration that § 1983 gives a private cause of action for deprivations of rights or privileges secured by federal *laws.*

Furthermore, as applied to federal spending programs it can be argued that *Thiboutot* "surpris[ed] participating States with postacceptance or 'retroactive' conditions"—something which the Court a year later, in *Pennhurst,* supra, held may not be done. The *Pennhurst* majority (albeit in dictum) even recited several reasons to doubt the feasibility of third-party program beneficiary actions under § 1983. 451 U.S. at 27–30.

Third-party enforcement suits against states themselves—if the *Hans* barrier were removed—should not face the problem presented for § 1983 suits by the distinction between rights secured by contract and those secured by law. Although it is contract rather than federal "law" that secures them, the determination and application of rights under federal contracts present federal questions, cf. Clearfield Trust Co. v. U.S., 318 U.S. 363 (1943); thus third-party actions to enforce federal grant or contract obligations should be regarded as "arising under" the "laws" of the United States for the *jurisdictional* purposes of both Article III and 28 U.S.C. § 1331.

§ 8.09 The Necessary and Proper Clause and Spending

Certainly the generic concept of the necessary and proper clause must apply in the context of the spending power no less than in connection with any other enumerated federal power. That concept is applicable, however, only insofar as there is a telic relation to some matter *within* the circle of legitimate federal concerns. This means that Congress may pass laws to facilitate the process of spending; but it does *not* mean that Congress may pass laws to ensure that any *extraneous end* toward which its spending might be aimed will be achieved.

Of course this is no different from what has been observed regarding the necessary and proper clause in other contexts. See § 5.03. There is less occasion for proper application of the necessary and proper clause in connection with spending, however, because compared with most of the other federal powers the mere act of "spending" (or more precisely, "tendering" or offering to spend, since the spending power itself imports no power to compel acceptance, and the money will not be "spent" unless someone accepts it) is extremely simple. There is less involved in doing it; and consequently there is less that can be done to facilitate doing it. Commercial paper may be used as an instrument of disbursement, and therefore defining the rights and liabilities of parties on such paper (see the discussion of *Clearfield Trust* in § 8.06) is to that extent a means to effectuate the spending power. Other illustrations, however, are difficult to find.

Because the necessary and proper clause—so significant elsewhere—has so little proper application here, it is particularly easy in the spending power context to slip into the bootstrap error illustrated by Figure 7 in § 4.06.

Buckley v. Valeo, 424 U.S. 1 (1976), provides a recent example. Discussing provisions authorizing payments to help finance political party conventions and campaigns, the Court there observed per curiam that the scope of Congress' spending power

> is quite expansive, particularly in view of the enlargement of power by the Necessary and Proper Clause. *McCulloch v. Maryland,* 4 Wheat. 316, 420 (1819). * * * Congress has concluded that the [spending] means are "necessary and proper" to promote the general welfare * * *.

§ 8.10   *CONGRESS' BORROWING POWERS*   199

424 U.S. at 90–91. If all the Court meant in this curious passage were that Congress' power to spend "is not limited by the direct grants of legislative power found in the Constitution"—the Hamiltonian thesis quoted from *Butler* in the same passage of the *Buckley* opinion—all reference to the necessary and proper clause would have been superfluous. In context, the quoted sentences seem to indicate rather that the Justices conceived of that clause as giving general power to promote an *extraneous end* with measures "necessary and proper" thereto, merely because that end was being promoted in part by spending. If that *is* what the Justices thought, of course, they were plainly mistaken.

On the other hand, one could take this passage in *Buckley* as based wholly on the premise that (as the Court also said) "Congress has power to regulate Presidential elections and primaries," 424 U.S. at 90. On that premise as well, however, any reference to the necessary and proper clause would have been superfluous; for without any assistance at all from *that* clause, Congress may spend as it pleases to promote ends within its constitutional powers—just as surely as to promote extraneous ends.

§ 8.10 The Source and Uses of Congress' Borrowing Power

Article I, § 8, cl. 2 authorizes Congress "[t]o borrow Money on the credit of the United States

* * *." Government borrowing has been significant since the earliest days.

Before the Constitution, both the several states and the Continental Congress experienced fiscal needs in excess of what the states could satisfy by taxation or the Congress could satisfy by requisitions from the states. Commercial banking was virtually unknown in this country at that time; apart from foreign countries, the only source of borrowed funds was the American public. In exchange for money borrowed, states and the Continental Congress alike issued negotiable notes promising repayment in specie. These were called "bills of credit," and circulated as currency in lieu of coin.

Bills of credit depended for their value in the marketplace upon faith in the issuing governments' ability eventually to redeem them in specie; and therefore, because of the desperate economic condition of most state governments during and for years after the Revolutionary era, most of these bills of credit plummeted in value. Because of this bitter experience, the Constitution forbade states to "emit Bills of Credit," Art. I, § 10, cl. 1. A similar prohibition on the federal government was considered in the Constitutional Convention, but rejected; the delegates nonetheless made clear their expectation that the expedient should be avoided if at all possible. The desire both to provide a ready source for federal borrowing and to provide a paper currency the value of which would not depend upon public confidence in the tenuous governments of the time was a principal reason why the Bank of the United States was established in 1791 as a private corporation, only a minority of its shares to be owned by the United States.

The details of the evolution of the paper currency system—involving note issues by the first and second Bank of the United States and by state chartered banks, the National Bank Act of the Civil War era, and ultimately the Federal Reserve System—are not material here. Financial exigencies of the Civil War led the federal government to issue several varieties of Treasury notes as borrowing devices, some of which were declared by law to be legal tender; and similar Treasury notes circulated as currency until a few decades ago. The paper currency in circulation today, however, consists exclusively of Federal Reserve notes.

While it no longer is the basis of the paper currency system, however, federal borrowing continues to occur constantly. The most commonplace examples are United States Savings Bonds, and Treasury bills with various periods of maturity which now are offered at weekly auctions and at other times. What is worth noting for constitutional purposes is that this continuous federal borrowing, particularly in the form of Treasury bills, is not designed merely for financing the costs of government.

Since World War II, Treasury bills have been employed extensively as instruments for the implementation of national monetary policy. The size and terms of each issue can be adjusted not merely to meet fiscal needs such as refinancing maturing issues, financing federal deficits, and smoothing out the uneven flow of tax receipts, but also (because of the way the Federal Reserve and banking systems work) to influence the money supply, and thus impact the economy as a whole. In other words the borrowing power, like other federal powers, is used constantly on the generic principle elucidated in Chapter Four, as a means to promote ends extraneous to the circle of legitimate federal concerns.

Of course the necessary and proper clause also applies to facilitate the borrowing power (but not the extraneous ends toward which any use of that power might be aimed); again, see the discussion of *Clearfield Trust* in § 8.06.

CHAPTER NINE

EXCEPTIONS AND QUALIFICATIONS TO ENUMERATED POWERS DOCTRINE: THE FOREIGN AFFAIRS AND PROPERTY POWERS

§ 9.01 National Power and Foreign Affairs

As mentioned in § 2.01, even before the Constitution was adopted it had been determined that the relevant political unit for diplomatic and other international purposes was to be the United States, not any or all of the states separately. In the vocabulary of international relations, "sovereignty" is ascribed only to such independent national political units.

Our own *internal* political theory, of course, posits sovereignty in "the people," who delegate some governing authority to the nation while reserving the rest to their respective states; that is why, *internally,* the doctrine of enumerated powers is fundamental. We should not expect that doctrine to have the same significance regarding international affairs, however; for our posture among the nations of the world is not something we alone can define.

By international custom and practice, "sovereigns" are considered competent to deal with each other in an unlimited variety of ways and regarding an unlimited variety of subjects. There is nothing in international law like a doctrine of enumerated powers. And of course, "[a]s a member of the family of nations, the right and power of the United States in that field are equal to the right and power of other members of the international family. Otherwise, the United States is not completely sovereign." U.S. v. Curtiss-Wright Export Corp., 299 U.S. 304, 318 (1936). Thus, our national government's legal competence on the international plane is determined by *international* rather than domestic law.

Consequently, while the Constitution alludes to only a few techniques of international relations (such as treaty-making, the exchange of ambassadors, and war), this nation cannot be denied the use of other techniques merely because they are unmentioned in the Constitution. Likewise, while the Constitution refers to only a few matters (such as commerce) concerning which this nation might deal with others, it is not forbidden to deal concerning matters as diverse as extradition, wildlife preservation, ocean mining, space exploration, and human rights merely because the Constitution does not designate them as matters of legitimate federal concern. "As a nation with all the attributes of sovereignty, the United States is vested with all the powers of government necessary to maintain an effective control of international relations." Burnet v. Brooks, 288 U.S. 378, 396 (1933).

§ 9.01 *FOREIGN AFFAIRS* 205

One certainly could not catalogue all possible concerns of the community of nations in a finite list. All that is necessary to make a matter one of international concern is that nations are interested in dealing with one another about it. Since our federal government is competent to deal with any matter of international concern, this means that all manner of subjects beyond the scope of the enumerated federal powers (and thus otherwise reserved to the states) come within the scope of federal authority if they become matters of international concern. Even such matters as sports and cultural activities, domestic relations, property rights, inheritance, and periods of limitation for initiating court proceedings, at least potentially are matters of international concern, and therefore potentially within the competence of the federal government.

The subjects of international concern, as well as the methods by which nations deal with each other regarding them, are subject to change over the course of time. Consequently, "a panoply of important powers is to be determined from unwritten, uncertain, changing concepts of international law and practice, developed and growing outside the constitutional tradition and our particular heritage." L. Henkin, Foreign Affairs and the Constitution 25 (1972).

Only rarely has it been suggested that the vast array of national powers with regard to foreign affairs might be traced to specific grants in the

Constitution. See, e.g., Fong Yue Ting v. U.S., 149 U.S. 698, 711–12 (1893). At the opposite extreme, it has been argued that international sovereignty at the moment of American independence devolved not upon the respective colonies but upon the conglomerate of them all, and that consequently no constitutional investiture of the national government with international competence was required. *Curtiss-Wright,* supra, 299 U.S. at 315–18; for a critique, see Levitan, *The Foreign Relations Power: An Analysis of Mr. Justice Sutherland's Theory,* 55 Yale L.J. 467 (1946).

The better view, intimated in a number of judicial opinions, is that the Constitution *does* "vest" comprehensive power over foreign affairs in the national government, but that it does so inexplicitly—the inference to be drawn from those few allusions and specific references that the text does contain. See, e.g., Mackenzie v. Hare, 239 U.S. 299, 311 (1915); Jones v. U.S., 137 U.S. 202, 212 (1890); Chae Chan Ping v. U.S., 130 U.S. 581, 603–04 (1889). While this reconciles federal power over foreign affairs with the notions of popular sovereignty and "delegated" powers, however, it leaves it a plain exception to the doctrine of "enumerated" powers.

Yet this does not make the doctrine of enumerated powers any less significant; for matters otherwise "extraneous" become matters of international (and thus of federal) concern only *insofar as* there is interest in dealing with them internationally.

Interest in particular matters may wax or wane, may be limited in scope, or may never arise at all. As a practical matter, as to most extraneous matters the potential of international interest (and thus federal power) never will be realized; and if it is, the federal government will not gain complete authority over the matter, but only the power to control it pro tanto according to the international interest therein.

§ 9.02 Foreign Affairs and the Necessary and Proper Clause

Even though federal competence in foreign affairs is an exception to the doctrine of enumerated powers, it is useful to consider it in terms of the diagram introduced in Chapter Two as illustrating the application of that doctrine. In terms of that diagram, of course, whatever happens to be of international concern falls within the circle of legitimate federal concerns (although there may be separation of powers questions—generally beyond the scope of this book—as to how and by which organ of the federal government any such concern might be dealt with). Given this, the diagram serves to illustrate the power which Congress can exercise with respect to foreign affairs by virtue of the necessary and proper clause.

A moments' reflection on the language of this clause together with Figure 2 in § 3.01 should make it apparent that even when *another* organ of government is competent as to a given aspect of foreign affairs, Congress may legislate to help that other organ perform its task. Also, once another federal organ authorized to do so sets a policy in the realm of foreign affairs, that is a policy objective within the circle of legitimate federal concerns so that action by Congress adapted to promote it is supported by the necessary and proper clause.

More significantly, however, Congress itself can frame foreign affairs policy and then legislate, by virtue of the necessary and proper clause, to carry that policy into effect. Immigration policy and legislation is the most obvious illustration.

There is some significant confusion regarding *Congress' own* foreign affairs power, as a result of the opaque opinion of Justice Holmes for the Court in Missouri v. Holland, 252 U.S. 416 (1920). The United States and Great Britain had concluded a treaty establishing close seasons and other provisions for the protection of migratory birds, and committing each party to take further steps by internal legislation to effectuate the treaty's goals. Thereafter Congress enacted the Migratory Bird Treaty Act. The Court held both the Act and the treaty valid. That holding certainly was correct; the opinion, however, obscures instead of revealing the reason why.

Two unappealed lower court decisions had held a comparable statute enacted *before* the treaty beyond Congress' power; and while not declaring those holdings right or wrong, Holmes wrote in *Holland:* "It is obvious that there may be matters * * * that an act of Congress could not deal with, but that a treaty followed by such an act could * * *." 252 U.S. at 433.

That, however, is not obvious at all. In fact, it is quite wrong; and Holmes' statement has fostered serious misunderstanding.

The premise of federal power over foreign affairs is that any matter which comes to be of international concern is therefore pro tanto within the circle of legitimate federal concerns—even if in the absence of international concern it could have been dealt with only by states. In 1916 the matter of migratory birds was plainly a matter of international concern, for in that year the treaty was made; but execution of a treaty is not the only possible evidence of international concern. It should be sufficiently persuasive that the matter is a subject of pending negotiations, or perhaps even that it is a matter capable of exacerbating or alleviating international tensions. One need not have a litmus test.

Insofar as the matter of migratory birds was a matter of international concern, Congress could legislate about it as freely as the President, with the advice and consent of the Senate, could make treaties about it. It would make no difference whether the legislation followed or preceded the treaty, or whether any treaty were concluded at all. Therefore, the decisions holding the earlier federal act invalid probably were wrong; and at least Holmes' suggestion that the treaty itself made a difference was clearly wrong. What made the Act valid was that it dealt with a matter of legitimate federal (because international) concern; the treaty was no more than evidence of that concern.

Holmes' opinion, unfortunately—to the extent it suggests any rationale at all—seems to reason that, (1) because the Constitution does not delimit the matters concerning which treaties may be made, they may be made even about matters extraneous to the circle of legitimate federal concerns; and (2) thereafter Congress can legislate to effectuate the treaty's extraneous ends. That is a great example of the utterly unsound and unsupportable "bootstrap" rationale illustrated in Figure 7 and discussed in § 4.06.

§ 9.03 Treaties and Federal Laws

Treaties are made by the President with Senate ratification; the House of Representatives is not involved. Federal statutes are made by both houses of Congress with presidential acquiescence or by overriding a veto. Given these very different processes by which policy on foreign affairs properly can be made, it is not surprising that conflicts sometimes arise. These are conflicts which nothing on the face of the Constitution resolves; for supremacy clause purposes, treaties and federal statutes have equal rank.

When presented with a federal law and a treaty regarding the same matter "the courts will always endeavor to construe them so as to give effect to both." Whitney v. Robertson, 124 U.S. 190, 194 (1888). If the conflict is unavoidable, however, "the last expression of the sovereign will must control." Chae Chan Ping v. U.S., 130 U.S. 581, 600 (1889). See also *Whitney,* supra, 124 U.S. at 194; The Cherokee Tobacco, 11 Wall. (78 U.S.) 616, 621 (1871). In other words, even though they are made by different organs of the government, a statutory rule can be superseded by treaty and a treaty provision can be abrogated by statute. (For a contemporary illustration in the context of treaties and statutes concerning American Indians, see U.S. v. Dion, 106 S.Ct. 2216 (1986).

Of course, in addition to being law for domestic purposes, treaties typically create obligations under international law. The Supreme Court, however, has not let this interfere with the rule that the "last expression of the sovereign will" must govern any question arising in domestic courts. As between nations, a treaty

> depends for the enforcement of its provisions on the interest and the honor of the governments which are parties to it. If these fail, its infraction becomes the subject of international negotiations and reclamations, so far as the injured party chooses to seek redress, which may in the end be enforced by actual war. It is obvious that with all this the judicial courts have nothing to do and can give no redress.

Edye v. Robertson (The Head Money Case), 112 U.S. 580, 598 (1884).

§ 9.04 State Law and Foreign Affairs

The Constitution contains several specific provisions debilitating states in various aspects of foreign affairs; e.g., Art. I, § 10, cls. 2 & 3. Negative inferences also are sometimes drawn; see, e.g., §§ 11.1, 11.16. On the other hand, subject to a requirement of congressional consent formal agreements between states and foreign nations are specifically contemplated by the Constitution, Art. I, § 10, cl. 3, and several today are actually in force. More important, there are countless ways in which the ordinary operation of state law impacts foreigners and thus, at least potentially, international relations.

A federal statute dealing with foreign affairs supersedes any contrary provision of state law by virtue of the supremacy clause. That clause also declares treaties made "under the Authority of the United States" to be "the supreme Law of the Land." Thus, even if it deals with a matter not otherwise within the federal government's control—such as contract obligations, limitation periods, or local business licensure—the terms of a treaty supersede contrary state law. This rule has been applied consistently from the beginning. See, e.g., Asakura v. Seattle, 265 U.S. 332 (1924); de Geofroy v. Riggs, 133 U.S. 258 (1890); Baldwin v. Franks, 120 U.S. 678, 683 (1887); Hauenstein v. Lynham, 100 U.S. 483 (1879); Chirac v. Chirac, 2 Wheat. (15 U.S.) 259 (1817); Hopkirk v. Bell, 3

Cranch (7 U.S.) 454 (1806); Ware v. Hylton, 3 Dall. (3 U.S.) 199 (1796).

Certainly "the language of a treaty wherever reasonably possible will be construed so as not to override state laws or to impair rights arising under them," Guaranty Trust Co. v. U.S., 304 U.S. 126, 143 (1938); but if the two are not reconcilable, the treaty will control.

While the supremacy clause on its face refers only to those international arrangements properly described as "treaties," state law is held to be superseded as well by less formal international arrangements, such as executive agreements. U.S. v. Pink, 315 U.S. 203 (1942); U.S. v. Belmont, 301 U.S. 324 (1937). The explanation given in *Belmont* was that "complete power over international affairs is in the national government and is not and cannot be subject to any curtailment or interference on the part of the several states." 301 U.S. at 331.

§ 9.05 Classic Doctrine Regarding Federal Enclaves Within States

Article I, § 8, cl. 1 of the Constitution provides that Congress shall have power "To exercise exclusive Legislation in all Cases whatsoever over such District * * * as may * * * become the Seat of the Government * * *, and to exercise like Authority over all Places purchased by the Consent of the Legislature of the State in which the Same shall be, for the Erection of Forts, Magazines, Arsenals, Dock-Yards, and other needful Buildings." Such places are referred to as "federal enclaves," and this provision can be referred to either as the "Article I property clause" or as the "enclave clause."

It is plain from the language that this clause applies to some places within the geographic borders of a state. On the other hand, it applies only to such places within states as have been "purchased with the Consent" of the state legislature. Consequently, not every tract of real estate owned by the United States—and not even every military facility or "other needful building" site—is an enclave; for as to many of those sites, there never has been the requisite state consent. The legal situation with respect to these non-enclave properties is discussed in §§ 9.07–9.08.

This enclave clause actually deals in one breath with two very different kinds of places. It must have been contemplated that the "District" which would become the "Seat of the Government," being permitted to be as large as ten miles square, almost certainly would contain a great deal of *privately owned* real estate, in addition to any the title to which the government might acquire. (In fact that was and is true of the District of Columbia, eventually established pursuant to this clause.) On the other hand, no "Place" outside that "District" could come within this clause unless it had been "purchased," and thus was *federally owned.*

Regarding the "District" for the seat of the government, this clause speaks in terms of "Cession" from a state and "Acceptance" by Congress. (In historical fact, the ten-mile-square at the mouth of the Potomac was ceded in part by Maryland and in part by Virginia; but the part from Virginia later was retroceded.) Regarding the other "places" the clause speaks in terms, not of "cession," but rather of state "Consent;" yet it provides that as to *all,* the Congress is to "exercise like Authority * * *." Since the "District" would contain property the legal rights consequent to ownership of which would be vested already in private hands, the "Authority" contemplated by this enclave clause must have to do with governing competence, rather than proprietorship rights; and the same governing competence is declared to be present whether title be in the United States or not. Therefore the "Cession" contemplated with respect to the "District" must have reference to governmental authority (without any disruption of private title), and the "Consent" to federal acquisition of *other* property must contemplate such a cession of governing authority as well.

A part, at least, of the governing authority consequent to such a cession is articulated on the face of the enclave clause: Congress may "exercise exclusive Legislation in all Cases whatsoever" there. This is a rather cumbersome phrase, but the Convention chose it over two alternatives which were proposed: To exercise "the exclusive right of soil and jurisdiction," and "to exercise exclusively legislative authority."

The language selected seems an inept way to confer exclusive legislative authority over the enclaves, and an even more inept way to confer exclusive governmental jurisdiction in general—legislative, executive, and judicial. That language seems quite appropriate, however, to give Congress power to legislate "exclusively" (that is, to pass laws superseding otherwise applicable state law), not merely as to enumerated matters but "in all Cases whatsoever."

On the latter view, "enclaves" would remain geographically and politically a part of the states wherein they were located, so that state governing jurisdiction would not automatically cease; but Congress legislatively could supersede state competence in any or every realm, as it chose, including matters of local police, regardless of relation to any (other) enumerated power. This would be ample to prevent such embarrassments as occasionally occurred under the Articles of Confederation (when national institutions and installations were dependent upon such protection as a state could or would give them) while at the same time preserving for any residents of an enclave their privileges, immunities, and rights as citizens of the enclave's host state.

Among the relatively recent cases involving enclaves, a few seem compatible with this sensible construction. (They are discussed briefly in § 9.08.)

§ 9.05 *FOREIGN AFFAIRS* 217

The traditional view, however, has been very different. Almost since the beginning, the prevailing view with regard to the enclaves has been the notion of "extraterritoriality." On this view the enclaves, in effect, are eliminated both politically and geographically from the states within whose borders they might be located, so that they are no more a part of that state than is a foreign country. See Reily v. Lamar, 2 Cranch (6 U.S.) 344, 356–57 (1800); U.S. v. Cornell, 25 F.Cas. 650, 653 (No. 14,868) (C.C.D.R.I.1820). Thus the phrase "exclusive Legislation" has been treated as if it were an incompetent draftsman's attempt to say "exclusive jurisdiction;" see, e.g., James v. Dravo Contracting Co., 302 U.S. 134, 141 (1937); Surplus Trading Co. v. Cook, 281 U.S. 647, 652 (1930); U.S. v. Bevans, 3 Wheat. (16 U.S.) 336, 388 (1818); and the federal government's power over these enclaves has been characterized as "in essence complete sovereignty," S.R.A. v. Minnesota, 327 U.S. 558, 562 (1946).

In any case, however, whether one takes the traditional "extraterritoriality" view, or the more conservative "power to legislate exclusively" view suggested here, the power of Congress to legislate for the enclaves is not limited to matters otherwise within the scope of the enumerated powers; it reaches to "all Cases whatsoever." In this sense, Congress' power over federal enclaves might be considered an "exception" to the doctrine of enumerated powers.

§ 9.06 Classic Doctrine Regarding Territory Outside Any State

The acquisition, governance, and disposition of territory has been a fact of international practice since the time when political groupings of humans first were called nations. A nation's capacity and limitations in these matters cannot be determined unilaterally. As an equal among international sovereigns, the United States is competent in this regard *by virtue of international law and practice;* it does not (and never did) require any provision in this nation's own organic law to make it so.

Thus, for example, the United States acquired, governed, and disposed of territory outside the boundaries of its constituent states even under the Articles of Confederation, although the Articles were silent as to such matters and explicitly confined the national government to powers "expressly" conferred. That limiting language in the Articles simply could not constrain the nation as an international sovereign; and neither can the doctrine of enumerated powers under the Constitution. See § 9.01.

It therefore is superfluous, for example, to justify the acquisition of territory through capture or negotiation by extrapolation from the constitutional provisions regarding war and treaties, as the Supreme Court tried to do in American Insurance Co. v. Canter, 1 Pet. (26 U.S.) 511, 541 (1828). Likewise it is superfluous to justify the governance and disposition of territory outside state boundaries, once it has been acquired, by reference to Article IV, § 3, cl. 2 of the Constitution, which provides that "[t]he Congress shall have power to dispose of and make all needful Rules and Regulations respecting the Territory or other Property belonging to the United States."

To say that any reference to this Article IV property clause is "superfluous" where extra-state territory is involved, however, is not to say that the clause does not contemplate such territory. Unquestionably, a part of the reason this clause was included (and placed in Article IV instead of Article I) was that several states already had ceded to the nation their claims in the so-called "Northwest Territory" with the expectation that new states would be erected there. Thus the property clause does apply to United States territory *outside* any state; but as to *such* territory it does not (indeed it could not) alter the rules which apply *by virtue of international law.*

International law precludes interference there by other international sovereigns; and states are incompetent simply because the territory lies outside their bounds. Unless and until it is organized and admitted to the Union as a state, therefore, any such territory simply has no government at all apart from the federal government (and such subordinate governing organs as the United States might choose to recognize or create). In *extra-state* territory, therefore, the federal government has more than its constitutionally enumerated powers;

simply by default, it has *general* governmental jurisdiction there.

This comprehensive, complete federal authority over extra-state territory is appropriate as an exception to the doctrine of enumerated powers; for precisely *because* such territory is *beyond* the states its governance presents none of the issues of federalism with which that doctrine is designed to deal. Indeed, it induces confusion to consider this authority as anything *other* than an exception to that doctrine. Specifically, to attribute federal power over such extra-state territories to the Article IV property clause (rather than to extra-constitutional, international law) is to invite profound confusion; for that same clause applies to "other Property belonging to the United States."

There are two reasons why extra-state territory and "other Property belonging to the United States" must be distinguished for constitutional purposes notwithstanding that this one clause contemplates both. First, when the nation acquires extra-state territory it does not necessarily acquire title to the land; ownership interests established under a prior civilized regime ordinarily are recognized. Thus, while such territory "belongs to" the United States in the political sense of being subject to its governing authority, it (or much of it) might not "belong to" the United States at all in an ownership sense. Second, as to property "belonging to the United States" in an ownership sense but located *within* a state, the issues of federalism with which the doctrine of enumerated powers is designed to deal are very much present; thus as to such property, unlike as to extra-state territory, *general* governmental jurisdiction in the federal government can neither be reconciled with, nor admitted as an exception to, the doctrine of emumerated powers.

§ 9.07 Classic Doctrine Regarding Other Federal Property

When the vast territories now comprising most of the nation's land area were acquired during the nineteenth century, they were populated for the most part by "uncivilized" natives in whom the federal government recognized no ownership rights; very little of the land was privately owned under the law of prior "civilized" regimes. Consequently, in addition to general governmental jurisdiction, the United States by default acquired title to virtually all of the land.

Through a variety of grant and homestead programs, the United States conveyed title to some of this property into private hands. In addition, as new states were created and admitted to the Union, ownership of certain property (such as river bottoms, and shore lands below high tide) passed from the United States to the new state by operation of law. See New Orleans v. U.S., 10 Pet. (35 U.S.) 662 (1836); Pollard v. Hagan, 3 How. (44 U.S.) 212 (1845). Some other land was voluntarily given to the new states. As to most of the land in the

West, however, the United States retained ownership despite the creation of new states.

But ownership is one thing, and governmental jurisdiction is quite another. According to the rationale of the *New Orleans* and *Pollard* cases, supra, whenever a state was created out of what had been extra-state territory, general governmental jurisdiction (which had been vested theretofore by default in the United States) was automatically transferred to the new state; this transfer occurred inexorably by operation of law, and the state and the United States were powerless even by agreement to prevent it. The reasons for this automatic and unavoidable transfer of governing authority were the "equal footing" doctrine and the doctrine of enumerated powers.

The "equal footing" doctrine actually antedates the Constitution. Its origin is in Article V of the Northwest Ordinance of 1787, which declared as national policy (later reiterated as to other territories) that the territory it covered would be formed into new states to be admittted "on an equal footing with the original States in all respects whatever * * *." The original states before the Constitution enjoyed general governmental jurisdiction over all the land within their respective limits, regardless by whom it was owned; and the new Constitution changed this no further than to give certain enumerated powers of governance to the national government. Consequently, except with regard to "enclaves"—where in addition to having title the United States had been ceded governmental jurisdiction (see § 9.05)—the states' competence to govern behavior and activities within their borders was in no way diminished because the United States happened to own the land. See *Pollard,* supra, 3 How. (44 U.S.) at 223; *New Orleans,* supra, 10 Pet. (35 U.S.) at 737. If it were otherwise, the "public land" states of the West would have only preemptible and concurrent general governing authority over 30% to 95% of their respective land areas (for that is the amount that is federally owned); and in this respect they would stand on a footing distinctly *un* equal to that of the other states.

Of course, even federal property as to which there had been no jurisdictional cession sufficient to make it an enclave could be used as a means for executing some enumerated federal governing power (e.g., for a courthouse or a military base); and obviously no state or local measure could interfere with such use. See Fort Leavenworth Railroad Co. v. Lowe, 114 U.S. 525 (1885); Kohl v. U.S., 91 U.S. 367 (1875). This, however, was not because of the *property* clause, or *that* clause combined with the supremacy clause; instead it was because of the necessary and proper clause (see Chapter Three) and the related doctrine of "federal immunity" examined in § 14.02.

As a proprietor, however, the United States (just like any other landowner) could permit the use of its property for purposes quite unrelated to its governance role—purposes such as hunting, grazing, or public recreation. When the United States did so, according to classic property clause doctrine, its permittees (no less than those of any other landowner) were fully subject to governance by the states. See, e.g., Wilson v. Cook, 327 U.S. 474, 487–88 (1946); Omaechevarria v. Idaho, 246 U.S. 343 (1918); Ward v. Race Horse, 163 U.S. 504 (1896). Before Colorado ceded governmental jurisdiction over Rocky Mountain National Park, for example, that state's law controlled even in the face of contrary policy established by the park administrator pursuant to authority expressly delegated to him by an act of Congress. Colorado v. Toll, 268 U.S. 228 (1925).

Such priority for state law over the federal will is entirely consistent with the supremacy clause, because according to the classic doctrine the property clause confers, not any power of sovereignty or governmental jurisdiction, but only the powers of control and utilization associated with ownership. Although they might be prescribed by a legislative body in its accustomed statutory form, the "needful Rules and Regulations" authorized by this clause are merely the policies of a proprietor, rather than "laws" in the sense of legislative assertions of governmental jurisdiction. See Butte City Water Co. v. Baker, 196 U.S. 119, 126 (1905). (Remember that the *governing* authority of the United States over territory *outside* any state derives not from this clause, but from international law.) Because

Congress' power to manage federal property within states, conferred by this clause in Article IV, was *different in kind* from the truly *legislative* powers conferred in Article I, it was held to be freely delegable to administrators even when the Supreme Court was keeping a tight rein on Congress' delegation of legislative powers. U.S. v. Grimaud, 220 U.S. 506, 515–16 (1911).

In two respects, the classic doctrine does countenance more than conventional proprietorship powers for the United States with respect to property within states that is covered by this Article IV clause. First, state law cannot affect the acquisition of adverse rights in federally owned lands: Title (or lesser interests) can be acquired from the United States only as Congress allows, regardless of state conveyancing, adverse possession, or condemnation law. This rule, which has no exception, traces its origin to express language in the 1787 Northwest Ordinance (and language with equivalent effect in the enabling acts providing for admission of new western states) saving to the United States the power of "primary disposal of the soil." Second, since Camfield v. U.S., 167 U.S. 518 (1897), the United States has been afforded unusual latitude for self-help in the protection of federally owned property.

It is not necessary to detail or document the classic property clause doctrine more elaborately here. For further study, see Engdahl, "State and Federal Power Over Federal Property," 18 Ariz.

L.Rev. 283 (1976), reprinted in 14 Pub. Land & Res. Law Digest 269 (1977); Engdahl, "Some Observations on State and Federal Control of Natural Resources," 15 Houston L.Rev. 1201, 1208–11 (1978); Comment, "The Property Power, Federalism, and the Equal Footing Doctrine," 80 Colum.L. Rev. 817 (1980).

§ 9.08 The Scrambled Egg: Enclave and Property Clause Doctrine in Disarray

There probably exists no better illustration of how radical and dysfunctional, even though unrecognized, changes in organic constitutional doctrine can occur inadvertently as a result of mistaken preconceptions, shortfalls in analysis, and shallow study of precedents, than what has happened under the enclave and property clauses. Unfortunately, the process of progressive conceptual confusion involved is too complex to be briefly explained; tracing and untangling it occupies more than fifty pages in the article, "State and Federal Power Over Federal Property," cited supra. It can be given only conclusory treatment here.

In sum, what has happened is that the Supreme Court has largely confounded and substantially merged the concepts and cases appropriate to the two separate clauses.

It has been held, for example, that federal jurisdiction over places purchased pursuant to the Article I enclave clause need not be even substantially exclusive, and that states may retain over enclaves any degree of governmental jurisdiction that Congress is willing to allow them. This had been deemed true as to Article IV property since 1885, but it became the rule as to enclaves only when the Court witlessly commingled the two clauses in the late 1930's.

Retention of any substantial state jurisdiction obviously cannot be reconciled with the classic "extraterritoriality" view of enclaves. Unsurprisingly, therefore, that extraterritoriality view was deliberately discarded (after careful briefing on the specific point) in Howard v. Comm'rs, 344 U.S. 624 (1953). Then, however, inexplicably and without elaboration, it was applied again in Paul v. U.S., 371 U.S. 245 (1963). Seven years later, when counsel in their briefs reminded the Court of *Howard, Paul* was ignored and *Howard's* rejection of the extraterritoriality view was unanimously reaffirmed in Evans v. Cornman, 398 U.S. 419 (1970), which held enclave residents to be residents of the enclave's host state. Yet three years later, on briefs mentioning neither *Howard* nor *Evans,* the Court speaking through the *same Justice* who had written the *Evans* opinion unflinchingly applied the enclave extraterritoriality view again as its premise of decision in U.S. v. Mississippi Tax Comm'n, 412 U.S. 363 (1973). (Explaining that he did not expect the Supreme Court to be consistent, counsel for Mississippi declined this author's suggestion that he petition for rehearing on the basis of *Howard* and *Evans.*)

If *Evans* were indeed to be followed, one could make a very credible argument that the long disenfranchised citizens of the District of Columbia enclave are entitled to vote for federal Senators and Congressmen as citizens of the state of Maryland. The stunning novelty of this suggestion should drive home the point that the ground rules of governing authority as to federal enclaves today are very unclear. No one—and, it would seem, least of all any Supreme Court Justice—can predict what might happen in the next enclave case. One can observe from experience, however, that fate should favor the lawyer who knows what's gone on, and can use that knowledge skilfully in a brief.

Even more significant than the muddle which has been made of the enclave clause is what has been done with Article IV property clause doctrine. In 1976, with an opinion that displays darkest ignorance of what had been established for two centuries before, the Supreme Court unanimously (albeit unawares) revolutionized its doctrine under that clause. Kleppe v. New Mexico, 426 U.S. 529 (1976). The briefing on behalf of New Mexico was inept; and for its part, the Court conspicuously failed to deal with many of the relevant cases, and demonstrably misunderstood the others. *Kleppe* is critiqued at pages 349–358 of the article, "State and Federal Power Over Federal Property," cited supra.

§ 9.08   *FOREIGN AFFAIRS*   229

Kleppe held that "Congress exercises the powers both of a proprietor and of a legislature over the public domain." 426 U.S. at 542. This holding would be consistent with classic doctrine only if Congress' power as a *legislature* over the public domain were conceived as confined to the exercise of otherwise enumerated powers, the "property power" itself being non-legislative in character; but the Court in *Kleppe* had no such conception. It viewed the property clause as independently vesting *general* legislative jurisdiction over federal property, *not* confined to the exercise of otherwise enumerated powers. On this view, Congress can make rules for federal property which have no relation whatever to any matter otherwise of legitimate federal concern, and *any* such rule, being *legislative* in character, "necessarily overrides conflicting state laws under the Supremacy Clause." 426 U.S. at 543. Nothing of this sort can be reconciled with the classic doctrine.

The Court did point out that the legislative power thus given to Congress "without limitations" (426 U.S. at 539) does not by itself preclude state legislation; it conceded that states retain *concurrent* jurisdiction over Article IV property. The *Kleppe* view of Congress' Article IV property power thus is distinguishable from the "exclusive jurisdiction" which classic Article I doctrine had given Congress with regard to the enclaves. It is not so distinguishable, however, from Congress' power over the enclaves under the more recent, more muddled cases which compromise the classic enclave rules.

In effect, *Kleppe* makes the Article IV property power another exception to the doctrine of enumerated powers. Oh, to be sure, that doctrine nominally is satisfied so long as one accepts the Court's proposition that the power conferred by the Article IV clause is legislative, or governmental in character, and not merely a proprietorship power; but as to property located within the boundaries of states, that is a profoundly novel proposition which makes a mockery of the basic purpose of enumerated powers doctrine. In this regard one should note that a material factor contributing to the *Kleppe* Court's error was its belief that this clause of the Constitution—rather than international law—is the source of the national government's general and comprehensive governing authority over "Territories" outside the bounds of any state, 426 U.S. at 540–541. See § 9.06.

What *Kleppe* really means is that, over all the vast federal public domain *within* states, the United States has plenary, general governmental jurisdiction, and is not confined to those enumerated powers which it may exercise elsewhere in the country. It means that as to the east and the middle west, enumerated powers doctrine remains the foundation for constitutional power analysis, but as to roughly half of the country from the Rocky Mountain states westward it has absolutely no significance at all.

§ 9.08 *FOREIGN AFFAIRS* 231

Once the profound potential of this absurd proposition had begun to sink in, ten western state governors joined in an amicus brief urging the Court to accept for full briefing and argument a certain case in which *Kleppe's* premises could have been reconsidered; but the Court declined the request, summarily affirming the *Kleppe*-based ruling without accepting briefs and without issuing any opinion. Ventura County v. Gulf Oil Corp., 445 U.S. 947 (1980). The time for sober reflection had not yet come.

Probably, however, that time will come. A seed whose ultimate fruit should be *Kleppe's* destruction was sown only seven months after *Kleppe* itself was decided, in Oregon v. Corvallis Sand & Gravel Co., 429 U.S. 363 (1977). There a 6–3 Court overruled a 7–1 decision barely three years old, and arguably another seven Justice opinion (an eighth Justice concurring) only nine years old. All three cases concerned title; but the avowed premise of the *Corvallis* decision was the ancient and venerable "equal footing" doctrine. That doctrine, of course, is not and never was confined in its application to questions of title; it is a premise from which the classic doctrine regarding governmental jurisdiction over federally owned property inexorably flows. See § 9.07.

Kleppe's misallocation of governing authority over Article IV federal property is irreconcilable with the "equal footing" doctrine revitalized in *Corvallis* just seven months later. One who has learned from the study of two centuries of organic constitutional doctrine that sound principles most often ultimately return can assert confidently that *Kleppe* must eventually be overruled.

When that might occur, however, depends heavily upon the perspicacity of litigating lawyers, as the earlier discussion of the enigmatic state of enclave doctrine surely shows. Little significant assistance has been offered from the academic side; no contemporary casebook troubles to explore this subject competently, and few Constitutional Law teachers are even conversant with it. As attention refocuses on federalism law issues in the coming years, this (one should hope) might change.

Meanwhile, so long as the *Kleppe* precedent stands one should expect that inferior judges and administrators will dutifully and uncritically follow it. Thus, one must calculate the costs and benefits of taking an adverse stand.

CHAPTER TEN

CONGRESS' ENFORCEMENT POWER

§ 10.01 The Enforcement Clauses of Certain Amendments

The thirteenth, fourteenth, and fifteenth amendments (adopted during the Reconstruction era), as well as several adopted later, contain sections providing (in these or equivalent words) that "Congress shall have power to enforce, by appropriate legislation, the provisions of this article." All of the amendments in which these "enforcement clauses" appear are self-executing at least in some degree: Without any legislation, the substantive provisions of each are judicially enforcible at least to the extent that acts in violation of them may be declared unconstitutional should that question arise in a case. The enforcement clauses plainly indicate, however, that this was not thought enough.

The most miserly conceivable construction of these clauses would authorize Congress at least to enact statutes prescribing civil or criminal sanctions for actual violations of these amendments' restrictions or requirements. See, e.g., Civil Rights Cases, 109 U.S. 3 (1883). The interesting question, however, is whether (or to what extent) these clauses enable Congress to impose requirements or restrictions beyond those imposed by the amendments themselves.

§ 10.02 The Necessary and Proper Clause Analogy

The language of these several enforcement clauses is strikingly similar to the language of the necessary and proper clause. Moreover the Supreme Court, since shortly after the first three of them were ratified, has described their operation in terms equivalent to John Marshall's classic explanation of the necessary and proper clause. Compare Ex parte Virginia, 100 U.S. 339, 345–46 (1879), with McCulloch v. Maryland, 4 Wheat. (17 U.S.) 316, 421 (1819); see also South Carolina v. Katzenbach, 383 U.S. 301, 326–27 (1966); Rome v. U.S., 446 U.S. 156 (1980).

There is a difference between the clauses, in that the enforcement clauses deal with effectuating *rights* (in large part, against government actions) while the necessary and proper clause deals with effectuating the federal government's *power* to act. This difference, however, does not diminish the importance of the analogy.

Few scholarly discussions of the enforcement clauses have exploited this analogy; but that probably is because constitutional rights scholars generally have neglected to study the necessary and proper clause with care. The more accurate one's understanding of classic necessary and proper

§ 10.02 CONGRESS' ENFORCEMENT POWER 235

clause doctrine, the more compelling a generous view of Congress' enforcement clause power becomes.

As the discussions in Chapter Three and elsewhere have shown, however, the necessary and proper clause frequently has been misconstrued, some of the power it confers upon Congress being wrongly attributed to other sources such as the commerce clause. Thus it should not be surprising that Justices, both past and present, frequently have misunderstood these enforcement clauses, most often understating (but occasionally overstating, see § 10.03) the power which they give to Congress.

Following the analogy to the necessary and proper clause, the basic requisite for legislation under an enforcement clause is a telic relation to some end the reviewing judiciary considers within the substantive scope of the relevant amendment. Each particular provision of an "enforcement" measure, to be valid, must separately satisfy this telic requirement; but great latitude is left for Congress to choose by what means to effectuate the amendments' ends.

Thus, for example, the majority in the 1883 *Civil Rights Cases,* supra, was wrong in restricting Congress to correcting after the fact, or providing modes of redress for, actual violations by state government officials of fourteenth amendment standards. (The dissenting opinions in *Rome,* supra, can be criticised on the same grounds.) Just as the necessary and proper clause enables Congress to regulate extraneous matters to achieve constitutionally legitimate ends, these enforcement clauses enable Congress (1) to outlaw practices, themselves not unconstitutional, as a means to eliminate or prevent practices which are, or (2) to impose requirements which it otherwise would lack power to impose, so long as they are imposed as means to implement the substantive provisions of one of these amendments.

The most prominent illustrations of this are the cases upholding federal legislation suspending or abrogating valid state laws in order to diminish the risk of unconstitutional interference with rights to vote; e.g., *South Carolina, Rome,* and *Ex parte Virginia,* supra. Of particular interest is the first of the two rationales used in Katzenbach v. Morgan, 384 U.S. 641, 650–53 (1966), to uphold a federal act prohibiting enforcement against certain persons of state laws which made English literacy a prerequisite for voting. Such literacy requirements had been upheld as constitutional in themselves; but enfranchising the persons which this federal act concerned, without regard to their literacy, could give them a political influence likely to diminish the prospect that they might suffer discrimination in the provision of government services—discrimination which would violate the fourteenth amendment. This rationale illustrates not only that a practice which in itself is permissible may be banned as a means under an enforcement

§ 10.02 *CONGRESS' ENFORCEMENT POWER* 237

clause, but also that enforcement clause measures may be prophylactic. See also *Rome*, supra. Analogously, the Supreme Court had said in *Jones & Laughlin* that "Congress was entitled to foresee and to exercise its protective power to forestall." 301 U.S. at 43. In addition, further demonstrating the close analogy to necessary and proper clause doctrine, this first *Morgan* rationale illustrates the use of a "filiation of necessities" argument in an enforcement clause context; cf. § 3.02.

Another example of enforcement clause legislation prohibiting what is not itself unconstitutional, but valid because it serves as a prophylaxis against what an amendment does forbid, is the federal law forbidding racial discrimination in the private sale or rental of housing. That law was upheld in Jones v. Alfred H. Mayer Co., 392 U.S. 409 (1968). Racial discrimination by private persons does not violate the Constitution, so the law could not be justified on grounds which the 1883 *Civil Rights Cases* majority would have thought sound. The thirteenth amendment, prohibiting slavery, does apply to private individuals; but to discriminate in the sale or rental of housing is not to make anyone a slave. Therefore the acts prohibited by this statute could not be said to be unconstitutional in themselves. However, discriminatory treatment and prejudicial exclusion from opportunities and benefits which others commonly enjoy can be said to be among the characteristic accompaniments— the "badges" and "incidents"—of slavery; and by outlawing these characteristic accompaniments Congress can help ensure that slavery—what the Constitution forbids—will not recur. As it was put by a floor manager of the bill, quoted by the Court in *Mayer,* "[a] man who enjoys the civil rights mentioned in this bill cannot be reduced to slavery." 392 U.S. at 443–44. For another example, see Griffin v. Breckenridge, 403 U.S. 88, 104–05 (1971).

The necessary and proper clause analogy also provides the rationale needed to reach private acts with statutes enforcing those amendments which, by their terms, only put limits on state action; for banning certain kinds of private action might be an appropriate means to prevent such state action as the amendment forbids.

As with respect to the necessary and proper clause, so when one of these enforcement clauses is employed it is not for the judiciary to second guess Congress or to satisfy itself that the requisite telic relation truly is there. All that the judiciary properly may do is inquire whether a rational basis for Congress' determination can be found. See, e.g., *Morgan,* supra, 384 U.S. at 653.

In analogy to the "class basis" feature of necessary and proper clause doctrine, enforcement legislation may comprehend within its reach particulars as to whom the need for its application in order to attain the end sought cannot be shown. See *South Carolina,* supra; *Rome,* supra.

§ 10.03   *CONGRESS' ENFORCEMENT POWER*   239

In §§ 3.09 and 3.10, the significance of an actual congressional determination of the telic purpose requisite to application of the necessary and proper clause was discussed. By analogy the same issue must arise under the enforcement clauses. It is arguable that where the objective is the enhancement of individual rights rather than the enlargement of government power, there should be less hesitancy to impute telic purposes that might not unequivocally appear. On the other hand, enforcement legislation frequently does involve an enlargement of federal control over matters otherwise left to states, or the imposition of costly obligations upon states; and arguably such consequences should not be countenanced unless Congress' enforcement purpose is made quite clear. There continues to be some dispute over how evident Congress' purported reliance on an enforcement clause must be. See the discussions of this point, e.g., in the majority opinion in Pennhurst State School & Hosp. v. Halderman, 451 U.S. 1 (1981), and the majority and dissenting opinions in EEOC v. Wyoming, 460 U.S. 226 (1983).

§ 10.03   Much Ado About Nothing: The Furor Over *Morgan's* Second (or "Substantive") Rationale

The Katzenbach v. Morgan case, 384 U.S. 641 (1966), was cited in the preceding section for the first of the two alternative rationales articulated by Justice Brennan for the majority in that case;

that first rationale was analogous to necessary and proper clause doctrine, and is sound.

Brennan's second rationale in *Morgan* is called by some writers a "substantive" theory of the enforcement clauses, to provide a verbal contrast with the "remedial" theory. But once the necessary and proper clause analogy is understood, such labelling becomes inadequate. It strains the language to call anticipating and acting to prevent possible constitutional violations "remedial." Furthermore, the adjective "substantive" gives no hint at all as to what *Morgan's* second rationale might be or might mean. It is best to disregard such unhelpful labels.

To judge the constitutionality of an English literacy prerequisite for voting (such as that involved in *Morgan*), a court must consider various practical factors. As Justice Harlan acknowledged in his *Morgan* dissent, "[d]ecisions on questions of equal protection and due process are not based on abstract logic, but on empirical foundations," and any relevant factual determinations by Congress "are of course entitled to due respect." 384 U.S. at 668. Brennan's second rationale, however, went dramatically beyond this: Observing that numerous factors were involved, he declared that "it was *Congress'* prerogative to weigh these competing considerations. * * * [I]t is enough that we [the judiciary] perceive a basis upon which *Congress* might predicate a judgment that the application of New York's English literacy requirement * * *

§ 10.03   CONGRESS' ENFORCEMENT POWER

constituted an invidious discrimination in violation of the Equal Protection Clause." 384 U.S. at 656 (emphasis added).

This quite radical proposition baldly asserts that Congress can declare unconstitutional a practice which the judiciary already has upheld, and that Congress' judgment then must prevail so long as any basis for its judgment can be judicially perceived. Despite Brennan's footnote ipse dixit to the contrary (384 U.S. at 651 n. 10), it seems logically to follow that Congress must likewise be able to override a judicial judgment holding some practice unconstitutional. *Morgan's* second rationale was the articulated basis on which Congress enacted a statute lowering the voting age to 18, although confining the vote to those over 21 had been held constitutional by the courts. It also has been the basis of arguments in support of bills to overturn or curtail the results of constitutional rulings by the Supreme Court regarding criminal procedure and abortion.

Brennan cited no authority for this second rationale. Indeed, there was none he could cite.

When the voting age statute, premised on that rationale, was challenged in Oregon v. Mitchell, 400 U.S. 112 (1970), the rationale did not survive. The splay of opinions produced an impractical outcome holding the lowered age requirement valid for federal but not state elections, which prompted fast adoption of the twenty-sixth amendment. More significant, not one of the Justices endorsed the role for Congress which *Morgan's* second rationale had been understood to contemplate. Since then, an argument that Congress may narrow the judicially ascertained scope of the amendments' guarantees has been rejected, in Mississippi University for Women v. Hogan, 458 U.S. 718 (1982); and a majority has never even agreed with the suggestion that Congress may broaden that scope.

All that arguably survives of that rationale is the "revised version" of it which Brennan articulated, with only White and Marshall concurring, in his separate opinion in *Oregon v. Mitchell,* the voting age case. (In fact this seems to be an entirely different theory, but Brennan put it forward as an elaboration of what he had meant in *Morgan*—but which no one had understood.)

Brennan's reformulation begins with the premise that the basic criterion of "equal protection" as established by the Supreme Court is whether the state measure under consideration is a means to a legitimate state end. That, he then reasoned, calls for a factual determination: Does the measure indeed conduce to the supposed end? When the *judiciary* makes this determination, Brennan argued, institutional constraints generalized as "the nature of the judicial process" dictate deference to the state legislature's finding unless it is "so clearly wrong that it may be characterized as 'arbitrary,' 'irrational,' or 'unreasonable.'" But "[l]imitations stemming from the nature of the judicial process * * * have no application to Con-

§ 10.03   *CONGRESS' ENFORCEMENT POWER*   243

gress. * * * Should Congress * * * undertake an investigation in order to determine whether the factual basis necessary to support a state legislative discrimination actually exists, it need not stop once it determines that some reasonable men could believe the factual basis exists. Section 5 [of the fourteenth amendment] empowers Congress to make its own determination on the matter." 400 U.S. at 248.

On this view, the voting age statute represented a congressional finding adverse to the respective states' findings that higher voting age limits promote certain state interests. Thus, "[t]he core of dispute * * * is a conflict between state and federal legislative determinations of the factual issues upon which depends decision of a federal constitutional question * * *;" and the supremacy clause gives primacy to the congressional determination. 400 U.S. at 249.

Brennan's revised theory does not purport to enable Congress to declare the Constitution's meaning; but it does posit for Congress a prerogative which the Court has denied to itself, the prerogative of reviewing and declaring erroneous the admittedly rational determinations made by states as to how their legitimate state goals might be achieved.

This revised theory is ingenious, but fatally flawed in its initial premise. The basic criterion of "equal protection" according to the Court's relevant decisions is *not* whether the state measure under consideration *is* a means to a legitimate state end. The articulated criterion, rather, is whether a legislature might rationally have believed it a means to such end—regardless whether that rational belief be demonstrably erroneous. See, e.g., McGowan v. Maryland, 366 U.S. 420 (1961); Williamson v. Lee Optical Co., 348 U.S. 483 (1955); Railway Express Agency, Inc. v. New York, 336 U.S. 106 (1949).

The reason why the basic "equal protection" requirement has been made no more stringent than this really has nothing to do with the relative competence of legislative and judicial bodies to make the kind of factual determinations of telic relation that are called for. The reason instead is a disinclination to countenance any greater federal interference in matters of state concern than is clearly necessary to protect interests which the Constitution secures. This preference for the values of federalism would be offended as much by allowing *Congress* to override a rational state determination as it would be by allowing the federal *judiciary* to do so, whether the basis for overriding it were that the rational state determination was erroneous or merely that it was undesirable.

§ 10.04 Enforcement of Rights Not Derived From Amendments

There are federal constitutional rights which do not derive from any of the amendments containing an enforcement clause. Some are identified in §§ 9 and 10 of Article I; there is also the interstate privileges and immunities clause of Art. IV, § 2; and as to the federal government, there are the first eight amendments as well as the openended ninth.

As to these, there is no explicit grant of enforcement power to Congress. Some have been held correlative to the federal government's interest in its own continuance in a republican constitutional form; and the Supreme Court has reasoned that legislation protecting and enforcing such rights (such as the right to vote) is supported by the necessary and proper clause in conjunction with the various powers bearing upon self-perpetuation of the republican-constitutional regime. See U.S. v. Classic, 313 U.S. 299, 314–17 (1941); Ex parte Yarbrough, 110 U.S. 651, 658–67 (1884); cf. Burroughs v. U.S., 290 U.S. 534, 544–48 (1934).

Extrapolating from these cases, Justice Stewart in his separate opinion in *Oregon v. Mitchell* (joined by Burger and Blackmun) resorted to the necessary and proper clause as general enforcement authority, 400 U.S. at 286; and he seems to have had the same notion in mind when he wrote for the Court in Griffin v. Breckenridge, 403 U.S. 88, 106 (1971). The problem with this thesis, of course, is that the necessary and proper clause deals only with the effectuation of *powers,* not of *rights.*

At least as regards the federal government, however, any legislation to be "proper" in effectuating its powers must respect and arguably might ensure ample safeguards for those constitutional rights. In addition, every enumerated power certainly is available for use, insofar as it might be effective, to promote respect by the states for every constitutional right—and indeed, for any extra-constitutional right; see Chapter Four.

While on the one hand there are these *constitutional* rights for which there is no "enforcement power" as such, however, it is interesting to note on the other that the enforcement clause of the fourteenth amendment might arguably be used to support the enforcement of rights which are *not* constitutional at all. The "privileges and immunities" clause of the fourteenth amendment was virtually emptied of *constitutional* meaning more than a century ago in the Slaughter-House Cases, 16 Wall. (83 U.S.) 36 (1872). But that clause need not necessarily be understood as referring only to rights of constitutional stature. The words "privileges" and "immunities" and equivalent terms of high-level generality had been used commonly in English and American law for six and a half centuries before the fourteenth amendment was written, to embrace rights some of which grew out of immemorial custom but some of which arose out of parliamentary *legislation*. Under our polity, of course, federal legislation can be valid only if consistent with the doctrine of enumerated powers; but if any rights created by valid *statutes* can be considered "privileges" or "immunities" of United States citizens for purposes of the fourteenth amendment, that amendment's enforcement clause might enhance Congress' capacity to enforce them. It might, for example, justify prophylactic measures for such statutory, no less than for constitutional rights, to prevent violations before they occurred.

CHAPTER ELEVEN

NEGATIVE IMPLICATIONS OF FEDERAL POWER

§ 11.01 Exclusivity *Vel Non*

One should expect that when Congress actually *exercises* its power state law to the contrary must yield. The operations of the supremacy clause (examined in detail in Chapters Five and Twelve) are more complicated than might first appear, but its basic thesis is hardly surprising.

However, there is room for uncertainty whether state laws can be precluded by the mere existence of federal power even when that power lies *dormant*. As to a few matters within federal competence the Constitution expressly disables the states: Certain aspects of foreign relations, for example, and the issuance of currency and coinage; see Art. I, § 10. On the other hand, there are some powers as to which concurrent authority seems plainly contemplated. The clearest example is the power to tax: That Congress taxes some activity makes no difference to the states' competence to regulate, prohibit, require, or simultaneously tax that same activity. See, e.g., Pervear v. Commonwealth, 5 Wall. (72 U.S.) 475 (1867); Gibbons v. Ogden, 9 Wheat. (22 U.S.) 1, 198–200 (1824).

§ 11.01   *FEDERAL POWER*   249

In other instances, however, the issue is less clear. It was long debated, for example, whether Congress' power regarding naturalization excluded equivalent power in the states. See, e.g., Chirac v. Chirac, 2 Wheat. (15 U.S.) 259 (1817). Even more controversial before Congress enacted adequate bankruptcy legislation was whether Congress' largely dormant power in that field prevented states from enacting insolvency laws. See, e.g., Sturges v. Crowninshield, 4 Wheat. (17 U.S.) 122 (1819); Ogden v. Saunders, 12 Wheat. (25 U.S.) 213 (1827). Even today some uncertainty remains regarding state competence to enforce laws impacting foreign affairs. See, e.g., Clark v. Allen, 331 U.S. 503 (1947). Since virtually everything is *potentially* a matter of international concern, see Chapter Nine, a negative inference from dormant federal power here would jeopardize the whole spectrum of state competence; and no such suggestion ever has been made. It has been held, however, that an application of state law which "affects international relations in a persistent and subtle way" deemed intolerable by the Justices is implicitly negatived by the dormant federal power over foreign affairs. Zschernig v. Miller, 389 U.S. 429, 440 (1968). The *Zschernig* case was the first to so hold, and its significance still is uncertain.

The predominant area of "negative implications" debate, however, always has been Congress' power over interstate and foreign commerce; and that is the focus of this Chapter.

§ 11.02 The Dormant Commerce Clause From 1789 to *Cooley*

There are some textual reasons why no negative on state power should be inferred from the commerce clause. Article I, § 10, cl. 2 restricts state imposts and duties on imports and exports; but if such exactions were to be precluded by implication anyway, this separate provision would be superfluous. Moreover, the same clause recognizes that states will have "inspection Laws," and uniquely subjects them to "the Revision and Controul of the Congress." When the Constitution was written, every port state enforced various health and quarantine laws against incoming ships, their crews, and their cargoes. These laws, the expenses of administering which were charged against ships' masters, generally provided for detention, health inspection, prohibition of landing in the event of disease, and even destruction of contaminated cargo. These "inspection Laws" plainly applied to ships and goods while they still were in commerce—whether local, interstate, or foreign. If the commerce clause were meant to carry any negative implication for state regulations of interstate and foreign commerce, it would be strange that this clause reads like a grant of special revisory power over authority admitted to remain in the states, rather than like a special concession to the states of an authority over commerce otherwise implicitly denied to them.

§ 11.02   FEDERAL POWER   251

For many years after the Constitution was adopted there seems to have been no serious doubt that states could continue to regulate interstate and foreign commerce, *insofar as it took place within their respective borders,* so long as they did not conflict with some actual exercise of Congress' power. In 1824, however, in *Gibbons,* supra, counsel attacking New York's steamboat monopoly law argued that the grant of the commerce power to Congress "implies in its nature, full power over the thing to be regulated, [and] excludes, necessarily, the action of all others that would perform the same operation on the same thing." This argument was immaterial because the steamboat monopoly's conflict with a federal statute on point actually decided the case; but in dictum Chief Justice Marshall responded that "[t]here is great force in this argument, and the Court is not satisfied that it has been refuted." 9 Wheat. (22 U.S.) at 209.

Thus encouraged, lawyers opposing various state laws increasingly argued that Congress' power over interstate and foreign commerce, even when dormant, is exclusive. One such effort was rebuffed by Marshall himself in Willson v. Black Bird Creek Marsh Co., 2 Pet. (27 U.S.) 245 (1829), where a state (to enhance property values and public health by draining swampland) had dammed a tidal creek theretofore navigated by a federally licensed sloop. Without elaborate discussion, Marshall noted that enhancing property values and health (and measures calculated to those ends) are within state competence absent collision with federal power, and that "under all the circumstances of the case," that state's action was not "repugnant to the power to regulate commerce in its dormant state * * *." Id. at 252.

A stronger case was presented in Mayor of New York v. Miln, 11 Pet. (36 U.S.) 102 (1837), involving a state law requiring ships' masters to report information about every passenger landed at the port of New York, or landed elsewhere with the intention of proceeding to New York. (The latter feature made the law applicable even to acts occurring outside the enacting state.) The case was first argued before Marshall died in 1835; but one seat was then vacant and the other Justices were evenly divided, so reargument was set for a later term. By 1837 the membership of the Court had changed significantly, and with only one dissent the state law was sustained.

Miln is important because of the different reasoning the several Justices employed. Justice Story (who had been present for *Gibbons*) was the lone dissenter in *Miln* (though he declared that the deceased Marshall had shared his view). Story insisted that New York's law was a regulation of interstate and foreign commerce, and claimed that *Gibbons* (by its dictum) had settled the point that Congress' commerce power is exclusive. He agreed that a state might pass laws to promote health and other "police" objectives, but claimed that no state could regulate foreign or interstate commerce even for such "police" ends "because it is a means withdrawn from its authority." Id. at 156–57.

Justice Thompson also had joined in the *Gibbons* decision; but he gave no force to its dictum. Concurring in *Miln,* he said instead that "the [state] law * * * not coming in conflict with any act of congress, is not void by reason of the *dormant power* [of Congress] to regulate commerce * * *." Id. at 149.

The other Justices voting to uphold the law in *Miln,* however, avoided discussing whether Congress' commerce power is exclusive. (In fact, they disagreed among themselves on this point.) Instead, they characterized the state law as a "regulation, not of commerce but police," its character as such being evident from "the end to be attained, and the means of its attainment;" and they declared that whether or not Congress' *commerce* power is exclusive of the states, the states' *police* power is exclusive of Congress. Id. at 132, 133, 139. This appears to have been the first clear endorsement of the "dual federalism" notion of mutually exclusive state and federal spheres of authority; and it made that notion an integral factor in future "negative implications" debate.

For more than a decade after *Miln* the question whether Congress' commerce power is exclusive (as the *Gibbons* dictum had suggested) remained in dispute. In the License Cases, 5 How. (46 U.S.) 504 (1847), the Court upheld state laws restricting sales of liquor introduced from other states or abroad; but there was a splay of opinions, with no single voice speaking for the Court. It appears, however, that at least a bare majority agreed that Congress' dormant commerce power carries *no* negative implication. The one Justice who expressly agreed with Story's contrary view rendered it inapplicable in any event by characterizing these laws (like the law upheld in *Miln*) as regulations of internal police; and he agreed with the others that an otherwise valid police regulation of a state could not be invalidated merely because it impaired—or even foreclosed—the local market for out-of-state goods, or made their importation futile or unprofitable. Id. at 577, 589–90, 609–11, 615–16. Two years later, again with a splay of opinions, a majority invalidated state taxes on alien passengers arriving at the ports of Massachusetts and New York. Passenger Cases, 7 How. (48 U.S.) 283 (1849). Only one Justice, however, based that conclusion on Story's "negative implication" view; the others insisted that whether Congress' commerce power is exclusive was not an issue in the case, and reached their conclusion on other grounds.

At last an uneasy and uncertain compromise was reached in Cooley v. Board of Wardens, 12 How. (53 U.S.) 299 (1851). There, seven of the nine Justices agreed that a Pennsylvania statute requiring ships to utilize a local pilot when navigating the waters surrounding Philadelphia ports was constitutional. Only one of those seven sought to

§ 11.02   *FEDERAL POWER*   255

distinguish between "police" and "commerce" regulations; the others acknowledged that the pilotage law was a regulation of interstate and foreign commerce by the state, but upheld it anyway.

To do so, however, they neither affirmed concurrent state power over *all* interstate and foreign commerce nor denied that Congress' dormant commerce power *ever* could be exclusive. Instead, the majority reasoned that interstate and foreign commerce embrace a vast array of "subjects"—problems, situations, and activities which a government might regulate—and that these are dissimilar in nature. "Whatever subjects of this power are in their nature national, or admit only of one uniform system, or plan of regulation, may justly be said to be of such a nature as to require exclusive legislation by Congress;" but those which are "local and not national" are "likely to be the best provided for, not by one system, or plan of regulations, but by as many as the legislative discretion of the several States should deem applicable to the local peculiarities of the ports within their limits." As to the *latter*, "until Congress should find it necessary to exert its power, it should be left to the legislation of the States * * *." Id. at 319.

Pilotage, they found, was one of these "local" subjects of interstate and foreign commerce. That did not preclude federal regulations of pilotage; otherwise Congress could not combat "[c]onflicts between the laws of neighboring states, and discriminations * * * deeply affecting that equality of commercial rights, and the freedom from state interference, which those who formed the Constitution were so anxious to secure * * *." Id. at 317. It did mean, however, that with regard to "local" aspects of interstate and foreign commerce, although state regulations could be preempted they were not to be foreclosed by any negative inference from the dormant federal power.

One dissenter in *Cooley* denounced it as the first decision ever to countenance state laws frankly acknowledged as regulations of interstate or foreign commerce. That may be true, but the *Cooley* opinion also was the first majority opinion clearly to affirm—even to a limited extent (i.e., "national" subjects of commerce)—the Story thesis that Congress' dormant commerce power could be exclusive.

What the *Cooley* majority said about "national" subjects of commerce, of course, was dicta; and it specifically declined to elaborate, or even to give examples of, what subjects of interstate or foreign commerce "are within the exclusive control of Congress," or what subjects other than pilotage "may be regulated by the States in the absence of all congressional legislation * * *." Id. at 320. Four years before *Cooley,* in his separate *License Cases* opinion, Justice Woodbury had suggested that Congress' power is necessarily exclusive "so far as regards the uniformity of a regulation reaching to all the States," "no State being able to prescribe rules for others * * *." 5 How. (46 U.S.) at 624. Woodbury's extraterritoriality criterion, however, was based on principles of jurisdiction, not on the commerce clause; see the discussion of taxing jurisdiction in § 11.13. The *Cooley* "rule" was attributed to the commerce clause, and it gave such latitude that judges eventually would be able to declare subjects "national" on the basis of substantive policies of their own choosing.

Woodbury, for example, considered the purchase and sale even of imported goods to be regulable by states, even though such regulation (or prohibition) might diminish consumption of foreign goods or discourage their importation. The *Cooley* formulation, on the other hand, soon induced arguments that the marketing, no less than the movement, of interstate or foreign goods is a "national" subject of commerce, foreclosed from regulation by states. (Indeed, eventually it would be considered sufficient to render a subject "national" that uniformity was "necessary in the * * * sense of useful in accomplishing a permitted [national] purpose." Morgan v. Virginia, 328 U.S. 373, 377, 386 (1946).)

§ 11.03 Evolution Under *Cooley*

The burgeoning of industry, transportation, communication, and trade after the Civil War induced hundreds of challenges to new and old state regulations, scores of which reached the Supreme Court; and within decades after *Cooley,* dormant commerce power cases accounted for a major share of the Justices' workload. In the mass of decisions rendered between the Civil War and the 1920's, a few principal traits can be discerned.

The Justices tended routinely to rely upon the dual federalism dichotomy between "police" and "commerce" regulations, reiterating that the "police" power resides exclusively in the states and characterizing those state laws they were disposed to uphold as "police" regulations and thus valid despite even severe impacts on interstate or foreign commerce. Notwithstanding their crucial influence on interstate grain movement, for example, pricing practices at Chicago's grain elevators were held regulable by the state. Munn v. Illinois, 94 U.S. 113 (1877). On the other hand, this reliance upon the dual federalism dichotomy made it easier ultimately to concede that the states could not avowedly regulate or tax interstate commerce itself at all. See, e.g., Wabash, St. L. & P.R. Ry. Co. v. Illinois, 118 U.S. 557 (1886); Robbins v. Shelby County, 120 U.S. 489 (1887); Leloup v. Port of Mobile, 127 U.S. 640 (1888).

As the latter proposition hardened, Justices attuned to the interests of large scale enterprise broadened the scope of the "national" aspect of interstate commerce (to use the *Cooley* term), so that soon it was held in broad terms that "interstate commerce, consisting in the transportation, purchase, sale and exchange of commodities, is national in its character, and must be governed by a uniform system * * *." Leisy v. Hardin, 135 U.S. 100, 109 (1890); see also Welton v. Missouri,

§ 11.03 FEDERAL POWER 259

91 U.S. 275, 280 (1876). This, plus relaxation of the concept of "articles of commerce" so as to include within the scope of the commerce power persons, electronic communications, meandering cattle, and non-vendible items, enlarged the significance of negative implications doctrine substantially beyond what had been contemplated half a century before.

As laissez faire economic theory came to the fore, there were recurrent assertions to the effect that "the entire freedom of commerce among the States" was "deemed essential to a more perfect union by the framers of the Constitution * * *." *Wabash Ry.*, supra, 118 U.S. at 573. Just as the Justices by the turn of the century were employing the due process clauses of the fifth and fourteenth amendments as rubrics under which to review the substantive wisdom of legislative measures, see, e.g., Allgeyer v. Louisiana, 165 U.S. 578 (1897); Lochner v. New York, 198 U.S. 45 (1905), so they were employing the commerce clause as a rubric under which they could discard, without congressional sanction, state acts interfering with the policy of free interstate trade to which they ascribed constitutional status. On the eve of the New Deal it was even suggested that the proper judicial role under "substantive due process" and under the dormant commerce clause is exactly the same. Gavit, The Commerce Clause 23, 26 (1932). (For a curiously anachronistic suggestion that negative implications decisions today should conform to the substantive due process pattern, see Tushnet, "Rethinking the Dormant Commerce Clause," 1979 Wis. L. Rev. 125.)

A handful of relatively discrete factors with surviving significance emerge from the Court's foray into economic policy under the guise of the commerce clause during the pre-New Deal era. All of them reduce ultimately to the dubious notion— given expression as early as *Cooley*—that the commerce clause reflects a policy (having *constitutional* dimension) of interstate free trade.

One such factor was "discrimination:" State laws treating interstate commerce less favorably than intrastate commerce were held void. The antidiscrimination precept is best illustrated among nineteenth century cases by decisions invalidating discriminatory state taxes. E.g., *Welton,* supra; *Robbins,* supra. It was applied, however, to non-revenue regulations as well. Serious difficulties are often encountered when one tries to apply this precept in concrete cases; but that problem will be discussed in a subsequent section.

Another such factor was the incompatibility, or potential incompatibility, of different states' regulations. In 1878 the Court invalidated a Reconstruction era statute of Louisiana *forbidding* racial discrimination in accommodations on riverboats and other passenger conveyances in interstate commerce. Hall v. DeCuir, 95 U.S. 485 (1878). At that time no one conceived that the equal protection clause of the fourteenth amendment might inhibit

§ 11.03 *FEDERAL POWER* 261

state-ordered racial segregation, and since adjacent states required segregation Louisiana's prohibition was deemed disruptive of commerce by necessitating a sort of "musical chairs" game as state borders were crossed. The same dormant commerce clause rationale was used two generations later to invalidate a Virginia statute *requiring* racial segregation on buses (there still being no barrier perceived at that time in the equal protection clause). Morgan v. Virginia, 328 U.S. 373 (1946).

A third relatively discrete factor was the precept that one state may not promote its own or its citizens' economic advantage at the expense of other states or their citizens, or exclude competitive operators for economic reasons alone. E.g., Buck v. Kuykendall, 267 U.S. 307 (1925); Foster-Fountain Packing Co. v. Haydel, 278 U.S. 1 (1928); Baldwin v. G.A.F. Seelig, Inc., 294 U.S. 511 (1935). Consistently with the dual federalism dichotomy between the police power and power over interstate commerce, however, regulations found to have health or safety rather than economic aims were upheld even though they might impede interstate trade. E.g., Bradley v. Public Utilities Comm'n, 289 U.S. 92 (1933); Mintz v. Baldwin, 289 U.S. 346 (1933).

Many of the cases employing the dual federalism dichotomy used the vocabulary of "direct" and "indirect" impacts on interstate commerce: It was said that state measures otherwise valid which impacted interstate or foreign commerce only "indirectly" must be sustained. The roots of this verbal distinction can be traced as far back as the several opinions in the *License Cases,* supra. However, there were other cases in which the Court seemed simply to consider the relative magnitude of the imposition placed upon interstate or foreign commerce by the state. E.g., compare Southern Ry. v. King, 217 U.S. 524 (1910), with Seaboard Airline Ry. v. Blackwell, 244 U.S. 310 (1917).

§ 11.04 The (Justice) Stone Foundation of the Modern Approach

Leadership in formulating the modern approach to negative implications doctrine was assumed by Justice Harlan Fiske Stone. Regarding the language of earlier cases, Stone observed that the Court had been "doing little more than using labels to describe a result rather than any trustworthy formula by which it is reached." In substance, he said, approved state laws were upheld

> because a consideration of all the facts and circumstances, such as the nature of the regulation, its function, the character of the business involved, and the actual effect on the flow of commerce lead to the conclusion that the regulation concerns interests peculiarly local and does not infringe the national interest in maintaining the freedom of commerce across state lines.

DiSanto v. Pennsylvania, 273 U.S. 34, 44 (1927) (dissenting opinion).

§ 11.04   *FEDERAL POWER*   263

Essentially this was a reformulation and elaboration of the old *Cooley* rule. The *Cooley* suggestion that the commerce power should be considered in terms of its "subjects" and that those subjects could be classified as either "national" or "local" had proven unworkable because subject classification was too artificial when applied to practical affairs. However, on a less exacting level, the observation that different occasions for regulation implicate different considerations of local and national interest has merit. Stone recognized that the Justices had been weighing these different considerations in reaching their dormant commerce clause judgments.

It is as shorthand for this observation, and not for the "subject classification" methodology, that *Cooley* continues to be cited today. E.g., Japan Line, Ltd. v. Los Angeles, 441 U.S. 434, 457 (1979); Ray v. Atlantic Richfield Co., 435 U.S. 151, 186 (1978) (concurring opinion). It is in this sense, also, that *Cooley* has been used in considering arguable negative implications in other contexts, such as the copyright power. See Goldstein v. California, 412 U.S. 546 (1973)

Stone's *DiSanto* reformulation of *Cooley,* however, was only the first step toward a more disciplined judicial approach.

In South Carolina State Highway Dept. v. Barnwell Bros., 303 U.S. 177 (1938), the Court in an opinion by Stone upheld a South Carolina statute limiting the size and weight of trucks using state highways. Larger or heavier trucks were barred even if they were moving interstate. Stone described the dormant commerce clause inquiry as "whether the state legislature in adopting regulations * * * has acted within its province, and whether the means of regulation chosen are reasonably adapted to the end sought." Id. at 190.

This of course resembles the classic judicial inquiry regarding *federal* legislation under the necessary and proper clause, which had begun to emerge from decades of confusion only the year before in *Jones & Laughlin;* see Chapter Three. Even more closely, and more significantly, it resembles the "reasonably adapted to legitimate state end" standard articulated four years earlier as the proper limit of substantive inquiry by the judiciary under the due process clause of the fourteenth amendment. Nebbia v. New York, 291 U.S. 502, 537 (1934). That standard had replaced a far more intrusive habit of "substantive due process" evaluation of the "reasonableness" of legislative policy choices. *Barnwell* reflects the same reawakening to the primacy of the legislative branch in matters of ordinary public policy.

The *trial* court in *Barnwell* had recognized the new, narrower boundaries of judicial inquiry under the due process clause, but had "proceeded upon the assumption that the commerce clause imposes upon state regulations * * * a standard of reasonableness which is more exacting * * * than that required by the Fourteenth Amendment."

§ 11.04 FEDERAL POWER 265

303 U.S. at 184. Upon this assumption the commerce clause still would afford great latitude for judicial disapproval of legislative policy choices; therefore the trial court had taken evidence concerning the effects of truck size and weight upon road durability and traffic safety, the relative advantages of different methods of weight measurement, and the actual capacity of South Carolina highways, resolving the conflicts and making its own judgment on these matters. The Supreme Court, however, held that such judicial inquiry is just as improper under the commerce clause as under the due process clause: Under both clauses, "fairly debatable questions as to its reasonableness, wisdom and propriety are not for the determination of courts, but for the legislative body * * *." Id. at 191.

Stone's *Barnwell* formulation, however, was not quite adequate to account for the judicial role approved in cases soon to follow. In Milk Control Board v. Eisenberg Farm Products, 306 U.S. 346 (1939), the Court upheld a Pennsylvania law applied to control prices paid to Pennsylvania milk producers by a New York dealer all of whose purchases were for resale in New York. Applying the *Barnwell* test the Court found that the end ("to reach a domestic situation in the interest of the welfare of the producers and consumers of milk in Pennsylvania") was legitimate for the state, and that the regulations in dispute were "appropriate means to the end in view;" but then it put an additional question: "[W]hether the prescription of prices to be paid producers in the effort to accomplish these ends constitutes a prohibited burden on interstate commerce, or an incidental burden which is permissible until superseded by Congressional enactment." This third question, the Court said, "can be answered only by weighing the nature of the respondent's activities, and the propriety of local regulation of them, as disclosed by the record." Id. at 352.

This third level of inquiry undertaken in *Eisenberg* must not be confused with the repudiated role assumed by the *trial* court in *Barnwell:* Stone, who had written for the Supreme Court in *Barnwell,* joined in the *Eisenberg* opinion, and also took account of this third level of inquiry in his own opinions in Duckworth v. Arkansas, 314 U.S. 390 (1941), and Parker v. Brown, 317 U.S. 341 (1943). The *Eisenberg* opinion, however, did not make the distinction clear; it was clarified later when Stone (by then elevated to Chief Justice) wrote the Court's opinion in Southern Pacific Co. v. Arizona, 325 U.S. 761 (1945).

Southern Pacific invalidated an Arizona law limiting the length of railroad trains. Interstate railroads crossing Arizona could comply with this law by breaking up their long trains before crossing the Arizona border; but that required elaborate switching facilities and switching crews, at significant expense. Alternatively, they could bear the substantial diseconomies of shorter trains from start to finish of any trip routed through Arizona.

The Arizona law was designed to reduce injuries from the "slack action" of long trains; and safety, of course, is a legitimate state end. The Arizona *trial* court had weighed the risk of slack action accidents against the increased risk of grade crossing accidents due to more, shorter trains, and invalidated the law. Arizona's *appellate* court then had reversed, applying its understanding of *Barnwell* and finding the safety end legitimate and the length limit reasonably adapted (whether or not the best means) to that end.

Although the Supreme Court conceded these points, it proceeded to the third inquiry suggested by *Eisenberg*—which now was more fully explained. Chief Justice Stone wrote:

> The decisive question is whether in the circumstances the total effect of the law as a safety measure in reducing accidents and casualties is so slight or problematical as not to outweigh the national interest in keeping interstate commerce free from interferences which seriously impede it * * *.

325 U.S. at 775–76. At this level of inquiry, Stone said, the problem is one of "appraisal and accommodation of the competing demands of the state and national interests involved." Id. at 769.

On the Southern Pacific record, "the Arizona Train Limit law, viewed as a safety measure, affords at most slight and dubious advantage, if any, over unregulated train lengths * * *," while "[i]ts undoubted effect on [interstate] commerce" is "preventing the free flow of commerce by delaying it and by substantially increasing its cost and impairing its efficiency." Id. at 779. Thus the law,

> admittedly obstructive to interstate train operation, and having a seriously adverse effect on transportation efficiency and economy, passes beyond what is plainly essential for safety since it does not appear that it will lessen rather than increase the danger of accident.

Id. at 781–82.

Justice Black, dissenting in *Southern Pacific,* missed the distinction between this and the role forbidden to courts by *Barnwell.* The *trial* courts in both cases had considered the problems addressed by the legislatures, evaluated possible solutions, and concluded that the ends sought could better be attained by different approaches—which might also interfere less with interstate commerce. *That* infringed the legislatures' prerogative to select from among alternative potential solutions, and was not warranted by the commerce clause. But the *Supreme* Court in *Southern Pacific,* in contrast, weighed the *effectiveness* of the regulation in promoting a concededly legitimate goal, against the gravity of that regulation's interference with the conceived national interest in facilitating interstate commerce.

Under this approach, a particularly effective measure might justify even substantial interference with interstate commerce, while if the impact on that commerce were modest enough even a measure rather poorly suited to the state's legitimate end might be found inoffensive to the commerce clause.

This third level of judicial inquiry, however, even though Black's criticism of it was based upon misunderstanding, is indeed subject to fair criticism. In practice it proves quite difficult to do much better than Black in keeping it distinct from the role forbidden to courts by *Barnwell.* Furthermore, even when the most blatant interference with state legislative choices is avoided, *Southern Pacific* does preserve to the judiciary much more control over substantive policy choices than the Constitution arguably allows. This point will be pursued further in § 11.11.

Before proceeding further with the main line of dormant commerce clause cases, notice should be taken of two relatively minor, but not unimportant, asides.

§ 11.05 Aside: The Market Participant Doctrine

Recently there has emerged a specialized doctrine permitting state impacts on interstate commerce which the normal rules would disallow. The scope, significance, and longevity of this new doctrine still are unknown.

In 1976 the Court rejected a dormant commerce clause challenge to a program by which Maryland gave bounties for scrap-processing abandoned auto hulks, despite features of the program which gave processors in Maryland an advantage over those outside. The Court held that Maryland in effect had entered the market as a purchaser, and that nothing prevents a state *as a "market participant"* from favoring its own citizens. Hughes v. Alexandria Scrap Corp., 426 U.S. 794 (1976).

By a somewhat different and smaller (5–4) majority four years later, the Court applied the same distinction between "market participant" and "market regulator" to hold that South Dakota's state-owned and operated cement plant could prefer local over out-of-state customers in a time of shortage. Reeves, Inc. v. Stake, 447 U.S. 429 (1980).

Seven Justices joined three years later in applying this doctrine to uphold a mayoral order requiring that all city-funded construction projects be performed by a work force composed at least 50% of residents of the city. White v. Massachusetts Council of Constr. Employers, Inc., 460 U.S. 204, 214–15 (1983).

However, in South-Central Timber Devel. v. Wunnicke, 467 U.S. 82 (1984), only two of the eight participating Justices found that doctrine applicable to Alaska's requirement that timber allowed to be cut from state-owned lands be processed in Alaska prior to export. Two others voted to remand for determination whether Alaska was indeed acting as a "market participant" on these facts; and indeed the case was remanded, the four other Justices arguing against that characterization and warning that "[u]nless the 'market' is relatively narrowly defined, the doctrine has the potential of swallowing up the rule that States may not impose substantial burdens on interstate commerce even if they act with the permissible state purpose of fostering local industry." Id. at 97–8. Justice Brennan took the occasion of this fracturing of opinion to note what he called "the inherent weakness of the doctrine." Id. at 101.

At the least it is true, as remarked in the *Wunnicke* plurality opinion (written by the only Justice who had dissented in all three of the prior cases), that "[t]he precise contours of the market-participant doctrine have yet to be established * * *." Id. at 93.

§ 11.06 Aside: Alcoholic Beverages

In conjunction with its repeal of prohibition, the twenty-first amendment made exception to dormant commerce clause restrictions as they were conceived in the early 1930's by providing that

> The transportation or importation into any State * * * for delivery or use therein of intoxicating liquors, in violation of the laws thereof, is hereby prohibited.

For decades this provision was understood to make liquor regulation a special case, unaffected by dormant commerce clause doctrine generally. See Tribe, American Constitutional Law § 6–22 (1978). However, near the close of its 1985 Term the Supreme Court held that the twenty-first amendment must be considered in the light of the dormant commerce clause and that the Court must "reconcile the interests protected by the two constitutional provisions" case by case. Brown-Forman Distillers Corp. v. New York Liquor Auth., 106 S.Ct. 2080, 2087 (1986).

The Court characterized the New York liquor control provision invalidated in *Brown-Forman* as having extraterritorial effect. As so characterized, the measure could be viewed as raising jurisdictional ("due process") questions, quite apart from any dormant commerce clause questions: See Justice Woodbury's position in the *License Cases,* discussed near the end of § 11.02; see also § 11.13. It might actually be best to regard *Brown-Forman* in those terms.

On its face, however, *Brown-Forman* is a "commerce clause" case; and considered as such, it demonstrates the amazing tenacity of the "negative implications" notion, for the Court there insisted upon applying it even in the teeth of express amendment language which seems to have been designed specifically to render it inapplicable.

§ 11.07 The Modern Approach: Preface

There have been hundreds of Supreme Court decisions regarding the "negative implications" of the commerce clause; to reconcile them all is impossible, and to organize them meaningfully is exceedingly difficult. Chief Justice Burger in 1986 referred with apt metaphor to "the cloudy waters of this Court's 'dormant Commerce Clause' doctrine * * *." Wardair Canada, Inc. v. Florida Dept. of Rev., 106 S.Ct. 2369, 2378 (1986) (concurring opinion).

There have been a few refinements since 1945, however, and the formulation recited most frequently since 1970 has been:

Where the statute regulates evenhandedly to effectuate a legitimate local public interest, and its effects on interstate commerce are only incidental, it will be upheld unless the burden imposed on such commerce is clearly excessive in relation to the putative local benefits. * * * If a legitimate local purpose is found, then the question becomes one of degree. And the extent of the burden that will be tolerated will of course depend on the nature of the local interest involved, and on whether it could be promoted as well with a lesser impact on interstate activities.

Pike v. Bruce Church, Inc., 397 U.S. 137, 142 (1970).

A further refinement seemed hinted in one 1986 opinion when Justice Marshall declared for the majority:

This Court has adopted what amounts to a two-tiered approach to analyzing state economic regulation under the Commerce Clause. When a state statute directly regulates or discriminates against interstate commerce, or when its effect is to favor in-state economic interests over out-of-state interests, we have generally struck down the statute without further inquiry. * * * When, however, a statute has only indirect effects on interstate commerce and regulates evenhandedly, we have

followed the *Pike* approach. *Brown-Forman,* 106 S.Ct. at 2084. Less than three weeks later, however, Justice Blackmun for the majority (which included Marshall) wrote of Marshall's first "tier" that such cases merely are

subject to more demanding scrutiny. * * *

* * * A State must make reasonable efforts to avoid restraining the free flow of commerce across its borders, but it is not required to develop new and unproven means of protection [of its own interests] at an uncertain cost.

Maine v. Taylor, 106 S.Ct. 2440, 2448, 2453 (1986). In that case the Court, 8–1, *sustained* a state law which "restricts interstate trade in the most direct manner possible, blocking all inward shipments of live baitfish at the State's border." Id. at 2447. Marshall himself had confessed in *Brown-Forman* that

there is no clear line separating [the two "tiers" he described]. In either situation the critical consideration is the overall effect of the statute on both local and interstate activity.

106 S.Ct. at 2084.

During the few days' interval between *Brown-Forman* and *Taylor,* Justice Brennan for a majority of 7 (including Marshall, but with Blackmun dissenting in favor of a *tougher* stance) made his own attempt at encapsulation, referring to "the policy of uniformity, embodied in the Commerce Clause, which presumptively prevails when the Federal Government has remained silent." *Wardair Canada,* supra, 106 S.Ct. at 2373.

Plainly the Court's dormant commerce clause jurisprudence defies concise summation. It does seem to be an accurate observation, however, that with certain refinements the Court continues to follow the approach illustrated in *Southern Pacific,* making the two inquiries approved in *Barnwell* and then (if these are answered affirmatively) proceeding to the third level of inquiry as articulated by Chief Justice Stone. The following discussion (in §§ 11.08–11.10) is organized in terms of those three stages of inquiry, and along the way indicates how the refinements alluded to in the *Pike* formulation arose. Through it all the student would do well to wonder whether this entire unhappy enterprise is one which the judiciary properly should engage in at all.

§ 11.08 The Modern Approach: Stage One

The first *Barnwell* inquiry is whether the end at which the state regulation is aimed is legitimate for the state, considering among other things the "free trade" bias attributed to the commerce clause. The Court has denounced economic "rivalries and reprisals that were meant to be averted by subjecting commerce between the states to the power of the nation," on the premise that the Constitution "was framed upon the theory that the peoples of the several states must sink or swim together * * *." Thus it has voided state laws which it deemed designed to "neutralize the economic consequences of free trade among the states." Baldwin v. G.A.F. Seelig, Inc., 294 U.S. 511, 522–23, 526 (1935). The commerce clause is said to constitute the nation a "federal free trade unit." H.P. Hood & Sons v. DuMond, 336 U.S. 525, 538 (1949). Consequently a state's end has been held illegitimate when it acted to hoard its natural resources; to afford its own residents special advantages in the exploitation of those resources; to require that resources be utilized preferentially to meet local demands; to require that local consumers or processors purchase from local rather than out-of-state producers; or to apply economic coercion to force industries to relocate there. E.g., *Wunnicke,* supra; New England Power Co. v. New Hampshire, 455 U.S. 331 (1982); *Pike,* supra; Polar Ice Cream & Creamery Co. v. Andrews, 375 U.S. 361 (1964); *Hood,* supra; Toomer v. Witsell, 334

U.S. 385 (1948); *Seelig,* supra; Foster-Fountain Packing Co. v. Haydel, 278 U.S. 1 (1928); Pennsylvania v. West Virginia, 262 U.S. 553 (1923). See also Hicklin v. Orbeck, 437 U.S. 518, 531–34 (1978). "[W]here simple economic protectionism is effected by state legislation, a virtually per se rule of invalidity has been erected." Pennsylvania v. New Jersey, 437 U.S. 617, 624 (1978).

A few older cases had allowed states to be selfish with certain natural resources such as water, Hudson County Water Co. v. McCarter, 209 U.S. 349 (1908), and game, Geer v. Connecticut, 161 U.S. 519 (1896). *Geer,* however, was expressly overruled in Hughes v. Oklahoma, 441 U.S. 322 (1979); and while *Hudson* was not squarely overruled, it was substantially elided in Sporhase v. Nebraska, 458 U.S. 941 (1982), considered further below.

It has been held that the commerce clause "precludes the application of a state statute to commerce that takes place wholly outside of the State's borders, whether or not the commerce has effects within the state," and that protection of the interests of non-residents cannot be claimed as a legitimate state end. Edgar v. Mite Corp., 457 U.S. 624, 642–43 (1982). For the same reason—the long accustomed denial of extraterritorial competence—a state may not protect its own consumers from relatively higher prices by a rule against price differentials which, in practical effect, controls prices charged elsewhere. *Brown-Forman,* supra.

However, the commerce clause "does not elevate free trade above all other values." *Maine v. Taylor,* supra, 106 S.Ct. at 2455. While economic isolation or commercial "balkanization" is considered illegitimate, enhancement of public health, safety, security, ecology, and quiet have been held to be legitimate ends. See, e.g., *Maine v. Taylor,* supra; Huron Portland Cement Co. v. Detroit, 362 U.S. 440 (1960); Breard v. Alexandria, 341 U.S. 622 (1951); Bradley v. Public Utilities Comm'n, 289 U.S. 92 (1933); Mintz v. Baldwin, 289 U.S. 346 (1933).

It also has been held legitimate for states to protect or promote their respective business economies, so long as they do not seek to advance themselves by imposing disadvantages on persons or businesses in other states. See, e.g., Parker v. Brown, 317 U.S. 341 (1943); cf. *Pike,* supra. It has been held legitimate, also, to promote conservation of resources (as distinguished from selfish reservation of them.) *Maine v. Taylor,* supra; Cities Service Gas Co. v. Peerless Oil & Gas Co., 340 U.S. 179 (1950).

At least once, however, anachronistic allusion to the old dual federalism dichotomy and its accompanying prohibition against state regulations of interstate commerce per se has appeared in a poorly reasoned modern opinion: Allenberg Cotton Co., Inc. v. Pittman, 419 U.S. 20 (1974). That dichotomy and the interstate commerce per se prohibition (see § 11.03) had remained the avowed premise of decision with respect to state *taxes* even after it had been abandoned with respect to non-revenue regulations—constituting the so-called "formal rule" against state taxation of interstate commerce itself. The "formal rule" in tax cases, however, seems now to have met its demise: See § 11.14, and see generally Lockhart, "A Revolution in State Taxation of Commerce?" 65 Minn.L.Rev. 1025 (1981). The rationale of *Allenberg Cotton* surely cannot survive this development.

Even if it could, however, *Allenberg Cotton* is defective on another ground. While it relied on a 1921 case holding delivery for the purpose of interstate transit to be itself a part of interstate commerce, and described the "intricate interstate marketing mechanism" for cotton in detail, the so-called "stream of commerce" cases it relied upon to show dormant federal power over that whole marketing process actually illustrate Congress' power under the *necessary and proper* clause, not under the commerce clause itself. See §§ 6.04 & 6.05. Thus the failure to recognize the distinction between these two clauses induced in *Allenberg Cotton* an unprecedented negative implication *from the necessary and proper clause.*

Similarly the Court declared in Lewis v. BT Investment Managers, Inc., 447 U.S. 27, 39 (1980), that "the same interstate attributes that establish Congress' power to regulate" commercial activities which, by themselves, are intrastate, "also support constitutional limitations on the powers of the

States." Here again, insofar as those "interstate attributes" technically are regulable by Congress by virtue of the necessary and proper clause, the Court's failure to distinguish the two clauses led it unwarrantably to draw a negative inference from *that* clause rather than from the commerce clause itself.

§ 11.09 The Modern Approach: Stage Two

The second inquiry authorized by *Barnwell* is into the aptness of the state's regulation as a means to the legitimate state end. As previously noted, *Barnwell* was decided shortly after the Court had begun its retreat from the superlegislative role it had played for some decades under the aegis of "substantive due process," and illustrates the same reawakening to the primacy of the legislative branch in matters of ordinary public policy. The Court since has reaffirmed that, so long as there is a basis in reason for believing a measure will promote the legitimate end, courts must not resolve disputes as to whether it will do so in fact, or reject the legislature's judgment for lack of such evidence as a court might find persuasive if the question were for it to decide. Brotherhood of Locomotive Firemen & Enginemen v. Chicago, R.I. & Pac. RR Co., 393 U.S. 129 (1968). As will soon be discovered, however, the Court has seriously compromised this prohibition against judicial interference with legislative judgment.

In *Sporhase,* supra, the Court invalidated a statute prohibiting export to another state of ground water from Nebraska wells except to other states permitting water from their own wells to be used in Nebraska. The Court stopped short of denying that a state may reserve this peculiar resource—so critical to health and survival and so carefully guided in its development by the state's own efforts—for its own citizens in times of severe shortage; and it conceded for the sake of argument that this end might justify some measures of state control. The *reciprocity* requirement, however, fell far short of the close fit of means to legitimate end required to justify a complete ban on transport out of state. (Several years earlier the Court had held a reciprocity provision regarding milk inspection and grading, which would admit milk from a reciprocating state even though of lower quality than what would be excluded from a non-reciprocating state, to be inapt as a means to the plainly legitimate objective of public health. Great A & P Tea Co. v. Cottrell, 424 U.S. 366 (1976).)

Of course discrimination for its own sake against out-of-state persons or products generally is an illegitimate end; but "the evil of protectionism can reside in legislative means as well as legislative ends." Philadelphia v. New Jersey, 437 U.S. 617, 626 (1978). Hence the stipulation in the *Pike* statement quoted earlier, and constantly referred to in more recent cases, that the state must regulate "evenhandedly." However legitimate and important the state's objective, it may not be promoted by discriminating against interstate commerce—unless there is some peculiar reason, apart from the interstate factor itself, to treat that commerce differently. *BT Investment,* supra, 447 U.S. at 36; *Philadelphia v. New Jersey,* supra, 437 U.S. at 626–27; *Hughes v. Oklahoma,* supra, 441 U.S. at 338–39; cf. *Maine v. Taylor,* supra.

Discrimination is most apparent when persons are permitted or forbidden to engage in the same activity depending upon their relationship to the state, as in *BT Investment,* supra; but it is present also when the state's own citizens and businesses as much as others are restrained by a regulation which disfavors out-of-state as compared to in-state marketing or consumption, as in *Maine v. Taylor,* supra, and *Hughes v. Oklahoma,* supra; cf. *Sporhase,* supra. Moreover, a regulation which is neutral on its face might be found discriminatory in one or more concrete applications, and if not thus rendered wholly invalid it will be invalid at least as so applied. See, e.g., Hunt v. Washington State Apple Advertising Comm'n, 432 U.S. 333 (1977); *Pike,* supra.

It is in connection with this rule against discrimination that the Court most clearly has compromised its prohibition against judicial interference with matters of legislative judgment. In 1951 the Court held that, "even in the exercise of its unquestioned power to protect the health and safety of its people," a state (or city) cannot discriminate

§ 11.09   *FEDERAL POWER*   283

against interstate commerce "*if reasonable nondiscriminatory alternatives, adequate* to conserve legitimate local interests, are available." Dean Milk Co. v. Madison, 340 U.S. 349, 354 (1951) (emphasis added).

The precedents cited by the Court in *Dean Milk* did not support this rule: One involved a regulation the claimed health effect of which was deemed remote and merely a matter of "faith," *Seelig,* supra, 294 U.S. at 524; the other involved a regulation which excluded admittedly wholesome meat simply because it was slaughtered out-of-state, Minnesota v. Barber, 136 U.S. 313, 328–29 (1890); in both a *sufficient* relationship to some *legitimate* state end was lacking, and *neither* suggested that the regulation in question might have survived if no better means of accomplishing the state's goal could be found. Nonetheless, as the *Pike* formulation quoted earlier indicates, judicial inquiry into supposed "reasonable nondiscriminatory alternatives" has become a highly prominent characteristic of modern dormant commerce clause discussions. See, e.g., *Maine v. Taylor,* supra; Minnesota v. Clover Leaf Creamery Co., 449 U.S. 456, 473–74 (1981); *Hughes v. Oklahoma,* supra, 441 U.S. at 337–38; *Washington Apple Comm'n,* supra, 432 U.S. at 353–54; *Great A. & P. Tea,* supra, 424 U.S. at 376–77.

The basic vice of this inquiry into supposed alternatives remains that identified by Justice Black in his *Dean Milk* dissent, 340 U.S. at 358–60: Without reliable information on the practical factors which might have conditioned the legislature's choice, and with nothing to guide them but scant judicial knowledge, speculation of counsel, and hunches, appellate judges in estimating the "reasonableness" and "adequacy" of alternatives play a superlegislative role even less restrained than that for which the trial courts in *Barnwell* and *Southern Pacific* had been rebuked.

Tempering this only slightly, the Supreme Court now says that *appellate* courts must not inquire into alternatives de novo; relevant trial court findings are to be overturned only if they are "clearly erroneous." *Maine v. Taylor,* supra, 106 S.Ct. at 2451. At the trial court level, however, the vice of such inquiry into the reasonableness and adequacy of alternatives is compounded by the fact that a challenger is not obliged to demonstrate any adequate means to the state's end; instead, "the burden falls on the State" to show "the *un* availability of nondiscriminatory alternatives adequate to preserve the local interests at stake." *Washington Apple Comm'n,* supra, 432 U.S. at 353 (emphasis added). This onerous burden sometimes can be sustained: See, e.g., *Maine v. Taylor,* supra; *Clover Leaf Creamery,* supra, 449 U.S. at 473–74. However, the task of proving a negative is difficult enough that ordinarily one should not expect success.

Even apart from the superlegislative role entailed by the *Dean Milk* inquiry, there are other

§ 11.09   *FEDERAL POWER*

problems involved in applying the rule forbidding means which "discriminate" against interstate commerce. A modest embarrassment is that it frequently requires a determination as to whether a legislature acted with a discriminatory "motive:" E.g., compare the concurring with the dissenting opinions in Kassel v. Consolidated Freightways Corp., 450 U.S. 662 (1981), and the majority with the separate opinions in *Clover Leaf Creamery,* supra; and cf. *Washington Apple Comm'n,* supra, 432 U.S. at 353-54. (Indeed, at least once the Supreme Court has undertaken to declare that a state legislature had purposes other than those which the state's own judiciary had found it to have! See *Clover Leaf Creamery,* supra.) Legislative "purpose" or "motive" inquiries, of course, on some issues are inescapable and quite appropriate; see, e.g., § 3.10. It is ironic, however, that the very Justices *least* interested in genuine "purpose" inquiries where they *should* be made (as, e.g., for purposes of the necessary and proper clause, or to distinguish real from sham "taxes"), are the ones who have insisted most vigorously in the dormant commerce clause context that convincing indications of actual purpose must be shown, and that hypothetical legislative purposes suggested by counsel are not good enough. See *Kassel,* supra, 450 U.S. at 681-85 (Brennan, with Marshall, concurring); cf. id. at 702-03 (Rehnquist, with Burger and Stewart, dissenting). See Eule, "Laying the Dormant Commerce Clause to Rest," 91 Yale L.J. 425, 457 & n. 179 (1982).

A more serious problem with this antidiscrimination rule is that whether a regulation appears discriminatory often depends upon what comparisons are made. In Exxon Corp. v. Maryland, 437 U.S. 117 (1978), a Maryland statute forbidding petroleum producers or refiners to operate retail gas stations within the state was challenged as discriminatory because no companies produced or refined petroleum in that state, so that only interstate businesses were affected. But the Court reasoned that there were *other* interstate dealers who did *not* produce or refine their own products and who thus, just like Maryland dealers, would be *un* affected by the act; and it declared:

> The fact that the burden of a state regulation falls on some interstate companies does not, by itself, establish a claim of discrimination against interstate commerce.

437 U.S. at 126. The commerce clause, the Court said, protects "the interstate market," not particular interstate firms or any particular market structure or method of operations. Id. at 127. The Court even has said that an otherwise valid state regulation

> is not invalid simply because it causes some business to shift from a predominantly out-of-state industry to a predominantly in-state industry.

Clover Leaf Creamery, supra, 449 U.S. at 474.

Yet in Raymond Motor Transportation, Inc. v. Rice, 434 U.S. 429 (1978), and in *Kassel,* supra, the Court considered state truck length regulations only in terms of their impact on that single segment of the interstate transportation industry; there was no consideration of whether increased trucking expenses attributable to the regulations might simply shift business to other interstate carriers (such as railroads) with little or no detriment to interstate transportation as a whole. Similarly, the decision in *Allenberg Cotton,* supra, is criticizable as protecting only the particular method of operations preferred by those involved in the interstate marketing of cotton, and not necessarily that commodity's interstate market itself.

§ 11.10 The Modern Approach: Stage Three

When both the legitimacy of the state end and the appropriateness of the means are established, the Court proceeds to the third step of inquiry, articulated in *Southern Pacific:* Whether the effectiveness of the regulation as a means to the state's end is sufficient to justify the degree of burden placed upon interstate commerce. In considering the degree of the burden, the challenged state regulation need not be considered in isolation; other applicable regulations of the same and of other states—even if not inconsistent—may be considered also, the combination perhaps constituting "multiple" or "cumulative" burdens on the interstate commerce. See, e.g., Morgan v. Virginia, 328

U.S. 373, 382 (1946); Western Live Stock v. Bureau of Revenue, 303 U.S. 250, 255–56 (1938).

It is an oversimplification to call this a "balance-of-interests test," as the Court did in Arkansas Electric Cooperative Corp. v. Arkansas Public Comm'n, 461 U.S. 375, 390 (1983): That loose description better fits the approach which Professor Dowling urged in his "Interstate Commerce and State Power," 27 Va. L. Rev. 1 (1940). Most commentators seem to equate the two; e.g., Eule, supra, 91 Yale L. J. at 427–28, 474; Tushnet, "Rethinking the Dormant Commerce Clause," 1979 Wis. L. Rev. 125, 150; Nowak, Rotunda & Young, Constitutional Law ch. 8, espec. at 270 (3d ed. 1986); but the inquiry framed by Stone (and still pursued today) more specifically weighs against the interstate burden the *effectiveness* of the state measure toward the legitimate end, and also the relative importance of that end.

Some of the factors relevant to the legitimacy of an end or the aptness of a means may operate again at this third stage of inquiry; consequently, unless great care is taken in expression, on the face of an opinion the discrete steps can (and often do) appear to merge. See, e.g., *Great A. & P. Tea*, supra, 424 U.S. at 375–76.

In expressing the result of this third level of inquiry, majority opinions generally have been written so as to avoid the appearance of close calls. Typically the burdens have been declared quite minor as well as the local benefits ample, as in

Clover Leaf Creamery, supra, 449 U.S. at 472–73, and Ray v. Atlantic Richfield Co., 435 U.S. 151, 179–80 (1978); or else the burdens have been declared substantial as well as the seeming relation to legitimate ends illusory, as in *Kassel,* supra, 450 U.S. at 671. Where the demonstrated burdens are modest, the Court has refused to allow hypothetical possibilities of greater burdens to support a facial challenge. *Arkansas Electric,* supra, 461 U.S. at 395. Conversely, where the demonstrated burdens are substantial it has refused to consider as sufficient either speculative or merely presumed relations to legitimate state ends. *Mite Corp.,* supra, 457 U.S. at 644–45; *Raymond,* supra.

The presence of dissents and separate concurring opinions in many of the cases, however, suggests that sometimes the calls are close indeed; and when debatable choices must be made among competing public interests, or between public and competing private interests, one might well wonder whether they ought not be made through the political rather than the judicial process.

A judicial calculus of effectiveness against burdens requires that choices of substantive policy be made. This is well illustrated by the cases involving incompatible regulations of different states applicable to the same interstate activity. Conceivable but improbable differences certainly may be disregarded as merely conjectural burdens on commerce, see, e.g., Colorado Anti-Discrimination Comm'n v. Continental Air Lines, 372 U.S. 714,

721 (1963); Bob-Lo Excursion Co. v. Michigan, 333 U.S. 28, 37, 39 (1948); and so, perhaps, may less improbable differences which are not shown to exist in fact, see, e.g., *Huron Cement,* supra, 362 U.S. at 448. However, the actual coexistence of incompatible regulations—even though compliance with all might be possible at some cost in money or convenience—frequently has been acknowledged as a severe burden on interstate commerce not outweighed by claimed benefits to the states. See, e.g., *Kassel,* supra; *Raymond,* supra; Bibb v. Navajo Freight Lines, 359 U.S. 520 (1959); *Morgan v. Virginia,* supra; Hall v. DeCuir, 95 U.S. 485 (1878).

In cases of the latter description, the Court's modern approach clearly gives it a major policymaking role. Under older theory, although technically only the particular law under challenge was ruled invalid the rationale was that such conflict among state laws showed the subject to be "national" in character (in *Cooley* terms), suitable only for a nationwide, uniform rule, so that *all* state laws on the point (whether consistent or inconsistent) were precluded. See, e.g., *Hall,* supra, 95 U.S. at 489. That certainly is how the rulings in *Hall* and *Morgan v. Virginia* were perceived: See *Bob-Lo,* supra, 333 U.S. at 43 (Jackson, with Vinson, dissenting); see also *Morgan v. Virginia,* supra, 328 U.S. at 390 (Burton, dissenting). However, now that *Cooley's* reference to the need for uniformity as the earmark of "national" facets of interstate commerce is construed to mean "nec-

§ 11.10 FEDERAL POWER 291

essary in the * * * sense of useful in accomplishing a permitted [national] purpose" (*Morgan v. Virginia,* supra, 328 U.S. at 377, 386), it no longer inexorably follows from the fact of incompatibility that the laws of *all* of the states on the point in question must fall.

Nevertheless, to condemn the first one challenged *only because* it is the first to be challenged—regardless how much wiser it might be—seems irrational; and to condemn one state's regulation *merely* because it is "out of step with the laws of all other" states in its region (cf. *Kassel,* supra, 450 U.S. at 671) could work to stifle innovations however dramatic their contributions to important state (or national) goals. No doubt it was for these reasons that the Court in *Bibb,* supra, declared that the merits of a particular state requirement "—out of line with the requirements of the other States—may be so compelling that the innovating State need not be the one to give way." 359 U.S. at 530.

That statement in *Bibb* was dicta; but it demonstrates a disposition to treat as judicial questions not only the determination of when foreclosing state regulation might promote what the Justices consider good policy for the nation, but also the determination of which of several states' inconsistent alternatives might better promote the objectives deemed legitimate for states. The latter is perilously close to the superlegislative role forbidden in *Barnwell;* and both are subject to Justice

Black's objection that "whether state legislation imposes an 'undue burden' on interstate commerce raises pure questions of policy, which the Constitution intended should be resolved by the Congress." *Morgan v. Virginia,* supra, 328 U.S. at 387 (concurring opinion).

§ 11.11 Critique of the Modern Approach

Even commentators who urge that the practice continue agree that, despite contrary pretensions, in dormant commerce clause cases "the Court performs an essentially legislative role by nakedly constructing policies for the particular case that are the product of the Court's own balancing of national versus state concerns." Choper, "The Scope of National Power Vis-a-Vis the States; The Dispensability of Judicial Review," 86 Yale L. J. 1552, 1585–86 (1977). Recognizing that this does not fit the traditional stereotype of constitutional adjudication, some argue that it illustrates an avowedly political theory of judicial review, which they enthusiastically embrace. E.g., Tushnet, "Rethinking the Dormant Commerce Clause," 1979 Wis. L. Rev. 125. Others suggest that the process be viewed, not as "true" constitutional adjudication at all, Choper, supra, at 1587 n. 194, but rather as a species of "federal common law." See Monaghan, "Constitutional Common Law," Foreword to "The Supreme Court 1974 Term," 89 Harv. L. Rev. 1, 17 (1975); see also O'Fallon, "The Commerce Clause: A Theoretical Comment," 61 Ore. L. Rev. 395, 408 (1982). The comparison to common

§ 11.11 *FEDERAL POWER* 293

law is not new: Dowling made it in his 1940 and 1947 articles, and urged that to candidly accept this characterization "might give the Court a larger freedom for its efforts." "Interstate Commerce and State Power—Revised Version," 47 Colum.L. Rev. 547, 559 (1947); cf. O'Fallon, supra, 61 Ore. L. Rev. at 414, 419.

The often inconsistent stumbling from case to case, emphasizing the factual peculiarities of each and occasionally tendering some reconciling explanation, is typical indeed of common law methodology. Moreover, while legislative change of rules judicially laid down is unorthodox (at least) for constitutional law, it certainly is appropriate for common law, and since 1945 the Court consistently has affirmed that Congress may "permit the states to regulate [interstate] commerce in a manner which would otherwise not be permissible * * *." *Southern Pacific,* supra, 325 U.S. at 769 (1945); see also Northeast Bancorp v. Board of Governors, 472 U.S. 159, 174 (1985); White v. Massachusetts Council of Construction Employers, 460 U.S. 204, 213 (1983); International Shoe Co. v. Washington, 326 U.S. 310, 315 (1945). (It will be explained in Chapter Thirteen how Congress' ability to supersede inferences from the dormant commerce clause evolved and is rationalized.)

Nonetheless the Court itself persists in describing these decisions as constitutional, and not "common law," in character. What apparently accounts for this is that the Court regards the policy of interstate free trade as a policy of constitutional stature. The truth is, however, that this so-called "constitutional" policy of free trade originated in the same era, and has its roots in the same extraconstitutional economic theories, as the old practice of scrutinizing business regulations on "substantive due process" grounds; and from the latter practice the Court long ago had the good sense to withdraw.

So far from ensuring that trade would be free, the Constitution enabled Congress to disrupt and obstruct interstate and foreign commerce however it might choose: Congress' discretion over that commerce was made plenary. See, e.g., *White,* supra, 460 U.S. at 213; *Morgan v. Virginia,* supra, 328 U.S. at 380; id. at 389 (Frankfurter, concurring). Certainly the founding generation was concerned about state selfishness and protectionism, and wished to eliminate undesirable barriers to national economic integration. The solution they settled upon, however, was vesting ample power in the national *legislative* body—not in the courts. See Eule, supra, 91 Yale L. J. at 434–35.

Since the days of Justice Stone, the expressed rationale for national intervention against state measures which impact interstate commerce has been that otherwise certain interests might promote their own advantage at the expense of others unrepresented, or underrepresented, in the relevant political process. *Barnwell,* supra, 303 U.S. at 184 n. 2; cf. *Carolene Products,* supra, 304 U.S.

at 152 n. 4. But this fails to justify any national *judicial* intervention; the interests locally disadvantaged *do* have political representation in Congress.

Defenders of judicial intervention therefore contend that Congress is too busy with other concerns, so that the judiciary must act lest mere political inertia allow centrifugal forces of localism to prevail. E.g., Tribe, supra, at 319; Choper, supra, 86 Yale L. J. at 1586–87. The argument is that, whereas few of them could attract Congress' attention, "one can expect that nearly every burdensome regulation will be the subject of judicial attention." Tushnet, supra, 1979 Wis.L.Rev. at 154. Yet Tushnet acknowledges that examining all of the material considerations is "a task beyond the Court's ability in general," 1979 Wis. L. Rev. at 160; and both he and Choper acknowledge that the absence or insufficiency of advocacy on behalf of diverse interests of the public often seriously impairs judicial deliberation. Id. at 161; 86 Yale L. J. at 1587 n. 194.

In any event, however, the claim that Congress is too busy is fanciful and unpersuasive. Congress has time for whatever its collective constituency deems important—and manages to deal with many other things besides. Policy for interstate commerce in fact has engaged a significant share of Congress' attention over the past century (quite aside from the many other matters, to influence which Congress has utilized its commerce power as a tool). And Congress can prioritize: If a fracturing of the national market were truly in prospect, there is no doubt it would receive ample attention; and if impacted industries or affected consumers cannot arouse congressional interest, perhaps that should be taken (by persons who profess some faith in democracy) to indicate that the state actions which trouble them do not really unsettle the nation.

Moreover, for problems too numerous, too varied, too complex, or too recurrent for continuous direct oversight by Congress itself, the routine solution for generations now has been delegation to administrative agencies, with provision for whatever method of accountability to Congress is deemed wise. See Eule, supra, 91 Yale L.J. at 435–36. See also Choper, supra, 86 Yale L.J. at 1587–88 n. 194. Many areas already have been dealt with this way.

In fact, as a practical matter "dormant" commerce clause arguments most frequently are employed by experienced counsel today merely as a secondary thesis to fall back on in case their primary argument—that Congress *has* acted materially (and preemptively)—should fail.

Despite all the efforts to rationalize and structure it, "the jurisprudence of the 'negative side' of the Commerce Clause remains hopelessly confused." *Kassel*, supra, 450 U.S. at 706 (Rehnquist, dissenting). The relevant private and public interests involved, the practical consequences to be considered, and the significant differences of fact are so multifarious that surely it will remain confused as long as the Justices continue to engage themselves in the process of accommodating, adjusting, and compromising these competing demands—a process far better suited (and constitutionally assigned) to the *political* arena.

It is unlikely that this bad judicial habit, of such long standing, and to which the Justices still seem so compulsively attached (see, e.g., § 11.06), will be broken suddenly. One might more realistically hope that, as federal legislation and agency jurisdiction continue to expand in scope, preemption will increasingly become the significant issue, and controversies over "negative implications" (at least as to state *regulations*) will just gradually fade away.

One should note in passing a possible alternative basis for reaching comparable results in *some* cases without resort to dormant commerce clause theory. When the Constitution was written, the concept of the business corporation was in its infancy; most local and interstate commerce, at least, was carried on by natural persons in sole proprietorship or partnership form. Thus it probably then was conceived that a sufficient constitutional barrier to parochial legislation and economic balkanization was provided by declaring that "[t]he Citizens of each State shall be entitled to all Privileges and Immunities of Citizens in the several States." U.S. Const. Art. IV, § 2.

As corporations became a more significant business form, however, they were held not to be "citizens" for purposes of this Art. IV privileges and immunities clause. See Bank of Augusta v. Earle, 13 Pet. (38 U.S.) 519 (1839); Paul v. Virginia, 8 Wall. (75 U.S.) 168 (1869). By the time corporations came to dominate the business world, therefore, the potential of this clause as an instrument for economic integration was small.

Recently an heroic effort to rehabilitate this Art. IV privileges and immunities clause, and to make it the focus of concerns otherwise dealt with under the aegis of the commerce clause, was made by Professor Eule in his Yale article cited repeatedly supra. However, even if the obstacles of language and precedent which hinder its application to corporations were surmounted, this clause probably could not support those aspects of the doctrine presently attributed to the commerce clause which consider factors other than the interests of out-of-state business in local resources and markets.

§ 11.12 Negative Implications for State Taxes: Preface

The foregoing discussion of negative commerce clause implications has focused primarily on state *regulations;* but the doctrine applies to state *taxes* as well, and here its application is even more complicated.

As to taxes, there is no practical issue as to the first two stages of current dormant commerce clause inquiry: Raising revenue to support state operations is plainly a legitimate end, and taxation plainly is an appropriate means to that end. The complicating factors appear at the third stage.

Taxing techniques are extremely varied; and the subjects of taxes—the items and activities which governments choose to tax—are enormously diverse and constantly changing. The number of relevant cases in the Reports already is enormous, and the Supreme Court itself has described them as a "quagmire" of decisions, "not always clear * * * consistent or reconcilable." Northwestern States Portland Cement Co. v. Minnesota, 358 U.S. 450, 458 (1959). "[E]specially in this field opinions must be read in the setting of the particular cases and as the product of preoccupation with their special facts." Freeman v. Hewit, 329 U.S. 249, 252 (1946). In 1980 the Court noted that litigation concerning negative implications for state taxes "appears to be undergoing a revival of sorts." Mobil Oil Corp. v. Commissioner of Taxes, 445 U.S. 425, 443 (1980). A major reorientation of doctrinal approach was announced in 1977; but as will be seen in due course, the new structure of inquiry has been of limited assistance in simplifying and clarifying this complicated field.

§ 11.13 The Tax Cases Before 1977

Although there had been relevant dicta earlier, the first time a state tax was held void by negative inference from the commerce clause was the Case of the State Freight Tax, 15 Wall. (82 U.S.) 232 (1873). Applying the *Cooley* "rule," the Court there held that interstate transportation of goods is a "national" aspect of interstate commerce, and thus no more taxable than it was regulable by states.

Soon not only transportation, but also the "purchase, sale and exchange of commodities," see Leisy v. Hardin, 135 U.S. 100, 109 (1890); see also Welton v. Missouri, 91 U.S. 275, 280 (1876), and even "[t]he negotiation of sales of goods which are in another state, for the purpose of introducing them into the state in which the negotiation is made," Robbins v. Shelby County, 120 U.S. 489, 497 (1887), came to be regarded as "national" aspects of interstate commerce under *Cooley.*

In *Robbins,* in fact, albeit in dicta, the Court announced for state taxes an even more categorical rule, declaring that

> Interstate commerce cannot be taxed at all [by a state], even though the same amount of tax should be laid on domestic commerce, or that which is carried on solely within the state.

120 U.S. at 497.

Like *Cooley* itself, this proposition in *Robbins* was based on the dual federalism notion which had become predominant in the mid-nineteenth century. The significance of dual federalism thought for state *taxes,* however, remained obvious long after its lingering presence as the basis of dormant com-

§ 11.13   *FEDERAL POWER*   301

merce clause doctrine generally had become more obscure. Characterization of the matter being taxed remained the decisive factor. See, e.g., Spector Motor Service v. O'Connor, 340 U.S. 602 (1951); *Freeman,* supra. Because states could not tax interstate commerce, or the privilege of conducting it, states had to identify as the "subject" of any tax some distinct local activity separate from interstate commerce itself. See, e.g., Hope Natural Gas v. Hall, 274 U.S. 284 (1927); Heisler v. Thomas Colliery Co., 260 U.S. 245 (1922).

Denominated sometimes the "separation theory" and sometimes the "formal rule," this proposition that states could not tax interstate commerce per se challenged the ingenuity of tax law draftsmen but accomplished no real substantive goal. For example, a state was barred from imposing a license tax for doing an interstate business, or for doing an entire business a part of which was interstate, Leloup v. Port of Mobile, 127 U.S. 640 (1888); but the license tax would avoid the constitutional obstacle if it were drafted so as to apply only to the local, and not to the interstate, business in which the same licensee engaged, and it was quite immaterial that the redesigned tax (because of its higher rate or otherwise) might be far more onerous in practical effect. Compare Allen v. Pullman's Palace Car Co., 191 U.S. 171 (1903), with Pickard v. Pullman Co., 117 U.S. 34 (1886).

In time, however, it came to be recognized that interstate business should bear a fair share of the costs of the state governments whose benefits it shared: As the Court put it, "[e]ven interstate business must pay its way." Western Live Stock v. Bureau of Revenue, 303 U.S. 250, 254 (1938), quoting Postal Telegraph-Cable Co. v. Richmond, 249 U.S. 252, 259 (1919). Eventually the nominal prohibition against state taxation of interstate commerce came to be so qualified with caveats and riddled with exceptions that it hardly could be described as a rule at all. It operated instead as a wild card whose unpredictable play might upset the best calculations of state tax planners. Nonetheless this "formal rule" was not actually discarded until 1977.

Even when the matter taxed could not be described as interstate commerce, the Court in the post-Civil War era held state taxes which discriminated against interstate commerce to be void by negative implication. The rule against discrimination had been intimated in dicta in Woodruff v. Parham, 8 Wall. (75 U.S.) 123, 140 (1869). It was applied in Welton v. Missouri, 91 U.S. 275 (1876) to a tax which was discriminatory on its face, using the out-of-state origin of goods as a criterion of the tax. Then in *Robbins,* supra, the Court held that a tax drawing no facial distinction between internal and interstate commerce nonetheless was void with regard to the latter where its practical effect (given the circumstances of the interstate business involved) was to place interstate merchants at a disadvantage compared with local ones. This pro-

§ 11.13   FEDERAL POWER   303

hibition against state taxes discriminatory either in purpose or in effect remains a part of dormant commerce clause doctrine today.

Another limitation on states' taxing power originally was conceived only in jurisdictional terms, but later became confounded with dormant commerce clause doctrine. Hays v. Pacific Mail Steamship Co., 17 How (58 U.S.) 596 (1855), involved a California property tax assessed against certain steamships belonging to a company incorporated in, and having its principal place of business in, New York. In the course of their travels, each of the steamships spent a few days at a time in California ports to load and unload, and for refitting and repairs. The Court held that California could not tax the vessels because, being only temporarily in that state, they had no "situs" there. Their situs, the Court said, was "the home port, where the vessels belonged, and where the owners were liable to be taxed * * *." Id. at 600.

In other words, the vessels were not "present" in California, and the state had no jurisdiction to tax property outside its bounds. The proposition that a state cannot tax (or otherwise govern) beyond its borders was a proposition so fundamental in American jurisprudence (until the mid-twentieth century brought *International Shoe* and the idea of "minimum contacts") that from the beginning of our history it had been regarded as "constitutional" even though not written down. (This, in fact, and nothing about the commerce clause, is why Justice Woodbury in his separate opinion in the 1847 *License Cases* (discussed near the end of § 11.02) had noted the "extraterritoriality" limit, declaring that no state could "prescribe rules for others," and that consequently "so far as regards * * * a regulation reaching to all the States" Congress' power over commerce was necessarily exclusive.)

Hays was decided (and Woodbury reasoned in the *License Cases*) on that jurisdictional basis more than a decade before the fourteenth amendment was adopted. Once that amendment was ratified, however, this concept of territorial limits to state jurisdiction came to be associated with its "due process" clause. Cf. Pennoyer v. Neff, 95 U.S. 714 (1878), holding Oregon court proceedings antedating the fourteenth amendment defective for lack of jurisdiction over an extra-state defendant, and noting that since adoption of that amendment the defect could be expressed in terms of due process.

Later the Court distinguished California's attempt to tax steamships from a tax which it treated as a property tax on railroad cars, in Pullman's Palace Car Co. v. Pennsylvania, 141 U.S. 18 (1891). Like the steamships, each Pullman car passed in and out of the state, none remaining constantly within it; but the Court found that the cars, unlike the steamships, had no fixed situs in the state of their owner's domicile. Instead, the Court considered their situs to be the place of their physical location; and it would follow that a state, "without regard to the place of the owner's domicile, could tax the specific cars which at a given moment were within its borders." 141 U.S. at 26 (dictum). What merits notice here is the curious fact that the Court in *Pullman's Palace-Car* treated the situs issue not as one of due process, but rather as one arising under the commerce clause: "The only question of which this court has jurisdiction," it said, "is whether the tax was in violation of the clause * * * granting to Congress the power to regulate commerce among the several States." 141 U.S. at 21–2.

Over the past half-century, the concept of "presence" as prerequisite to state jurisdiction for purposes of adjudication and regulation has yielded to the concept of "contacts," see International Shoe Co. v. Washington, 326 U.S. 310 (1945); and likewise the concept of "situs" as a prerequisite to taxing jurisdiction has yielded to the concept of "nexus." This concept remains important to the constitutionality of state taxation; but considerable equivocation remains as to whether it is a due process or a commerce clause concept—or both. (Even in *International Shoe,* supra, the argument was cast in both due process and commerce clause terms.)

Another factor was the risk of multiple taxation. The Court in *Hays,* supra, had observed that

 if the State of California possessed the authority to impose the [steamship] tax in question, any other State in the Union, into the ports of which the vessels entered in the prosecution of their trade and business, might also impose a like tax.

17 How. (58 U.S.) at 599. This risk of multiple taxation was perceived as unfair; and the *Hays* court—thinking only in terms of jurisdiction—addressed it with the dictum (quoted supra) that jurisdiction to tax the vessels should be found only at their "home port." This "home port doctrine," as the Court noted recently in Japan Line, Ltd. v. Los Angeles, 441 U.S. 434, 442 (1979), was a corollary of the maxim of medieval law that "moveables follow the person." The home port doctrine is *not* the principal rule followed with regard to taxation of moving equipment today.

Neither, however, is the *Pullman's Palace-Car* dictum to the effect that a state may tax any moving equipment that is within its borders at a given moment. This proposition likewise presents risks of multiple taxation; for "tax days" vary from state to state, and equipment which happened to be in different states on their respective tax days thus could be taxed several times.

On its facts, however, *Pullman's Palace-Car* did not involve a tax on the cars within the state at some particular moment; technically, it was not even a property tax. Rather Pennsylvania had imposed a tax on the company *measured* by the *average* number of its cars within the state during the period for which the tax was assessed and the proportion which that number bore to the total number of cars which the Pullman Company owned. The Court treated this as, *in effect,* a tax imposed on a fraction of the Pullman cars, apportioned with other states where they might be located from time to time; and the Court reasoned that if every state through which Pullman cars ran were to adopt the same method of assessment, there would be no multiple taxation at all. (Of course other states were not obliged to adopt the same method, so complete protection against multiple taxation was not actually guaranteed.)

In *Hays* the risk of multiple taxation had conditioned a ruling on jurisdiction—in modern terminology, a due process issue. In *Pullman's Palace-Car* the same risk was discussed, not in terms of due process, but in terms of the commerce clause. In more recent cases prior to 1977, due process and commerce clause considerations frequently were commingled in discussions of multiple taxation problems; the concept of "situs" or "nexus" thus did double duty as both a due process and a commerce clause concept.

Sometimes the commerce clause issue remained, however, even where the due process requirement was found satisfied. See, e.g., *Western Live Stock,* supra. It was held that sufficient situs in a state to justify taxation could be established by showing that the taxpayer's vehicles were regularly and habitually present there, even though the particular vehicles present from time to time might not be the same. E.g., Braniff Airways, Inc. v. Nebraska

State Board of Equalization, 347 U.S. 590 (1954). Since those same vehicles, however, on the same basis, must have a situs elsewhere as well (in fact, at several other places), the risk of multiple taxation could be avoided only by requiring something more. The Court therefore held that moving property must be *apportioned* among the several states through which it might move, and allowed each state to tax only its apportioned share.

While requiring apportionment, however, the Court did not require that every state use the same apportionment formula; nor did it require that the apportionment accomplished by any particular formula be exact. The Court gave relief, however, when a formula was shown to yield a grossly distorted result in a particular case. Norfolk & Western Ry. v. Missouri State Tax Comm'n, 390 U.S. 317 (1968).

Of course "[t]he rule which permits taxation by two or more states on an apportionment basis precludes taxation of all of the property by the state of the domicile." Standard Oil Co. v. Peck, 342 U.S. 382, 384 (1952). The domicile, however, still could be the default situs, permitted to tax any part of such property not shown to have established a tax situs elsewhere even though it was continuously outside the domiciliary state. Central R.R. Co. v. Pennsylvania, 370 U.S. 607 (1962). (But see the 1980 opinion in *Mobil Oil*, supra, 445 U.S. at 444–46.)

§ 11.14 The Tax Cases Since 1977

In 1977 the Supreme Court repudiated the "formal rule," recognizing that its greatest effect had been to promote semantic quibbles and reward ingenuity in draftsmanship. Complete Auto Transit, Inc. v. Brady, 430 U.S. 274 (1977). The Court emphasized that what should matter is "not the formal language of the tax statute but rather its practical effect;" and it summarized the bulk of the prior cases as having

> sustained a tax against Commerce Clause challenge when the tax is applied to an activity with a substantial nexus with the taxing State, is fairly apportioned, does not discriminate against interstate commerce, and is fairly related to the services provided by the State.

430 U.S. at 279.

Subsequent cases, involving several different kinds of taxes, have treated this passage in *Complete Auto Transit* as the operative restatement of dormant commerce clause doctrine for taxes. E.g., Wardair Canada, Inc. v. Florida Dept. of Rev., 106 S.Ct. 2369, 2373 (1986); Commonwealth Edison Co. v. Montana, 453 U.S. 609, 615–16 (1981); Maryland v. Louisiana, 451 U.S. 725, 754 (1981); Mobil Oil Corp. v. Commissioner of Taxes, 445 U.S. 425, 443 (1980); Washington Dept. of Revenue v. Association of Washington Stevedoring Companies, 435 U.S. 734, 750 (1978). See generally Lockhart, "A Revolution in State Taxation of Commerce?" 65 Minn.L.Rev. 1025 (1981).

The tendency has been to treat this summary as a "four-pronged test." The factors thus identified, however, are not discrete; they commingle and coalesce. Moreover, several of these factors have been discussed in some recent cases in terms of due process instead of—or as well as—in commerce clause terms. The four factors are discussed here in a sequence different from their recitation in *Complete Auto Transit,* for three reasons: To facilitate perception of the relations among them; to emphasize the limitations of this new formulation; and to encourage isolation of the due process from the commerce clause considerations involved.

1. The tax must not discriminate against interstate commerce. This is one of the oldest negative inferences drawn from the commerce clause, and it seems to have no due process coloration at all. The precept is simple in statement; but there are great difficulties in its application, for various tax measures, alone or in combination, (like various regulations) combine with a multitude of other factors to produce the complex mix of relative advantages and disadvantages enjoyed by local and interstate competitors in the marketplace.

Despite statements to the effect that dormant commerce clause questions are to be decided by practical consequences rather than form, the question of "discrimination" seems to be heavily influenced by appearances. A state severance tax on coal was held not to discriminate against interstate commerce even though 90% of the coal mined in the state was shipped elsewhere and the economic effect of the tax was thus shifted primarily to out-of-state utilities and their customers; the tax was computed at the same rate regardless of the destination of the coal, and the Court therefore found no differential in tax treatment as between interstate and intrastate commerce. *Commonwealth Edison,* supra. On the other hand, a wholesale gross receipts tax from which local manufacturers were exempt was held to discriminate against interstate commerce even though the exempt local manufacturers were subject to a far higher tax on manufacturing measured by wholesale price; for "manufacturing and wholesaling are not 'substantially equivalent events' such that the heavy tax on in-state manufacturers can be said to compensate for the admittedly lighter burden placed on wholesalers from out of state." Armco Inc. v. Hardesty, 467 U.S. 638, 643 (1984). See also *Maryland v. Louisiana,* supra.

The out-of-state manufacturers might be (although they might not be) subject to a manufacturing tax at home, in which case the wholesale tax would be a burden in addition to that which the in-state manufacturers bore. But the Court in *Armco* refused to require a showing that such was the case. Instead (borrowing a standard from a case discussing fair apportionment and not discrimination) it required that the tax be such that, if applied by every jurisdiction, there would be no impermissible interference with free trade. Thus the non-discrimination and apportionment requirements were effectively merged: "A tax that unfairly apportions income from other States is a form of discrimination against interstate commerce." 467 U.S. at 644. The Court deemed it irrelevant that other combinations of different states' taxing schemes might produce identical economic results.

2. The tax must be applied to an activity having a substantial nexus with the taxing state. This is the modern counterpart of the old proposition that states cannot tax (or regulate) beyond their territorial bounds, "nexus" having replaced "situs" as the minimum requisite here just as "contacts" has displaced "presence" as the minimum requisite for jurisdiction over persons. Fundamentally, therefore, this "substantial nexus" requirement appears to be a due process requirement, not a requirement under the commerce clause.

The most frequent application of this requirement in the past several years has been with regard to state taxes on income, taxpayers with income both from within and from without a state objecting to that state's inclusion for tax purposes of any part of the latter. So long as there is a sufficient connection between the taxpayer and the state, there is no absolute *due process* bar to a tax by that state on the taxpayer's income—even that attributable to its out-of-state activities. See Exxon Corp. v. Wisconsin Dept. of Revenue, 447 U.S.

§ 11.14 *FEDERAL POWER* 313

207, 219–27 (1980); *Mobil Oil,* supra, 445 U.S. at 435–42; Moorman Mfg. Co. v. Bair, 437 U.S. 267, 271–75 (1978).

In *Mobil Oil* and in *Exxon,* supra, however, the Court elaborated that income from out-of-state could be included only insofar as it was generated by a "unitary business enterprise" of that taxpayer, that unitary enterprise having the requisite nexus with the taxing state; income from an entirely separate enterprise of the same taxpayer could not be taxed unless *that* enterprise had sufficient nexus with the state.

There might be considerations *other than* the due process requirement of nexus which would preclude a particular state from taxing *all* of such a taxpayer's unitary business enterprise income; for example, as will be discussed below, some sort of "apportionment" might be required. But the "nexus" requirement by itself does not require that the particular *aspects* of a taxpayer's enterprise being taxed be connected with the taxing state; it requires only that the taxpayer, and his particular enterprise being taxed (or the income from which is being taxed) have that sufficient nexus.

With respect to some other kinds of taxes, the nexus requirement might be satisfied even more easily. Most states impose sales taxes on many transactions, the tax being chargeable to the purchaser but the seller being obligated to collect and pay over the tax, and the seller being liable to pay the tax himself if he fails to collect it from the buyer. As a corollary to this tax, most sales tax states also impose a compensating "use tax" on the in-state user of goods bought out-of-state which would have been subject to the sales tax if bought within the state; and some of the use tax states—at least with regard to some taxable goods—impose use tax *collection* obligations equivalent to the sales tax collection obligations commonly imposed on sellers. That use tax collection obligation necessarily is imposed on sellers *outside* the state. (If the seller were in-state, the sales tax would apply instead.) The question thus arises, what kind of nexus between the out-of-state seller and the use-taxing state must be present to support jurisdiction to impose that use tax collection obligation?

National Geographic Society v. California Board of Equalization, 430 U.S. 551 (1977), involved such a use tax collection obligation. The Society maintained two offices in California soliciting advertising for its magazine; but those offices had nothing to do with the strictly mail-order sales of the Society's publications, on the use of which in California the use tax was imposed. All of the sales solicitation and order-filling activities occurred out-of-state, and the Society therefore contended that it could not be required to collect (or to pay if it did not collect) the California use tax with respect to publications sold by mail to California residents.

Without using the "unitary business rationale of *Mobil Oil* and *Exxon,* the Court held that the use tax obligation *could* be enforced against the Society

§ 11.14 FEDERAL POWER 315

because of its advertising sales offices in the state. It rejected the Society's argument that there must be a nexus not only between the seller and the state, but also between the particular taxable activity of the seller involved and his activity taking place in the state:

> However fatal to a direct tax a "showing that particular transactions are dissociated from the local business * * *," * * * such dissociation does not bar the imposition of the use-tax-collection duty.

430 U.S. at 560.

A disconcerting feature of the *National Geographic* opinion, written by Justice Brennan, is that it treats the nexus issue as one under the commerce clause as well as under the due process clause. A similar equivocation appears in the *Exxon* opinion, written by Justice Marshall. Probably this equivocation is due to the intimate connection between nexus and the requirement of apportionment (to be considered below); the apportionment requirement is basically a function of dormant commerce clause doctrine (although in some opinions it has been articulated in terms of due process as well). It would facilitate analysis, and better application in future cases, if the Justices would take greater care to isolate the due process and commerce clause issues; as this illustrates, however, they often fail to do so.

3. The tax must be fairly related to the services provided by the state. As the Court said in 1978,

> The Commerce Clause balance tips against the tax only when it unfairly burdens commerce by exacting more than a just share from the interstate activity.

Washington Stevedoring, supra, 435 U.S. at 748. Three years later the Court acknowledged that this requirement is closely related to the nexus requirement, but noted that it adds

> the additional limitation that the *measure* of the tax must be reasonably related to the extent of the contact, since it is the activities or presence of the taxpayer in the State that may properly be made to bear a "just share of state tax burden."

Commonwealth Edison, supra, 453 U.S. at 626.

This, however, does not mean that taxes must be proportional to particular governmental services provided, or that the revenue produced from an interstate business by a tax must equate (even approximately) with the costs a state incurs on account of that taxpayer's activities. Id. at 623–28. No analogy can be drawn to "user fees" or to assessments for particular benefits; for general taxes are assessed to support a broad spectrum of miscellaneous government activities, from which a particular taxpayer might gain nothing but the unspecific privilege of operating in an organized

§ 11.14   FEDERAL POWER   317

society. Rather, the notion behind this requirement is that

> [w]hen a tax is assessed in proportion to a taxpayer's activities or presence in a State, the taxpayer is shouldering its fair share of supporting the State's provision of "police and fire protection, the benefit of a trained work force, and 'the advantages of a civilized society.'"

Id. at 627, quoting from *Exxon,* supra, 447 U.S. at 228, in turn quoting from *Japan Line,* supra, 441 U.S. at 445. The extent of such general benefits to be provided, and the level of taxation required to support them, essentially are matters for legislative resolution, 453 U.S. at 627, which will vary from state to state. This makes it impossible to ascribe uniform taxable valuations to particular quanta of in-state activity. Consequently, only "when the measure of a tax bears no relationship to the taxpayers' presence or activities in a State" will the state be viewed as "imposing an undue burden on interstate commerce." Id. at 629.

While in *Washington Stevedoring* and in *Commonwealth Edison,* supra, this requirement was described as derived from the commerce clause, it was characterized instead as a requirement of due process in *Exxon,* in *Mobil Oil,* and in *Moorman,* supra. See also Standard Pressed Steel Co. v. Washington Dept. of Revenue, 419 U.S. 560, 562 (1975). Here again, the Court's equivocation over the source of the requirement is troubling; for the source of the requirement has crucial consequences for Congress' ability to control or override judicial decisions regarding it, as will be discussed in § 11.15.

4. The tax must be fairly apportioned. The essential function of apportionment is to prevent multiple taxation, which would "unduly burden" interstate business. See *Mobil Oil,* supra, 445 U.S. at 442 et seq. As already noted, the apportionment idea first appeared in 1891 in *Pullman's Palace-Car,* supra, where it was applied to a tax which the Court treated like a tax on moving property. See § 11.13. It also was there noted that the tax in that case technically was not a tax on the property, but rather a tax on the company "measured" by the average of Pullman cars within the state during the taxing period. The apportionment requirement is applied to a wide variety of taxes on interstate business. Most of the recent cases discussing apportionment happen to have involved state taxes on incomes.

Attempting recently to elucidate this requirement the Court observed that, in order to accomplish a "fair" apportionment, the allocation formula employed by a state for income tax purposes

> must be such that, if applied by every jurisdiction, it would result in no more than all of the unitary business' income being taxed.

Container Corp. of America v. Franchise Tax Board, 463 U.S. 159, 169 (1983). (The Court labelled this characteristic "internal consistency;" but the label is not very apt, and not at all illuminating.)

§ 11.14   *FEDERAL POWER*   319

With slight modification the same elucidation is applicable to various other kinds of taxes.

This fair apportionment requirement, however, does not preclude a state from including, in the total which is to be apportioned, those activities of the taxpayer which take place outside the taxing state—so long as they are part of a "unitary business enterprise" which the state, by virtue of satisfying the *other* requirements already discussed, may tax.

> [T]he entire net income of a corporation, generated by interstate as well as intrastate activities, may be fairly apportioned among the States for tax purposes by formulas utilizing in-state aspects of interstate affairs.

Northwestern States Portland Cement Co. v. Minnesota, 358 U.S. 450, 460 (1959). But "the linchpin of apportionability in the field of state income taxation is the unitary-business principle." *Mobil Oil,* supra, 445 U.S. at 439.

Thus a state for tax purposes may include in the apportionable income of an interstate business doing business in the state even its income in the form of dividends from *foreign* subsidiaries and affiliates, if those foreign activities are part of the same integrated business enterprise, *Mobil Oil,* supra; and income from all the sundry activities of a vertically integrated petroleum company (including exploration, production, and refining as well as marketing) may be taxed on a fair apportionment basis by a state in which nothing but marketing activity takes place—absent a showing by the taxpayer that those other activities constitute unrelated business activities (discrete enterprises) of the taxpayer, *Exxon,* supra.

But the "unitary business" principle precludes a state from including (even though apportioned) any income from subsidiaries which operate substantially autonomously rather than as integrated parts of the taxpayer's enterprise taking place in part in the taxing state. F.W. Woolworth Co. v. New Mexico Tax. & Rev. Dept., 458 U.S. 354 (1982); Asarco Inc. v. Idaho State Tax Comm'n, 458 U.S. 307 (1982). The parent's oversight of a subsidiary's capital structure and debt is not sufficient to satisfy this unitary business requirement, see *Woolworth,* supra; but on the other hand, the fact that a company segregates the activities for purposes of its internal accounting is not sufficient to establish that they are *not* all parts of the same unitary business enterprise, see *Exxon* and *Mobil Oil,* supra.

Although the apportionment formula chosen by a state must be such that, *if* it were applied by all states, no multiple taxation would occur, there is no requirement that all states actually *do* employ the same formula; and in fact, they do not. Moreover, it is not required that the apportionment accomplished even under any particular state's formula be exact. *Moorman,* supra, 437 U.S. at 278. A "rough approximation" is good enough. *Exxon,* supra, 447 U.S. at 223. Consequently, it

§ 11.14 FEDERAL POWER 321

obviously is quite possible that some degree of multiple taxation of interstate businesses will occur. The Supreme Court has approved the holding that

> an apportionment formula that is necessarily only a rough approximation of the income properly attributable to the taxing State is not subject to constitutional attack unless the taxpayer proves that the formula has produced an income attribution "out of all proportion to the business transacted" within the State.

Moorman, supra, 437 U.S. at 271.

As illustrating, again that the four factors identified in *Complete Auto Transit* commingle and coalesce, and do not really comprise a "four-pronged-test," it should be noted that this so-called "internal consistency" characteristic necessary to qualify an apportionment for tax purposes as "fair," also has been used as a test of whether a state tax is "discriminatory" against interstate commerce. *Armco,* supra, 467 U.S. at 644.

Moreover, as with others of the *Complete Auto Transit* factors, the Justices continue to equivocate as to whether the requirement of fair apportionment derives from the due process or the commerce clause. The old *Pullman's Palace-Car* case, supra, had discussed it under the commerce clause, and it was discussed in the same terms in *Complete Auto Transit* itself, 430 U.S. at 279, and in *Washington Stevedoring,* supra, 435 U.S. at 748, 749–50. But in *Asarco* and in *Woolworth,* supra, the Court discussed it only in terms of the due process clause. In several other recent cases the Court has discussed the apportionment requirement as associated with *both* the due process and commerce clauses. E.g., *Moorman,* supra, 437 U.S. at 274–75 (due process), and 276–81 (commerce); *Mobil Oil,* supra, 445 U.S. at 436–42 (due process), and 442–46 (commerce); *Exxon,* supra, 447 U.S. at 219–27 (due process), and 227–30 (commerce). See also *Container Corp.,* supra, 463 U.S. at 169.

Burden of proof. One point maintained consistently since repudiation of the old "formal rule" is that state taxes applied to interstate business are presumed to be valid, so that the taxpayer bears the burden of proving that one or another of the factors necessary to validate the tax as applied to it is missing. This is true whether the claim is that the tax discriminates against interstate commerce, see *Washington Stevedoring,* supra, 435 U.S. at 750; or that no sufficient nexus is present, see *Mobil Oil,* supra, 445 U.S. at 439–40; or that "extraterritorial values" are being taxed, see *Exxon,* supra, 447 U.S. at 221–22; or that an apportionment formula offends the "unitary business enterprise" principle, see *Exxon,* id. at 224; *Container Corp.,* supra, 463 U.S. at 175, or results in an allocation to the taxing state radically disproportionate to the business transacted in that state, see *Moorman,* supra, 437 U.S. at 274; *Container Corp.,* supra, 463 U.S. at 180; or that the apportionment results in multiple taxation, see *Standard Pressed Steel,* supra, 419 U.S. at 563.

§ 11.15 Critique of the Current Approach in Tax Cases

While the spate of recent litigation over state taxes has produced some improvement in dormant commerce clause doctrine (particularly the demise of the "formal rule"), its principal effect has been to demonstrate even more convincingly the utter futility of looking to the judicial process for consistent and reliable guidance in this realm. Sound policy formulation regarding the interstate aspects of state taxation requires sophisticated inquiries into changing business structures and practices; state revenue needs, resources, and techniques; and the economic impacts of taxes. It requires comprehensive planning rather than ad hoc and particularized adjudication. The judiciary is unsuited satisfactorily to perform these tasks. The Supreme Court's elaboration of purported negative commerce clause implications for state taxes has created a great deal of lucrative work for lawyers; but little else good about it can be said.

Justice Black protested frequently against elaborating commerce clause restraints on state taxes; while he would have foreclosed discrimination, he otherwise would have left the protection of commerce to Congress. See his dissents, e.g., in *Northwestern States,* supra; McCarroll v. Dixie Greyhound Lines, Inc., 309 U.S. 176, 183 (1940); Gwin, White & Prince, Inc. v. Henneford, 305 U.S. 434,

442 (1939); J.D. Adams Mfg. Co. v. Storen, 304 U.S. 307, 316 (1938). Most Justices, however, oddly still feel it their duty to afford commerce protection when Congress does not. See, e.g., *Wardair Canada,* supra, 106 S.Ct. at 2372–73; *Japan Line,* supra, 441 U.S. at 454; *Moorman,* supra, 437 U.S. at 283 (Powell, joined by Blackmun, dissenting). Occasionally a citation to the old *Cooley* case belies the dual federalism basis of this curious compulsion. See, e.g., *Washington Stevedoring,* supra, 435 U.S. at 749. Bad habits of mind are difficult to break.

It really is the number of dollars paid out in taxes and related costs of compliance—not the number of jurisdictions to which taxes are paid or the "taxable incidents" upon which they are laid— that determines the burden a taxpayer bears. It hardly eases the actual burden, for example, if "fair allocation" is required but no limit is imposed on the rate or the level at which any state may tax what is fairly allocated to it. Yet, recognizing that "numerous and competing economic, geographic, demographic, social, and political considerations * * * must inform a decision about an acceptable rate or level of state taxation," the Court firmly insists that "questions about the appropriate level of state taxes must be resolved through the political process." *Commonwealth Edison,* supra, 453 U.S. at 628. Apart from questions of jurisdiction, why should not the political process equally be trusted to resolve the other questions about state taxation as well?

§ 11.15 *FEDERAL POWER* 325

The Court admits that Congress, by virtue of its power under the commerce clause, may supervene judicial rulings about tax impacts on interstate commerce; see generally Chapter Thirteen. Occasionally it has even refrained from imposing some proposed standard "[a]bsent some explicit directive from Congress * * *." See, e.g., *Mobil Oil,* supra, 445 U.S. at 448 (1980). Why should such occasional exceptions not become the standard rule?

Following the Court's decisions in *Northwestern States,* supra, and Scripto, Inc. v. Carson, 362 U.S. 207 (1960), Congress did launch a long and very comprehensive study of interstate taxation problems and solutions, leading to elaborate legislative proposals in the mid–1960's and 1970's. See *Mobil Oil,* supra, 445 U.S. at 448–49. No major resulting bill ever passed more than one house; but certainly part of the reason Congress has failed to take more action is that inaction is made tolerable by the Justices' willingness to continue legislating policy in this realm on their own—however inappropriate and unsuitable their efforts might be.

Most states now have joined in the Multistate Tax Compact promulgated late in 1966, which facilitates administrative resolution of many of the practical problems concerning taxation of interstate business. See U.S. Steel Corp. v. Multistate Tax Comm'n, 434 U.S. 452 (1978). (For more information about the "compact" device generally, see Chapter Fifteen). Interstate cooperation and accommodation, however, cannot eliminate the troublesomeness of judicial intrusions.

The Court's equivocation as to whether various of its precepts are attributable to the commerce or rather to the due process clause is particularly distressing. Obstacles attributable to the commerce clause can be relaxed (and others added) by Congress by virtue of its plenary power over interstate (and foreign) commerce; and with its commerce power supplemented by the necessary and proper clause, Congress can eliminate *any* state taxes it considers undesirable for such commerce even though due process requisites for state taxing jurisdiction are met. But Congress has no power to authorize what the due process clause forbids, see Chapter Ten. As noted in § 11.14, both the "fair apportionment" requirement and the requirement that a tax must be "fairly related to the services provided by the state" have been attributed in several recent opinions to the due process as well as the commerce clause. It would be most unfortunate if the Court's equivocation of theory, in a policy realm where it does not even belong, were to prove a barrier to better (and more appropriate) legislative solutions.

§ 11.16 State Taxes and International Commerce

With regard to foreign commerce, there is an *express* limitation on state taxes imposed by Art. I, § 10, cl. 2:

§ 11.16 *FEDERAL POWER* 327

> No State shall, without the Consent of the Congress, lay any Imposts or Duties on Imports or Exports, except what may be absolutely necessary for executing its inspection Laws: and the net Produce of all Duties and Imposts, laid by any State on Imports or Exports, shall be for the Use of the Treasury of the United States; and all such Laws shall be subject to the Revision and Controul of the Congress.

This *express* limitation is considered here because its construction and application historically have been closely related to the elaboration of negative *implications* for state taxes impacting foreign commerce. It has been the actual focus, however, of much less litigation: There have been more than three hundred Supreme Court cases considering state taxes under the commerce clause, but scarcely more than a dozen considering issues under this "import-export clause."

The reasons for this express restriction on state taxation of international trade are simple. In the first place, other original states sought an end to the peculiar fiscal opportunity enjoyed (at the expense of consumers in those other states) by seaboard states with major ports; that was a source of acrimony during the Confederation era. Second, even the authorization for *Congress* to impose duties and imposts requires that they "shall be uniform throughout the United States," Art. I, § 8, cl. 1. State imposts and duties would disrupt this uniformity, which seemed important not only to prevent undesirable interstate competition for trade, but also to enable the nation to speak with a single voice in matters of foreign trade. Thus the express restriction by the import-export clause complemented the grant of power to Congress concerning commerce with foreign nations and the conduct of international affairs generally.

At an early date, this clause was construed to reach beyond levies assessed at the port of entry, to preclude other taxes deemed specially disadvantageous to importers—such as taxes imposed on goods because they had been imported, and license taxes on the business of selling imported goods. Brown v. Maryland, 12 Wheat. (25 U.S.) 419 (1827). This made it important to determine at what point goods which had been imported lost their distinctive, insulating character as imports so as to become subject to ordinary taxation by a state. In *Brown* Chief Justice Marshall suggested that

> when the importer has so acted upon the thing imported, that it has become incorporated and mixed up with the mass of property in the country, it has, perhaps, lost its distinctive character as an import, and has become subject to the taxing power of the state; but while remaining the property of the importer, in his warehouse, in the original form or package in which it was imported, a tax upon it is too plainly a duty on imports, to escape the prohibition in the constitution.

12 Wheat. (25 U.S.) at 441–42. This passage gave rise to the "original package" test, which enjoyed a long history not only under the import-export clause, but also under the commerce clause once the negative implications view of that clause had taken firm hold.

In fact, during the post-Civil War era when dormant commerce clause doctrine was flourishing the Court broadened the scope of the import-export clause substantially, holding that even a non-discriminatory, general ad valorem property tax could not be applied to goods which still retained their character as "imports" under the original package test. Low v. Austin, 13 Wall. (80 U.S.) 29 (1872). *Low* offered no policy justification for this extension of the tax immunity; and in reality, instead of operating to spare imports from discriminatory disadvantage, it gave to imports (or to those who held them) a special advantage. For example, stockpiled supplies or materials destined for eventual use in a manufacturing enterprise would escape state taxation if they happened to be imported, while identical materials of domestic origin could be taxed. This tended to create artificial incentives to import supplies and materials, potentially destructive of domestic industries and disruptive of federal regulation of foreign trade.

This anomaly at last was ended when the Court overruled *Low* in Michelin Tire Corp. v. Wages, 423 U.S. 276 (1976). There, upholding a nondiscriminatory ad valorem property tax as applied to unsold tires, imported in bulk and remaining in the importer's warehouse, the Court emphasized the purposes of the import-export clause to prevent port states' profiteering on their favorable geographic location at the expense of other states' consumers, and to prevent interference with federal control over international commercial affairs. Id. at 285–86. The Court did not criticize Chief Justice Marshall's statement in *Brown,* but did observe that it only provided illustrations, rather than a formula, and that its proper application is only evidentiary; the ultimate question is whether the tax is applied without discrimination—that is, without regard to the foreign or domestic origin of goods. Thus the clause only bars state taxes selectively imposed so as substantially to impair or specially to profit from importation. Id. at 287–88, 297, 298–99.

After *Michelin Tire,* misuse of the "original package" formulation as a "test" for tax immunity should no longer be a factor either under the import-export clause or as to negative commerce clause implications.

In other recent negative implications cases, however, the Court has observed that special considerations do justify greater restraints when state taxes are applied to inter*national* rather than inter*state* commerce.

In Japan Line, Ltd. v. Los Angeles, 441 U.S. 434 (1979), it held that international considerations bring two additional factors into play. The first is an enhanced risk of multiple taxation, because one (or more) of the potential taxing bodies is a foreign sovereign over which neither the Court nor Congress can exercise control. Id. at 448. The second, borrowed from *Michelin* (an import-export clause case), is a special need for the nation to "speak with one voice." Thus, in addition to answering the questions posed in *Complete Auto Transit,*

> a court must also inquire, first, whether the tax, notwithstanding apportionment, creates a substantial risk of international multiple taxation, and, second, whether the tax prevents the Federal Government from "speaking with one voice when regulating commercial relations with foreign governments."

Id. at 451.

Considering these additional factors in *Japan Line* the Court (8–1) invalidated under the dormant commerce clause California ad valorem property taxes applied to cargo shipping containers temporarily present in the state but owned by Japanese companies and exclusively used for international commerce. Considering the same additional factors, however, the Court later (5–3) *upheld* a California corporate franchise tax geared to income, applied to an American corporation doing business in California and elsewhere, including abroad. The share of corporate income allocated for purposes of the tax was arrived at using the "unitary business" principle and a fair apportionment formula, but including in the apportionable income the corporation's income from its foreign subsidiaries. The taxpayer argued that *Japan Line* required exclusion of the foreign subsidiary income from the calculation; but the majority disagreed. Among the distinctions justifying the different result, the majority noted that this tax fell not on foreign owners or instrumentalities of foreign commerce, but on a domestic corporation headquartered in the United States; that it was a tax on income rather than on property; and that multiple taxation would neither *necessarily* result from the taxing scheme employed nor necessarily be avoided by an alternative scheme, and in any event would depend solely on the facts of the particular case. Container Corp. of America v. Franchise Tax Bd., 463 U.S. 159 (1983).

The "one voice" factor was considered again in Wardair Canada, Inc. v. Florida Dept. of Rev., 106 S.Ct. 2369 (1986). There a state tax on sales of fuel to common carriers (including airlines), applied to the full amount of fuel purchased in that state regardless of where the fuel might be used, was challenged as applied to fuel purchased by a foreign airline exclusively engaged in foreign commerce. The Court held, however, over a vigorous dissent, that this was not a "dormant" commerce clause case at all, inferring from the Nation's participation in a succession of international arrangements concerning aviation (none of which yet had forbidden such state taxes) that the federal government had opted, at least for the time being, to

§ 11.16 *FEDERAL POWER* 333

leave the states unrestrained. The Court declined to intimate how it might have decided were it not for the history of international dealings, but it said:

> In *Japan Line* * * * we explained that Foreign Commerce Clause analysis requires that a court ask whether a state tax "prevents the Federal Government from 'speaking with one voice when regulating commercial relations with foreign governments.'" But we never suggested in that case or any other that the Foreign Commerce Clause *insists* that the Federal Government speak with any particular voice.

Id. at 2375–76.

CHAPTER TWELVE

PREEMPTION

§ 12.01 Introduction

Preemption, (in some older works called "supersedure") is the displacement of one government's law on a point by the law of another. Under the federal Constitution, the foundation of preemption doctrine is the supremacy clause, Art. VI, § 2.

In considering preemption, one must always remember the limit of preemptive capability; see Chapter Five. The principles discussed in this Chapter can properly apply only where preemptive capability is present.

Preemption is a generic doctrine, operating with respect to every federal power. It happens, however, that most of the litigated cases, and most (but not all) which will be cited here, have involved federal legislation under the commerce power or under the necessary and proper power in conjunction therewith.

§ 12.02 Evolution of Preemption Doctrine

Early preemption doctrine was influenced by the longstanding debate as to whether federal power necessarily is exclusive of similar power in the states. It was influenced, also, by the attempt (integral to *Cooley's* tentative resolution of that

§ 12.02 *PREEMPTION* 335

dispute) to distinguish among discrete "subjects" of regulation.

Suppose Congress exercised its commerce and necessary and proper clause powers to enact a law which did nothing but require that all railroad cars moving on interstate rail lines be equipped with couplers meeting certain safety specifications: What was the "subject" or "field" which Congress thus regulated? Railroad car couplers? Only certain couplers? Railroad equipment generally? Railroad *safety* equipment generally? Railroads generally? Or what?

Now suppose that a state undertook to require safety handholds on the sides of all railroad cars used in that state. If there were no material federal legislation, insofar as it applied to cars used in interstate commerce this state requirement would raise a dormant commerce clause question, to be decided in *Cooley* terms; but should the federal *coupler* statute be considered material?

Under early preemption doctrine, the answer would depend upon what "subject" or "field" the federal law were regarded as reaching. If the federal law's "field" were only couplers, for example, it would be immaterial to the subject of handholds, and therefore the *Cooley* "rule" would control. But if its "field" were railroad safety equipment generally (or something broader), the handholds issue could not be analyzed in terms of "dormant" federal power; for then Congress would have acted, and its failure to make provision for anything but couplers would be taken automatically to import a considered decision that nothing should be required with respect to railroad safety equipment (or whatever broader field might be ascertained) except the specified couplers. In that event, the state's handhold requirement would be preempted. See, e.g., Napier v. Atlantic Coast Line RR, 272 U.S. 605 (1926); Oregon-Washington RR & Navig. Co. v. Washington, 270 U.S. 87 (1926); Pennsylvania RR v. Public Serv. Comm'n, 250 U.S. 566 (1919); Charleston & Western Carolina Ry. v. Varnville Furniture Co., 237 U.S. 597 (1915); Southern Ry. v. Railroad Comm'n of Indiana, 236 U.S. 439 (1915).

The question whether the absence of any federal provision on a particular point indicated a gap in the regulatory scheme which the states would remain free to fill, or indicated instead a silent determination that the point should remain unregulated, was regarded as a question of congressional intent, whether expressed or implied, to be answered by statutory construction; for

> when the question is whether a Federal act overrides a state law, the entire scheme of the statute must be considered and that which needs must be implied is of no less force than that which is expressed.

Savage v. Jones, 225 U.S. 501, 533 (1912). See also Atchison, Topeka & Santa Fe Ry. v. Railroad Comm'n, 283 U.S. 380, 391 (1931).

If it were determined that federal power *had* been exerted over the particular point in question, however—even if it had been exerted merely by deliberate silence—the rule which prevailed well into the twentieth century was that such exercise of the federal power was *inherently exclusive* of any state power to deal with that point. State laws could not be "applied in coincidence with, as complementary to or as in opposition to, federal enactments." Missouri Pacific Ry. Co. v. Porter, 273 U.S. 341, 346 (1927). "[C]oincidence is as ineffective as opposition; and a state law is not to be declared a help because it attempts to go farther than Congress has seen fit to go." *Varnville Furniture*, supra, 237 U.S. at 604.

In such a case the Court might say that Congress had "taken the particular subject-matter in hand * * *," *Varnville Furniture*, supra, 237 U.S. at 604; or it might say that Congress had "occupied the field," e.g., *Southern Ry.*, supra, 236 U.S. at 446–47.

Every act of Congress was considered to "occupy" some field—although the "field" might be small, or large like the whole realm of locomotive equipment on interstate trains. See *Napier*, supra; *Pennsylvania Railroad*, supra. The "field" might be covered completely, or gaps might be left unoccupied; one example of the latter was the federal law governing labelling of foods and drugs in interstate commerce. See, e.g., Corn Products Refining Co. v. Eddy, 249 U.S. 427 (1919); *Savage v. Jones*, supra.

The distinguishing characteristic of the old doctrine, however, was that whatever the limits of the field federally "occupied" that "occupation" inexorably and automatically precluded any exercise of power in the same field by the states. As the Court said, the federal power "is such that when exercised it is exclusive, and *ipso facto,* supersedes existing state legislation on the same subject." *Southern Ry.,* supra, 236 U.S. at 446. See also Southern Ry. v. Reid & Beam, 222 U.S. 444, 447 (1912); Southern Ry. v. Reid, 222 U.S. 424, 440 (1912). Thus, although the notion of exclusive *dormant* federal power was on the wane, the proposition that federal power *when exercised* inherently and inevitably precludes concurrent state power prevailed into the 1930's.

A great change in preemption doctrine is discernible in Mintz v. Baldwin, 289 U.S. 346, 351–52 (1933). There, even though the opinion treated the state and federal laws as regulations of the very same aspects of the same subject, the Court upheld the state law against a preemption challenge. The determining factor, it said, was whether Congress *intended* to preempt.

Of course congressional intent always had been explored for the purpose of defining the bounds of the "field" which Congress had reached; until *Mintz,* however, once it was determined what Congress *had* reached the conclusion of preemption had been automatic. *Mintz* appears to have been the first case in which a congressional *intent to preempt* states with regard to a particular matter (as distinguished from a congressional *intent to exercise* federal power over that particular matter, either expressly or by deliberate silence) was deemed a prerequisite to preemption. Certainly it was the first in which an intent *not* to preempt was taken to spare from preemption a state law which dealt with a particular matter which Congress itself had reached.

This change in doctrine was subtle enough that some Justices subsequently have denied that "inherent exclusiveness" or "automatic preemption" ever was the rule. See, e.g., Campbell v. Hussey, 368 U.S. 297, 315 (1961) (Black, dissenting); California v. Zook, 336 U.S. 725, 729 (1949). Demonstrably, however, it was; and the change in doctrine was both real and salutary. Without it, the increase of federal legislative activity during the New Deal indeed would have entailed sharp curtailment of the role of the states. Certain passages in opinions from that era are comprehensible only when one realizes that this change in preemption doctrine was not immediately assimilated by all of the Justices. An example is the majority's assertion in Carter v. Carter Coal Co., 298 U.S. 238, 299 (1936), that to admit the validity of the federal measure there at issue *necessarily* would diminish state power. That assumption—that the states *automatically* would lose competence, without any inquiry into Congress' preemptive intent—reflects the pre-*Mintz* doctrine of preemption.

Since under modern preemption doctrine *both* the scope of the subject dealt with and the preemptive effect of Congress' act depend upon congressional intent, the significance of the "subject" determination as a separate inquiry has completely disappeared. Modern preemption doctrine concerning interstate commerce, therefore, avoids the difficulties which plagued *Cooley's* old subject classification approach.

However, one must remember the change which took place in preemption doctrine in 1933 to avoid being misled when language from some of the older preemption cases is recited today. When Chief Justice Stone, for example, dissenting in Hines v. Davidowitz, 312 U.S. 52, 78 (1941), declared that "every Act of Congress occupies some field," that statement already was untrue; for under modern preemption doctrine, *many* federal acts do not "occupy" *any* field, at least in the sense that the older cases had used that term. Today, even the existence of explicit federal provisions on exactly the same point generally is insufficient to accomplish preemption unless, in addition, there is a congressional intent to preempt. See, e.g., Head v. New Mexico Bd. of Examiners, 374 U.S. 424 (1963); Florida Lime & Avocado Growers, Inc. v. Paul, 373 U.S. 132 (1963); Colorado Anti-Discrimination Comm'n v. Continental Air Lines, 372 U.S. 714 (1963); California v. Zook, 336 U.S. 725 (1949); Rice v. Santa Fe Elevator Corp., 331 U.S. 218 (1947). Consequently today, for example, *contrary* to the holdings in such cases as *Missouri Pacific Co. v. Porter* and *Varnville Furniture,* supra, even the "fact of identity does not mean the automatic invalidity of state measures." *Zook,* supra, 336 U.S. at 730, quoted in *Continental Air Lines,* supra, 372 U.S. at 722.

§ 12.03 Modern Preemption Methodology

The Supreme Court repeatedly in the modern era has declared that the initial assumption must be that state and federal laws can coexist and preemption is not lightly to be found. E.g., Jones v. Rath Packing Co., 430 U.S. 519, 525 (1977); New York State Dept. of Social Serv. v. Dublino, 413 U.S. 405, 413 (1973); Schwartz v. Texas, 344 U.S. 199, 202–03 (1952).

However, there are no preemption "formulas," and it is difficult even to distill meaningful "principles" from the mass of preemption cases. "[P]rior cases on preemption are not precise guidelines * * * for each case turns on the peculiarities and special features of the federal regulatory scheme in question." Burbank v. Lockheed Air Terminal, 411 U.S. 624, 638 (1973); see also Head v. New Mexico Board of Examiners, 374 U.S. 424, 430 (1963); California v. Zook, 336 U.S. 725, 731 (1949).

Because the last phrase of the supremacy clause speaks of state laws "to the contrary" of federal, Justice Harlan once observed that "conflict is the touchstone of pre-emption." San Diego Building Trades Council v. Garmon, 359 U.S. 236, 250

(1959). But this gives little guidance, for "the conflicts which may develop between state and federal action are as varied as the fields to which congressional action may apply." Goldstein v. California, 412 U.S. 546, 561 (1973).

Lawyers by disposition and training, however, are driven to systematize inquiry; and sometimes the Justices have succumbed. In Maryland v. Louisiana, 451 U.S. 725 (1981) (White for the Court), and Fidelity Federal Sav. & Loan Ass'n v. de la Cuesta, 458 U.S. 141 (1982) (Blackmun for the Court), near-unanimous majorities subscribed to nearly identical formulations which—put into outline form and, for simplicity, omitting citations—look like this;

I. State law is preempted if Congress so intends.

  A. There is a presumption against preemptive intent, but;

  B. Preemptive intent may be expressly stated, and

  C. Preemptive intent may be inferred whenever:

  1. A preemptive design is "implicitly contained in [the federal act's] structure and purpose;" or

  2. "The scheme of federal regulation [is] so pervasive as to make reasonable the inference that Congress left no room for the States to supplement it;" or

3. "[T]he Act of Congress * * * touch[es] a field in which the federal interest is so dominant that the federal system will be assumed to preclude enforcement of state laws on the same subject;" or
4. "[T]he object sought to be obtained by the federal law and the character of obligations imposed by it * * * reveal" the purpose to displace state law; or
5. "[T]he state policy * * * produce[es] a result inconsistent with the objective of the federal statute."

II. In addition, state law is nullified to the extent that it actually conflicts with federal law. Such a conflict arises:
   A. When "compliance with both federal and state regulations is a physical impossibility;" or
   B. When state law "stands as an obstacle to the accomplishment and execution of the full purposes and objectives of Congress."

In slightly truncated form this same formulation was endorsed unanimously in Hillsborough County v. Automated Medical Laboratories, 471 U.S. 707 (1985) (Marshall for the Court).

The impression of check-list methodology given by this nice formulation, however, is misleading. In the first place, so elaborate a formulation is set out infrequently; most often only one or two isolated factors are addressed by counsel or the Court. Second, specialized bodies of accumulated caselaw control preemption inquiries in certain fields, such as labor law; see, e.g., Golden State Transit v. Los Angeles, 106 S.Ct. 1395 (1986); Wisconsin Dept. of Industry v. Gould, Inc., 106 S.Ct. 1057 (1986).

Third, and most significant, this formulation intimates a clean demarcation between "preemption" based on "intent," and nullification of state law due to "conflict" with federal law. For a time in the 1960's and 1970's it appeared that doctrine might be moving in that direction, certain factors more commonly taken as grounds for inference of preemptive intent sometimes being recited as grounds for preemption without making the intermediate inference of intent explicit. One such factor was the frustration of federal purposes or objectives: Compare, e.g., Perez v. Campbell, 402 U.S. 637 (1971); Brotherhood of Railroad Trainmen v. Jacksonville Terminal Co., 394 U.S. 369 (1969); Compco Corp. v. Day-Brite Lighting, Inc., 376 U.S. 234, 237 (1964); Sears, Roebuck & Co. v. Stiffel Co., 376 U.S. 225, 231 (1964); Local 174, Teamsters v. Lucas Flour Co., 369 U.S. 95, 104 (1962). There also were other examples. Whether or not fairly, Justice Black in one case criticized the majority as "proceed[ing] from the bare fact of congressional legislation to the conclusion of federal preemption by application of a mechanistic formula which operates independently of congressional intent."

Campbell v. Hussey, 368 U.S. 297, 312 (1961) (dissent).

No such clean demarcation, however, has been observed. Nor could it be, without in some measure reviving the pre-1933 doctrine; for if preemption depends on the intent of Congress, then incongruity, incompatibility, and even plain frustration of federal objectives must be possible if Congress elects to allow it.

In fact, the more recent cases say just that. A state may pursue policies under its unemployment insurance program which operate to frustrate the cardinal policy of the federal labor laws, because the Court is persuaded that Congress "intended to tolerate the conflict * * *." Baker v. General Motors Corp., 106 S.Ct. 3129, 3137 (1986); New York Telephone Co. v. New York Labor Dept., 440 U.S. 519 (1979). There is tension (to say the least) between Congress' assertion of exclusive control over the safety aspects of nuclear energy and the persistence of state law punitive damage remedies for nuclear safety violations; but most of the Justices believe that "Congress intended to stand by both concepts and to tolerate whatever tension there was between them. We can do no less." Silkwood v. Kerr-McGee Corp., 464 U.S. 238, 256 (1984). If a state moratorium on the construction of nuclear power plants frustrates the expressed federal objective of promoting nuclear power, "it is for Congress to rethink the division of regulatory authority in light of its possible exercise by the

States to undercut a federal objective. The Courts should not assume the role which our system assigns to Congress." Pacific Gas & Electric Co. v. State Energy Resources Comm'n, 461 U.S. 190, 223 (1983).

Perhaps recognizing these defects in its appealing systematic formulation, late in its 1985 Term the Court stressed that "[t]he critical question in any pre-emption analysis is always whether Congress intended that federal regulation supersede state law." Louisiana Public Service Comm'n v. FCC, 106 S.Ct. 1890, 1899 (1986). In that case the majority ran a litany of material factors—but without intimating any clean demarcation. Omitting again for simplicity the citations to illustrative precedents:

> Pre-emption occurs when Congress, in enacting a federal statute, expresses a clear intent to preempt state law * * *, when there is outright or actual conflict between federal and state law * * *, where compliance with both federal and state law is in effect physically impossible * * *, where there is implicit in federal law a barrier to state regulation * * *, where Congress has legislated comprehensively, thus occupying an entire field of regulation and leaving no room for the States to supplement federal law * * *, or where the state law stands as an obstacle to the accomplishment and execution of the full objectives of Congress * * *.

Id. at 1898.

Three weeks later the Court characterized these as among "various verbal formulations" it had employed "throughout the years * * * in identifying numerous varieties of pre-emption," but said again:

> we have consistently emphasized that the first and fundamental inquiry in any pre-emption analysis is whether Congress intended to displace state law, and where a congressional statute does not expressly declare that state law is to be pre-empted, and where there is no actual conflict between what federal and state law prescribe, we have required that there be evidence of a congressional intent to preempt the specific field covered by the state law.

Wardair Canada, Inc., v. Florida Dept. of Rev., 106 S.Ct. 2369, 2372 (1986). In other words, virtually all of the verbalizations repeated in the litany or in the more systematic formulation—including the "obstacle to accomplishment" and the "comprehensiveness" or "occupation of the field" factors—are merely labels for "evidence" relevant to congressional intent. The only factor which *Wardair* seems to contemplate as possibly operating independently of congressional intent is "actual conflict" in the sense of state and federal regulations with which it is impossible simultaneously to comply.

Sometimes opposite premises have given rise to identical inferences regarding preemptive intent. For example, in *Zook,* supra, 336 U.S. at 736, a striking absence of state laws on a matter prior to federal action was found to imply that Congress intended merely to "fill a void" and not to preempt the states; but in other cases the fact that state statutes on the matter were common before Congress acted has been found to imply non-preemptive intent, e.g., *Dublino,* supra, 413 U.S. at 414; Hines v. Davidowitz, 312 U.S. 52, 79 (1941); see also the dissents in *Campbell v. Hussey,* supra, 368 U.S. at 316–17, and Pennsylvania v. Nelson, 350 U.S. 497, 514 (1956). Similarly, the comprehensiveness of a federal regulatory scheme has sometimes been taken to imply preemptive intent, see, e.g., *Burbank,* supra; Rice v. Santa Fe Elevator Corp., 331 U.S. 218, 230 (1947); but not always, see, e.g., *Dublino,* supra.

Every year a dozen or so new preemption cases are decided by the Supreme Court, and most of them turn on inferences concerning preemptive intent. Most frequently the Justices sharply disagree. Often it seems evident that what drives the majority even in a 5–4 decision is a strongly held view of sound policy for the matter at issue, more than a genuine appraisal of Congress' intent; see, e.g., Midlantic National Bank v. New Jersey Dept. of Environmental Protection, 106 S.Ct. 755 (1986); Transcontinental Gas Pipe Line Corp. v. State Oil & Gas Bd., 106 S.Ct. 709 (1986). It simply is impossible to reduce the process of judgment to formulae; and one cannot even get a feel for what the repeated verbalizations are taken to mean ex-

§ 12.03   PREEMPTION   349

cept by reading some score of the cases at length. For one to believe that he understands preemption because he is familiar with its vocabulary, is a delusion.

Most important, one must not be diverted from the focus on congressional intent by the Court's own continuing occasional use of catch phrases which long ago had independent significance. Both in *Pacific Gas & Electric* and in *Silkwood,* for example, the Court used that old expression, "occupation of the field;" but in both cases the context makes clear that congressional intent to displace states from the field—not merely Congress' own entry upon it—was considered the critical factor. Rejecting backhanded reliance on that metaphor in *Wardair,* the Court declared that "state law is not pre-empted whenever there is any federal regulation of an activity or industry or area of law." 106 S.Ct. at 2372.

Similarly, in *Hillsborough County* the Court answered reliance on that old catch phrase, "dominant federal interest," by declaring that it will not undertake to rank in importance matters which Congress deems sufficiently of national concern to warrant its legislative attention, but instead will find federal interests materially dominant only when there are "special features" of such magnitude as the constitutional priority of the national government with respect to foreign affairs. 105 S.Ct. at 2378.

§ 12.04 "Express" Preemptive Intent

One might reasonably hope that cases in which Congress has made "express" its intent regarding preemption would be simpler than cases where its intent must be inferred; but that hope is in great degree disappointed.

To be sure, there are instances when Congress makes its intent unequivocally clear; but such instances seldom appear in litigation. The litigated cases, instead, illustrate how drastically persons can differ in their impressions of what Congress "expressly" has said. They also indicate that even when construing express language the Justices can be influenced by considerations one might deem appropriate only when intent has to be inferred.

For example, seven Justices found express preemption in Exxon Corp. v. Hunt, 106 S.Ct. 1103 (1986); but the dissent found the language relied on to be "too opaque," and refused to "presume preemption unless Congress clearly identifies its intent." A minority of four in Offshore Logistics v. Tallentire, 106 S.Ct. 2485 (1986), found the clear language, avowed purpose, and explicit effect of an amendment approved during consideration of an enacted measure to negate the preemption which would have been accomplished by the original language of the bill; but a bare majority, looking to the underlying purposes and language "of the Act as a whole" and the desirability of uniformity in that area of law, found preemption anyway—in the dissenters' view imposing on the particular point a federal exclusivity "that Congress declined to enact."

§ 12.05 Preemption and Federal Administrative Agencies

The authority and actions of a federal administrative agency can be significant in determining whether the *statute that agency administers* preempts state law. For example, that an agency has been entrusted with administration of a complex and comprehensive regulatory scheme has been taken to support an inference of preemptive intent, see San Diego Bldg. Trades Council v. Garmon, 359 U.S. 236, 242 (1959), while a finding that only limited power in some area has been conferred on the agency has been taken to imply nonpreemptive intent, see Head v. New Mexico Bd. of Examiners, 374 U.S. 424, 431 (1963). An agency's own opinion as to the preemptiveness of the statute it administers may be persuasive to the Court, see Farmers Educational & Co-op Union v. WDAY, Inc., 360 U.S. 525, 532–33 (1959). That the agency has encouraged and assisted cooperative state action might serve to buttress an argument against preemption, see New York State Dept. of Social Serv. v. Dublino, 413 U.S. 405 (1973); *Head,* supra, 374 U.S. at 432; Parker v. Brown, 317 U.S. 341, 358–59 (1943); Mintz v. Baldwin, 289 U.S. 346, 351 (1933), although it might not outweigh contrary indications of Congress' intent, see Cloverleaf Butter Co. v. Patterson, 315 U.S. 148, 169 (1942).

In addition, however, authorized *regulations of the federal agency itself* can preempt state law. See Fidelity Fed. Sav. & Loan Ass'n v. de la Cuesta, 458 U.S. 141, 153 (1982). A regulation's preemptive force does not depend upon a showing that Congress intended the agency to act preemptively; it depends only on whether the regulation is within the agency's delegated authority and whether the *agency* intended it to preempt. Id. at 154.

The Court is less willing to *infer* preemptive intent in the case of agency regulations, however, than it is in the case of statutes. Regulations generally are more elaborate and detailed than statutes, and agencies can readily articulate their intentions not only through formal regulations but through interpretive statements and comments; consequently, especially in a field of traditional concern to states, the Court is unlikely to find "comprehensiveness" itself persuasive of a preemptive agency intent. Hillsborough County v. Automated Medical Laboratories, 471 U.S. 707, 717 (1985). Similarly, since an agency more easily than Congress can track closely for years the success in achievement of a federal program's goals and the impact of state laws upon it, and can act more readily than Congress to preempt if that should seem needed, the Court is unlikely to find the claim of "obstacle[s] to the accomplishment and execution of the full purposes and objectives of Congress" persuasive of a preemptive agency intent. Id. at 721.

§ 12.06 Permissive Licensure and Preemption

Much of the "regulation" accomplished by the federal government is in the form of licensure, or conditions which must be complied with in order to secure or retain a license federally required. Assuming the constitutional validity of any particular federal licensure requirement, if the licensed activity is one over which states also have some regulatory authority a question of preemption obviously can arise.

Licenses, however, ordinarily are only *permissive:* They permit, but do not require, that something be done. Normally, where the permission of more than one entity is needed, one would not proceed without the approval of all; but exaggerated notions of "federal supremacy" (and industry's impatience with multiple regulations) increasingly have induced arguments of preemption by federal licensure.

The courts have been quite inconsistent in their appreciation of the significance for preemption of the merely permissive character of many federal licenses. Often they have simply assumed that federal licensure is equivalent to full authorization to proceed, or even an expression of federal determination that the deed should be done. In such instances, state or local naysaying in the form of additional licensure or other legal requirements has evoked recitation of catch phrases like "obstacle to the accomplishment and execution of the full objectives of Congress," or "frustration of the federal purpose."

The Supreme Court, however, seems now to be paying more attention to whether particular federal licenses are merely permissive, and thus plainly non-preemptive, or are (and can be deemed valid as) something more. Although poorly articulated, this seems to have been a factor in the *Hillsborough County* case, supra. It was somewhat more evident as a factor in Blackmun's separate concurring opinion (joined by Stevens) in *Pacific Gas & Electric,* supra, 461 U.S. at 223. The decision in a case argued on December 2, 1986, California Coastal Comm'n v. Granite Rock Co. (decision below, 768 F.2d 1077 (9th Cir.1985)), might serve to illustrate the Court's current level of perception on this point.

§ 12.07 A Reminder About Preemptive Capability

The significance of the limit of preemptive capability in the particular context of Congress' spending power was discussed in § 8.06; and in § 8.07 it was demonstrated that only in the 1980's has the Court *begun* to realize the *contractual* character of obligations imposed under federal spending programs. This late-dawning awareness is still very imperfect, as one 1985 "preemption" case shows.

In Lawrence County v. Lead-Deadwood School District, 469 U.S. 256 (1985), the Court (with only Rehnquist and Stevens dissenting) held that a state

CHAPTER THIRTEEN

CONGRESSIONAL ENLARGEMENT OF STATE POWER

§ 13.01 State Actions Contingent Upon Federal Consent

The first clause of Art. I, § 10 specifies several things which states are forbidden to do. It would seem that Congress cannot authorize such actions; for Congress alone cannot amend the Constitution. The second and third clauses of the same section, however, only forbid the states to do certain things "without the Consent of Congress." In some particulars, in other words, the Constitution does clearly contemplate that Congress may enlarge the competence of the states.

The most significant of these conditional or categorical prohibitions have been mentioned in other Chapters. But by far the most significant realm in which congressional consent can enlarge state competence is not dealt with in these terms in the Constitution at all.

This is the realm of regulation and taxation of interstate and foreign commerce. The evolution and present state of "dormant commerce clause" doctrine has been examined already in Chapter Eleven. We return here to sketch the origins and scope of the notion that Congress may authorize state dealings with "commerce" which otherwise might be foreclosed.

§ 13.02 Congressional Enlargement of State Power Over Interstate and Foreign Commerce

A federal statute authorizing the state pilotage regulation challenged in Cooley v. Board of Wardens, 12 How. (53 U.S.) 299 (1851) was held by the Court to be insufficient to render the state statute valid; for

> [i]f the States were divested of the power to legislate on this subject by the grant of the commercial power to Congress, it is plain this act could not confer upon them power thus to legislate. If the Constitution excluded the States from making any law regulating commerce, certainly Congress cannot regrant, or in any manner reconvey to the States that power.

Id. at 318. Only for that reason did the Court go on to distinguish between "local" and "national" aspects of interstate and foreign commerce. If the majority at that time had regarded pilotage as a "national" aspect of such commerce, its view that the Constitution made federal power exclusive in that realm would have prevented it from upholding the state law notwithstanding Congress' consent.

§ 13.02   STATE POWER   359

That evident premise of *Cooley,* however, was abandoned in 1890—silently, and apparently without notice at the time. The Court declared:

> [A] subject matter which has been confided exclusively to Congress by the Constitution is not within the jurisdiction of the police power of the State, *unless placed there by congressional action.*

Leisy v. Hardin, 135 U.S. 100, 108 (1890) (emphasis added). Elaborating this dictum further, the Court reasoned that with regard to an aspect of interstate commerce which, in *Cooley* terms,

> is national in its character, and must be governed by a uniform system, so long as Congress does not pass any law to regulate it, *or allowing the States so to do,* it thereby indicates *its will* that such commerce shall be free and untrammelled.

Id. at 109–10 (emphasis added).

On this *Leisy* reasoning, what disabled the states from dealing with certain aspects of interstate commerce was not really a *constitutional* policy, but only the policy of Congress—a "negative implication" drawn, not really from the Constitution, but merely from congressional silence.

Leisy's contribution to the evolution of doctrine under *Cooley* was thus more complex than indicated earlier in § 11.03. Less than four months after the *Leisy* decision was announced, Congress relied upon its dictum in authorizing states to enact precisely the kind of regulations that had been held unconstitutional (in the absense of such consent) in *Leisy* itself. The congressional authorization, and the previously unenforcible state regulations, were upheld in Wilkerson v. Rahrer, 140 U.S. 545 (1891).

The subject of regulation in *Leisy* and *Rahrer* was intoxicating beverage. It was to be many years before Congress again made use of this curious power—so at odds with, and never reconciled with, the prevalent dormant commerce clause theory of the day. A federal law authorizing states to regulate interstate commerce in goods made by convict labor, however, was upheld on the basis of *Rahrer* in Whitfield v. Ohio, 297 U.S. 431 (1936).

The federal statutes upheld in *Rahrer* and *Whitfield* were cautious and limited responses to the *Leisy* dictum: They did no more than remove the "original package doctrine" as a barrier to specified state regulations; and they did so at a time when that doctrine was losing credence anyway. The fact that the *Rahrer* opinion contained some language seeming to restrict the novel *Leisy* thesis might help to explain why Congress for so long made no more dramatic attempt to authorize legislation otherwise subject to dormant commerce clause challenge.

Fifty years later, however, the climate had become hospitable to the full implications of *Leisy*'s dictum. A word of encouragement came from Chief Justice Stone in the midst of his reformulation of dormant commerce clause doctrine. As dictum in the Arizona Train Limit case he wrote for the Court:

> Congress has undoubted power to redefine the distribution of power over interstate commerce. It may * * * permit the states to regulate the commerce in a manner which would otherwise not be permissible.

Southern Pacific Co. v. Arizona, 325 U.S. 761, 769 (1945). Six months later he repeated the dictum:

> It is no longer debatable that Congress, in the exercise of the commerce power, may authorize the states, in specified ways, to regulate interstate commerce or impose burdens upon it.

International Shoe Co. v. Washington, 326 U.S. 310, 315 (1945).

After exactly another six months, the principle endorsed in these dicta became the actual ground of decision in Prudential Insurance Co. v. Benjamin, 328 U.S. 408 (1946). Two years before, in U.S. v. South-Eastern Underwriters Ass'n, 322 U.S. 533 (1944), the Court had broken with decades of precedent to declare the insurance business interstate commerce. *South-Eastern* provoked doubts whether state regulations and taxes long imposed on that business could survive dormant commerce clause scrutiny. To resolve the uncertainty, Congress enacted the McCarran Act, declaring itself opposed to any "barrier to the regulation or taxation of such business by the several States." 59 Stat. 33. (Stone's dicta in *Southern Pacific* and *International*

Shoe were hardly fortuitous; argument in *Southern Pacific* occurred less than three weeks after the controversial McCarran Act was approved.)

In *Prudential* the Court upheld the McCarran Act and a state tax authorized by it, firmly establishing that Congress may authorize states to do what dormant commerce clause doctrine otherwise would forbid. Speaking of Congress' commerce power the Prudential Court said:

> This broad authority Congress may exercise alone, * * * or in conjunction with coordinated action by the states * * *. Here both Congress and South Carolina have acted, and in complete coordination * * *. Clear and gross must be the evil which would nullify such an exertion, one which could arise only by exceeding beyond cavil some explicit and compelling limitation imposed by a constitutional provision or provisions designed and intended to outlaw the action taken entirely from our constitutional framework.

328 U.S. at 434–36.

Congress' power over interstate and foreign commerce, of course, is very broad; it even is referred to as plenary. Congress, for example—unlike the states, according to dormant commerce clause doctrine—may burden, restrict, or even discriminate against that commerce. Apparently whatever Congress itself could do with regard to such commerce, it now may authorize states to do, dormant commerce clause inferences notwithstanding.

States with Congress' consent, moreover, might even be able to do things which Congress itself could not do. Article I, § 9, cls. 5 & 6 prohibit *Congress* from taxing exports or preferring the ports of one state over those of another with regulations of commerce or revenue. In addition, Art. I, § 8, cl. 1 requires that *federal* taxes be uniform throughout the United States. However, because not every state acting pursuant to congressional consent will act the same, *state* measures which do not conform to these limitations should be sustained (unless, of course, they come into conflict with some constitutional restriction applicable to *state* action, *other than* the dormant commerce clause).

For example, state regulations could only be applicable to that state's own ports, and they might be applicable only to some of those ports; the effect could be a "preference" for some ports over others. *State* taxes on interstate or foreign commerce certainly would not be "uniform" throughout the country. Again, while the prohibition against *federal* duties on exports is absolute, Art. I, § 10, cl. 2 expressly allows *state* export duties with Congress' consent.

Congress' competence to consent to *state* measures therefore does not mean that constitutional prohibitions against certain actions by *Congress* may be circumvented by using states as Congress' surrogates; the measures consented to remain *state* laws, not federal. Rejecting the contrary suggestion, the Court said in *Prudential* that it

> obviously confuses Congress' power to legislate with its power to consent to state legislation. They are not identical, though exercised in the same formal manner.

328 U.S. at 438 n. 51.

For the same reason, federal consent to state measures otherwise subject to dormant commerce clause challenge cannot free them from any applicable *state* constitutional restrictions. The contrary has been suggested in some cases dealing with interstate compacts; but interstate compact law is a badly fouled, peculiar area of doctrine, still awaiting satisfactory analysis by the Court, see Chapter Fifteen. The compact cases should be given no force whatsoever by analogy here.

§ 13.03 Recent Cases on Congressional Consent to State Regulation and Taxation of Commerce

There remains unanimous agreement today that Congress unquestionably may authorize state or local interference with, or discrimination against, interstate commerce which otherwise would be invalidated under the commerce clause. See, e.g., White v. Massachusetts Council of Construction Employers, Inc., 460 U.S. 204, 213, 215 (1983). One 1985 case makes the point especially nicely. Few state restraints upon interstate commerce have received such short shrift in the recent cases as

§ 13.03 STATE POWER 365

reciprocity preconditions; see the discussion of Sporhase v. Nebraska, 458 U.S. 941 (1982), and Great A. & P. Tea Co. v. Cottrell, 424 U.S. 366 (1976), in § 11.09. However, in Northeast Bancorp v. Board of Gov., 472 U.S. 159 (1985), a reciprocity provision was unhesitatingly, and unanimously, enforced by the Court: The relevant federal law allowed the Federal Reserve Board to approve a bank acquisition only if such acquisition "is specifically authorized by the statute laws of the State in which such bank is located;" and the statutes of the state there in question allowed acquisition of in-state banks by out-of-state banks only from reciprocating states within a prescribed region.

On the other hand, some very recent opinions carry quite an anomalous connotation. It happens that the McCarran Act, which was enacted when nothing but *Leisy* and *Rahrer* yet could be cited for the proposition, was quite express and redundantly explicit in authorizing the state measures in question; and the Court in *Prudential* made passing reference to this specificity. However, *Prudential* did not impose any *requirement* of specificity or explicitness as a prerequisite for giving effect to congressional consent. Nonetheless the Court began moving in that direction in 1982.

First in New England Power Co. v. New Hampshire, 455 U.S. 331, 343 (1982), and then in *Sporhase,* supra, 458 U.S. at 960, the Court pointed out that, whenever the principle had been applied, Congress had "expressly stated" its consent. Two years later a majority agreed that "[t]here is no talismanic significance to the phrase 'expressly stated,'" but insisted that

> for a state regulation to be removed from the reach of the dormant Commerce Clause, congressional intent must be unmistakably clear. * * * Unrepresented interests will often bear the brunt of regulations imposed by one State having a significant effect on persons or operations in other States. * * * A rule requiring a clear expression of approval by Congress * * * reduces significantly the risk that unrepresented interests will be adversely affected by restraints on commerce.

South-Central Timber Devel, Inc. v. Wunnicke, 467 U.S. 82, 92 (1984). And again yet more recently:

> An unambiguous indication of congressional intent is required before a federal statute will be read to authorize otherwise invalid state legislation, regardless whether the purported authorization takes the form of a flat exemption from Commerce Clause scrutiny or the less direct form of a reduction in the level of scrutiny.

Maine v. Taylor, 106 S.Ct. 2440, 2448 (1986).

It might be that this new emphasis on unambiguous specificity really amounts to nothing more than a wholesome warning against strained conjecture and extrapolation, of the kind unsuccessfully attempted, for example, in *New England Power* and in Lewis v. BT Investment Managers, Inc., 447

§ 13.03   STATE POWER   367

U.S. 27 (1980). Seven Justices, after all, *inferred* sufficient federal (not even congressional!) consent from a congeries of bilateral and other international arrangements—none specific on the point—to surmount a foreign commerce clause challenge to a state tax in Wardair Canada, Inc. v. Florida Dept. of Rev., 106 S.Ct. 2369 (1986); and they did so over the vigorous dissent of Justice Blackmun, who wrote the perhaps overly forceful words of the *Maine v. Taylor* opinion delivered only five days later. Furthermore, the federal consent unanimously found in *Northeast Bancorp,* supra, cannot fairly be described as so explicit.

On its face, this new nominal emphasis on unmistakable clarity seems almost to begrudge Congress its prerogative of control over interstate and foreign commerce; and that is quite inappropriate. Not in *Leisy,* nor at any time since, has anyone reconciled Congress' prerogative to authorize state measures which otherwise would be held void under the commerce clause with the thesis that dormant commerce clause doctrine truly is *constitutionally* based. The fact, of course, is that it *cannot* be reconciled; for to acknowledge Congress' power to authorize state burdens is, ultimately, to concede that protecting commerce from state burdens really is *Congress'* job, and is not a proper function for the judiciary to undertake on its own at all. (Cf. the opinion of Justice Catron in the very early License Cases, 5 How. (46 U.S.) 504, at 608 (1847).)

CHAPTER FOURTEEN

INTERGOVERNMENTAL IMMUNITIES

§ 14.01 Introduction

"Intergovernmental immunities" insulate one level of government from regulation or taxation by another. This has nothing to do with "sovereign immunity," or with the tenth amendment, or with amenability to suit, or with liability for acts of governments or government officials. The potential for confusion from these different uses of the word "immunity" is unfortunate; but the usage is well established and unlikely to change.

Two aspects of "intergovernmental immunities" doctrine must be distinguished: "Federal immunity," which concerns the constitutional limits (if any) of state competence to regulate or tax the United States or its activities; and "state immunity," which concerns the constitutional limits (if any) of federal competence to regulate or tax the states or their activities.

"Federal immunity" was the earlier doctrine to emerge; but it has undergone changes, and still is somewhat confused. "State immunity" doctrine originated as a facet of "dual federalism," although it does have a basis logically independent of that classic fallacy. Its significance today, nonetheless, is uncertain.

§ 14.02 Constitutional Immunity For the United States and Its Instrumentalities: The *McCulloch* Rationale

The Constitution does not expressly immunize the nation from taxation or regulation by any state. However, in McCulloch v. Maryland, 4 Wheat. (17 U.S.) 316 (1819), the Supreme Court inferred such a constitutional immunity from the supremacy clause. It reasoned that

> the states have no power, by taxation or otherwise, to retard, impede, burden, or in any manner control the operations of the constitutional laws enacted by Congress to carry into execution the powers vested in the general government. This is, we think, the unavoidable consequence of that supremacy which the constitution has declared.

4 Wheat. (17 U.S.) at 436.

The state tax in that case was imposed upon a branch of the Bank of the United States—a private corporation in which the United States held only a minority ownership interest, but which Congress had created as its chosen tool or "instrumentality" to effectuate several federal powers. A fortiori, *McCulloch*'s immunity rule must apply to the various offices and agencies of the federal government itself.

It is essential, however, to ascertain just what *McCulloch*'s immunity rule *is*. In that same case Chief Justice Marshall articulated the classic formulation of necessary and proper clause doctrine, see § 3.01; and that was no accident, for these two doctrines are intimately related. *Both* build on the premise that the national government must be able to accomplish *what the Constitution contemplates that it should.* The difference between them is only that the doctrine of federal immunity limits state interference whether Congress has addressed that interference or not, while the necessary and proper clause cannot be invoked unless Congress affirmatively acts.

The fact that these doctrines share a common origin and original purpose should lead one to expect—or invite one to argue—that insights and developments regarding one of them should be mirrored with respect to the other. Therefore, before considering further the federal immunity doctrine, some points regarding the history of necessary and proper clause doctrine should be recalled.

As was shown in § 4.02, confusion persisted for many years between the principle of the necessary and proper clause (which enables Congress to accomplish *what the Constitution contemplates that the federal government should do*), and the very different principle permitting Congress to promote *extraneous* ends (i.e., to do *more* than the Constitution contemplates that the federal government

§ 14.02 *INTERGOVERNMENTAL IMMUNITIES* 371

should do). The distinction was not clearly recognized until the *Darby* case in 1941; see §§ 4.01, 4.03 & 4.04. Once that distinction was recognized, "preemptive capability" (see Chapter Five) for the first time became a cognizable constitutional issue.

Logically, federal immunity doctrine should have developed on a parallel line. At least heretofore, however, it has not: Federal immunity doctrine commonly is applied with thoughtless disregard for whether the federal agency or instrumentality involved is concerned with matters within the circle of legitimate federal concerns, or only with extraneous matters. In other words—although it makes no sense at all—federal *immunity* from state regulation or taxation sometimes has been found even where *preemptive* capability could not be.

Historically, most federal immunity holdings have involved activities within the circle of legitimate federal concerns. For example, it was held that even though a state retained governmental jurisdiction over land owned by the United States, it could not exercise that jurisdiction in such a way as to interfere with the use of that land as a fort (or with its use in some other way as a means to effectuate some enumerated federal power). Fort Leavenworth Railroad Co. v. Lowe, 114 U.S. 525, 539 (1885). It also was held that a state could not prosecute a federal marshal for homicide committed in the course of protecting a federal official. Cunningham v. Neagle, 135 U.S. 1 (1890). The selection of food rations for a federal military facility was held immune from state regulation. Ohio v. Thomas, 173 U.S. 276 (1899). When the Post Office was operated as a department of the government, a state could not require postal employees to secure drivers' licenses before driving vehicles transporting mail. Johnson v. Maryland, 254 U.S. 51 (1920). Federal immunity was held to preclude a state from requiring licensure of contractors selected by the federal government to construct defense facilities. Miller v. Arkansas, 352 U.S. 187 (1956).

There were dicta in Van Brocklin v. Tennessee, 117 U.S. 151 (1886), suggesting tax immunity for federal property regardless of the use to which it is put; but facts actually posing a federal immunity question in the context of federal activities extraneous to the circle of legitimate federal concerns never arose until 1939. Two cases decided in that year—Graves v. New York ex rel. O'Keefe, 306 U.S. 466, and Pittman v. Home Owners' Loan Corp., 308 U.S. 21—considered the application of the federal immunity doctrine to the Home Owners' Loan Corporation, a corporation created and wholly owned by the United States but the activities of which (providing emergency financial assistance to indebted homeowners) today would readily be perceived as extraneous.

While the facts in *Graves* and *Pittman* were appropriate, however, *in 1939* the Justices could not perceive the issue they posed. Two years were yet to pass before *Darby*, and the distinct concepts

§ 14.02 *INTERGOVERNMENTAL IMMUNITIES* 373

treated in Chapters Three and Four still were confounded in the Justices' minds. They could not treat those cases as involving *immunity* for *extraneous* federal activities, because they did not yet even acknowledge that extraneous federal activities could be *valid*. (The Home Owners' Loan Act was not held valid in *Graves;* its validity was merely assumed "[f]or the purposes of this case," 306 U.S. at 477.)

Thus the Court's statement in *Graves* that "all activities of government constitutionally authorized by Congress must stand on a parity with respect to their constitutional immunity from [state] taxation," 306 U.S. at 477, must be discounted in view of the Court's pre-*Darby* immaturity of theory.

One might expect that the error of this *Graves* statement should have become obvious once the distinction between legitimate (i.e., enumerated) federal concerns, and extraneous matters which might be influenced using federal powers as a means, was made clear in 1941. However, it did not; and the reason, apparently, is that everyone's attention was diverted by a different forensic squabble.

When *states* began dabbling in ventures comparable to private industry, the Court had responded by limiting *state* immunity to "governmental" as distinguished from "proprietary" activities. (This is discussed further in § 14.06.) By the 1930's the *federal* government was involved in similar enterprises (the Home Owners' Loan Corporation being one good example); and unsurprisingly, states tried to justify taxation and regulation of these new federal activities with the same proprietary-governmental distinction that had been applied against them.

The states' efforts, however, hit a snag. The Supreme Court took the doctrine of enumerated powers to preclude application of the proprietary-governmental distinction to the United States: "As [the federal] government derives its authority wholly from powers delegated to it by the Constitution, its every action within its constitutional power is governmental action * * *." *Graves,* supra, 306 U.S. at 477. "The federal government is one of delegated powers, and from that it necessarily follows that any constitutional exercise of its delegated powers is governmental." Federal Land Bank v. Bismarck Lumber Co., 314 U.S. 95, 102 (1941), citing *Graves.*

Of course this was a classic non-sequitur: Even assuming that a distinction can be drawn between "governmental" and "proprietary" powers, certainly nothing could prevent "we the people" from delegating some of the latter, as well as some of the former, to the federal government instead of to the states.

What is most significant, however, is not that the Justices thus confounded two unrelated dichotomies and treated them as one, but rather that these mental contortions apparently consumed everyone's attention so that the subtler and more

§ 14.02 *INTERGOVERNMENTAL IMMUNITIES*

significant distinction was overlooked. The first evidence of this came in 1943, when the Court on federal immunity grounds barred application of a state inspection system to fertilizer owned by the United States and held for distribution to farmers as part of a federal program to improve farm productivity and income. At least on its face, the objective of that federal program was clearly extraneous to the circle of legitimate federal concerns; and by 1943—two years *after Darby*—that fact and its arguable relevance to federal immunity should not have gone unnoticed. Yet not the slightest effort was made either to characterize the fertilizer program as a means to some constitutionally legitimate federal end, or to consider the consequences for federal immunity doctrine (given its *McCulloch* rationale) if no such constitutionally legitimate end could be shown. The Court merely reiterated the addlepated rationale of the 1939 cases, that in carrying out its fertilizer program the federal government was acting "in a governmental capacity." Mayo v. U.S., 319 U.S. 441, 444 (1943).

The *McCulloch* rationale for federal immunity is simply irrelevant to cases like *Mayo, Bismarck Lumber, Pittman,* and *Graves.* Marshall's whole purpose in *McCulloch* was to prevent state interference with the federal government's pursuit of ends placed by the Constitution *within* the circle of legitimate federal concerns. Certainly Congress is permitted (as has been freely acknowledged since *Darby*) also to use any or all of its powers as tools to promote *extraneous* ends; but Congress' will for extraneous matters has no preemptive capability (see Chapter Five), and equivalent reasoning should preclude immunizing extraneous federal activities against state interference. Certainly nothing in *McCulloch*—or in *any other* Supreme Court opinion—even whispers a hint of any *reason* for federal immunity under such circumstances.

§ 14.03 Constitutional Federal Immunity Dehors *McCulloch*

Although it has not yet restricted the doctrine to the scope of its *McCulloch* rationale (as is suggested here), the Supreme Court today does apply federal immunity with considerable restraint.

The last time the Court blocked a state tax or regulation with a "constitutional" rule of federal immunity was in Department of Employment v. U.S., 385 U.S. 355 (1966), where it found that the peculiar status and role of the American National Red Cross make it a federal instrumentality for tax immunity purposes. Eighteen months later, three Justices argued that modern "national banks" are so different in function and role from the bank involved in *McCulloch* that the tradition of immunizing them as "federal instrumentalities" is outmoded. First Agricultural Nat'l Bank v. State Tax Comm'n, 392 U.S. 339, 348 et seq. (1968) (Marshall, with Harlan and Stewart, dissenting). The majority in that case declined to discuss the immunity of modern national banks as a constitutional point, and pursued instead what has become the typical approach—considered in § 14.05—of resolving federal immunity questions by reference to statutes.

Most recently, after reconsidering the whole matter again, the Supreme Court concluded that a "constitutional" rule of

> tax immunity is appropriate in only one circumstance: when the levy falls on the United States itself, or on an agency or instrumentality so closely connected to the Government that the two cannot realistically be viewed as separate entities, at least insofar as the activity being taxed is concerned.

U.S. v. New Mexico, 455 U.S. 720, 735 (1982).

The immunity of the United States or its instrumentalities from state taxes can be waived by act of Congress. Also, instead of consenting to state taxation, Congress can utilize its spending power to authorize payments "in lieu of" taxes to states where federal property, facilities, or operations are found.

§ 14.04 Federal Immunity for Private Entities

For a time it was held that federal immunity as a constitutional doctrine extended far beyond the United States itself, to private persons and entities variously related to the Government. For example, persons contracting to supply goods or services to the Government were held immune from state taxes and regulations with respect to those activities; federal lessees were held immune from state taxes; and even the salaries of federal officials were held not to be taxable by states. Perhaps the most extreme case held immune from a state income tax the royalty income of private persons derived from patents issued by the United States. Long v. Rockwood, 277 U.S. 142 (1928); see Powell, "An Imaginary Judicial Opinion," 44 Harv. L. Rev. 889 (1931).

In the 1930's, however, this overgrown doctrine at last began to wither. The leading studies of the decline from extravagance are Thomas Reed Powell's "The Waning of Intergovernmental Tax Immunities," 58 Harv. L. Rev. 633 (1945), and "The Remnant of Intergovernmental Tax Immunities," 58 Harv. L. Rev. 757 (1945). Immunity from state regulations as well as from state taxes was narrowed; see Penn Dairies v. Milk Control Comm'n, 318 U.S. 261 (1943).

Until the 1980's, nonetheless, a significant immunity of constitutional stature remained for federal contractors. It was clear that the mere fact that the actual economic effects of taxes imposed on contractors passed through to the United States was not enough to justify immunity; see, e.g., Detroit v. Murray Corp., 355 U.S. 489, 494 (1958); U.S. v. Detroit, 355 U.S. 466, 472 (1958); Alabama v. King & Boozer, 314 U.S. 1, 8 (1941); James v. Dravo Contracting Co., 302 U.S. 134, 160 (1937). On the other hand, a tax would be held invalid "even though it does not fall directly on the United States if it operates so as to discriminate against the Government or those with whom it deals."

§ 14.04 *INTERGOVERNMENTAL IMMUNITIES* 379

U.S. v. Detroit, supra, 355 U.S. at 473; see also Phillips Chemical Co. v. Dumas Independent School Dist., 361 U.S. 376 (1960). In the absence of such discrimination, the technical incidence of the tax (regardless of practical economic effect) was considered of crucial significance.

This placed a premium on cleverness (or mere luck) in statute or contract draftsmanship, with no real policy justification. For example, a state could tax sales of materials to a contractor even though the materials were for use in constructing federal facilities—unless the contract were so written as to make the contractor appear to be, in effect, a purchasing agent acquiring the materials on behalf of the Government itself. Compare *King & Boozer,* supra, with Kern-Limerick, Inc. v. Scurlock, 347 U.S. 110 (1954). A tax would be valid even as applied to work done under a Government contract so long as the statutory language made it appear that the privilege of doing business as a contractor, and not the Government contract, was being taxed. *James,* supra. Taxes were valid if they could be viewed as imposed on the private party's benefit (rather than the Government's benefit) derived from a lease, procurement, or service contract with the United States. See U.S. v. Boyd, 378 U.S. 39 (1964); *Detroit v. Murray Corp.,* supra; U.S. v. Muskegon, 355 U.S. 484 (1958); *U.S. v. Detroit,* supra.

In 1982, however, the Court again surveyed the complex of precedents and virtually eliminated federal immunity for private entities as a constitutional doctrine. It said,

> [A] finding of constitutional tax immunity requires something more than the invocation of traditional agency notions: to resist the State's taxing power, a private taxpayer must actually "stand in the Government's shoes."

U.S. v. New Mexico, 455 U.S. 720, 736 (1982)—quoting a phrase used by Frankfurter in *Detroit v. Murray Corp.*, supra, 355 U.S. at 503.

The factual circumstances sufficient to constitute "stand[ing] in the Government's shoes" cannot be specified in advance. No catch phrase or formula can be sufficient. Some feeling for the concept might be gained by studying in detail the intricate facts of scores of cases; but in the end it's a judgment call.

This, however, did not deter Justice Blackmun, speaking for the Court in *U.S. v. New Mexico,* from venturing verbal formulations—some newly coined and some quoted with approval from earlier cases: E.g., "incorporated into the government structure;" "integral parts;" "virtually an arm of the government;" "so assimilated by the Government as to become one of its constituent parts," and "so intimately connected with the exercise of a power or the performance of a duty" by the Government that taxation of it would be "a direct interference with the functions of government itself."

§ 14.05 Federal Immunity Governed by Statute

In its 1982 opinion in *U.S. v. New Mexico,* supra, the Court declared that if federal immunity is to be expanded beyond the very narrow constitutional limits there described, "it is Congress that must take responsibility for the decision, by so expressly providing * * *." 455 U.S. at 737. In most of the earlier federal immunity cases involving private entities (and in some involving federal "instrumentalities," too), there had been relevant statutory language affirming the immunity; yet typically in those cases the Court had suggested that the immunity had constitutional stature. Now that the scope of "constitutional" federal immunity has been sharply curtailed, such statutory language has much greater significance.

For example, the majority in First Agricultural National Bank v. State Tax Comm'n, 392 U.S. 339 (1968), held it immaterial whether national banks as they now exist and function have any *constitutional* immunity from state taxes, because *Congress* had addressed the point: For more than a century, statutes had permitted such banks to be taxed in certain ways; and the majority construed that legislation as prescribing the *only* ways in which states could tax them. 392 U.S. at 341–44.

This assumes as a postulate, however, that Congress somehow has power to confer extra-constitutional immunities from state authority. Heretofore this postulate seems not to have been questioned; but in many applications, at least, it seems subject to serious doubt.

Certainly Congress may specify the terms on which it will contract for the goods and services it needs in order to accomplish its constitutionally prescribed functions; and state regulations cannot be allowed to stand in the way. See, e.g., U.S. v. Georgia Pub. Serv. Comm'n, 371 U.S. 285 (1963); Public Util. Comm'n of Calif. v. U.S., 355 U.S. 534 (1958). Whether this is described as a pro tanto immunization of contractors from state regulations, or instead as an instance of preemption (see Chapter Twelve), makes no practical difference.

It is not at all evident, however, why Congress should be able to free from state regulation any private entity it uses to promote *extraneous* ends; for in the pursuit of *such* ends even Congress itself is subject to state control and frustration, see Chapter Five.

Neither is it obvious why, whether, or when Congress should be able to immunize private entities from state taxation. Attempting an explanation in Carson v. Roane-Anderson Co., 342 U.S. 232, 234 (1952), the Court said that

> The power [to immunize] stems from the power to preserve and protect functions validly authorized [citing Pittman v. Home Owners' Loan Corp., 308 U.S. 21, 33 (1939), discussed in § 14.02]—the power to make all laws necessary and proper for carrying into execution the powers vested in the Congress.

§ 14.06   *INTERGOVERNMENTAL IMMUNITIES*   383

This explanation, however, is utterly inadequate, as anyone who has read this far must know: Certainly the necessary and proper clause supports immunizing anyone or anything from state taxation when Congress, on a rational basis, finds that immunization will promote its policy for some matter *within the circle of legitimate federal concerns;* but many entities statutorily immunized from state taxation (including the Home Owners' Loan Corporation considered in *Pittman*) are employed only to effectuate *extraneous* ends.

As suggested already in § 14.02, when *Pittman* was decided in 1939 the Court had not yet realized that many functions might be "validly authorized" by Congress and yet *not* invoke the necessary and proper clause "to preserve and protect" them, because their aims are extraneous to the circle of legitimate federal concerns. But by 1952, when *Carson* was decided, there had been plenty of time for that point to sink in. It is apparent from the inadequate explanation quoted above, however, that it had not.

The intervening years have brought no better explanation. Even today, the postulate that Congress may confer immunity by statute although all it advances is some *extraneous* end, is an assumption with no rationale to support it.

§ 14.06   State Immunity Before 1976

The *McCulloch* rationale for federal immunity rested on the supremacy clause, and plainly contemplated no comparable immunity for states. As dual federalism thought achieved dominance, however, intergovernmental immunity gained a reciprocal aspect. The Court reasoned in Collector v. Day, 11 Wall. (78 U.S.) 113, 125 (1871), that "the means and instrumentalities employed * * * [by state] governments for preserving their existence, and fulfilling the * * * duties assigned to them * * * should not be liable to be crippled" by the federal taxing power.

The particular measure invalidated in *Day* was a federal income tax as applied to a state judge's salary. From that beginning, state immunity doctrine within a few years grew into a substantial impediment to federal taxation and regulation—not only of states themselves, but of private persons and entities variously related to states and state activities. Eventually the extravagance of this doctrine provoked adjustments.

Late in the nineteenth century, states began engaging in activities amounting to business ventures such as private persons might undertake. The operation of railroads, of gas, water, and electric utilities, and of liquor dispensaries, are examples. With the character of state activities thus changing, the Court reconsidered its state immunity doctrine, and declared in 1905 that

> the exemption of state agencies and instrumentalities from national taxation is limited to those which are of a strictly governmental character, and does not extend to those which are used by

§ 14.06   *INTERGOVERNMENTAL IMMUNITIES*   385

the State in the carrying on of an ordinary private business.

South Carolina v. U.S., 199 U.S. 437, 461 (1905). The Court analogized to the proprietary-governmental dichotomy which long had been employed in the context of municipal tort liability.

That and other verbal dichotomies proved unworkable, however, in an age of increasing and diversifying government activities; and in 1946, new attempts to articulate state immunity principles were made. One of the 1946 cases involved a federal tax; the other two involved federal regulations applied to states.

In the tax case, New York v. U.S., 326 U.S. 572 (1946), two Justices (Black and Douglas) argued that *all* state activities should be tax-immune. None of the other Justices went that far; but they were unable to agree on a majority opinion. They did agree in substance, however, that the federal government cannot tax "the State as a state." As elaborated by Chief Justice Stone (whose opinion was joined by three other Justices), this meant that "a Federal tax * * * may * * * so affect the State, merely because it is a State that is being taxed, as to interfere unduly with the State's performance of its sovereign functions of government." 326 U.S. at 587. This concept of state immunity against "undue interference" did not depend upon verbal formulae; it called for case-by-case judgment.

The regulation cases almost simultaneously considered were Case v. Bowles, 327 U.S. 92 (1946), and Hulbert v. Twin Falls County, 327 U.S. 103 (1946). In both of these cases—as earlier in U.S. v. California, 297 U.S. 175 (1936)—the application of a federal regulation to a state, state subdivision, or state enterprise was *upheld*. This, plus the fact that Justice Black (who advocated categorical state immunity from taxes) himself was the author of the *Case* opinion, led some commentators to conclude that the state immunity doctrine pertained *only* to taxes, and not to regulations at all. A closer reading of the *Case* and *Hulbert* opinions, however, reveals an "undue interference" inquiry equivalent to that contemporaneously made in the tax case. See Engdahl, "Sense and Nonsense About State Immunity," 2 Const'l Commentary 93, 101–04 (1984).

§ 14.07 State Immunity: *Usery, Garcia,* and Beyond

For thirty years after *Case* and *Hulbert*, state immunity doctrine as applied to federal regulations was generally regarded as defunct. It proved to be no barrier, for example, to amending the Fair Labor Standards Act to cover state hospital and school employees. Maryland v. Wirtz, 392 U.S. 183 (1968). (Justice Douglas dissented in *Wirtz*, just as he had in *Case* and *Hulbert* twenty years before, arguing that the states should be immune from such regulations.)

§ 14.07 *INTERGOVERNMENTAL IMMUNITIES* 387

By a 5-4 vote in 1976 the Supreme Court overruled *Wirtz* and held that state immunity barred application of the Fair Labor Standards Act to state employees. National League of Cities v. Usery, 426 U.S. 833 (1976). The more fortunate passages in Justice Rehnquist's opinion for the *Usery* majority reflect the kind of case-by-case judgment suggested by Chief Justice Stone's opinion in *New York v. U.S.,* supra; and Justice Blackmun (who filed a short concurrence in addition to joining the majority opinion) described the majority as adopting "a balancing approach," 426 U.S. at 856. Some other passages in the majority opinion, however, are reminiscent of earlier unsatisfactory struggles to encapsulate reasoning in verbal dichotomies. Some even invite the accusation that the majority was reviving dual federalism views.

For nine years after *Usery,* in a succession of cases, lawyers for states sought to enlarge its significance; but their arguments never carried a majority of the Court. Some of those arguments *did* echo dual federalism, seeking to reserve various categories of activity exclusively for state regulation; but the Court pointed out that the principle applied in *Usery* pertained only to regulation of the states themselves, and not to federal regulation of third parties or activities also regulable by states. See, e.g., Hodel v. Virginia Surface Mining & Reclam. Ass'n, 452 U.S. 264, 287-88 (1981).

Even as to regulations of the states themselves, however, attempts to utilize *Usery* failed. In one case the Court was unanimous in finding reliance upon *Usery* misplaced, United Transp. Union v. Long Island RR Co., 455 U.S. 678 (1982); in two others, the Court divided 5–4, FERC v. Mississippi, 456 U.S. 742 (1982); EEOC v. Wyoming, 460 U.S. 226 (1983).

The argument for application of the state immunity doctrine was particularly strong on the facts of the latter two cases; and it probably would have prevailed had not some of the Justices been so resolute against *any* state immunity doctrine (at least as to regulations) that they determined to oppose every attempted application of *Usery* until a majority could be mustered to overrule it. That finally happened in Garcia v. San Antonio Metropolitan Transit Authority, 469 U.S. 528 (1985), when Justice Blackmun changed his position and wrote the opinion of the new majority.

Garcia on its face declares *Usery* overruled; but little else about it, or about its meaning for the future, is clear. The opinion of the new 5–4 majority asserts that "the political process" will ensure that federal laws which "unduly burden the States will not be promulgated;" yet at the same time it suggests (without explaining at all) a judicial role "tailored to compensate for possible failings in the national political process * * *." It discusses the efforts made earlier to express in verbal formulae a state immunity rule for *taxation,* and describes *New York v. U. S.* as acknowledging the failure of those efforts. (Ironically, equivalent

§ 14.07   *INTERGOVERNMENTAL IMMUNITIES*   389

shortcomings of language had not deterred Blackmun himself from venturing verbal formulations as to *federal* immunity—which is equally dependent upon case-by-case judgment—in *U.S. v. New Mexico*, see § 14.04.) But *New York v. U.S.* did not abrogate state immunity from taxation, and it does not appear that *Garcia* does, either. (For a post-*Usery* discussion of state immunity from federal taxes, seemingly untouched by *Garcia*, see Massachusetts v. U.S., 435 U.S. 444 (1978).)

The *Garcia* opinion is built on the premise that the Fair Labor Standards Act is an exercise of Congress' commerce power; but of course it is not. As applied to activities not themselves interstate commerce, it is an exercise of Congress' power under the necessary and proper clause. The dissent of O'Connor (joined by Powell and Rehnquist) recognized this. Since *McCulloch v. Maryland* (and even before then, since the writings of Hamilton on which John Marshall relied), the word "proper" in that clause has been taken to require an assessment of consistency not only with the letter, but also with the "spirit" of the nation's Constitution. See Engdahl, "Sense and Nonsense About State Immunity," supra. As more Justices reawaken to the importance of distinguishing commerce clause from necessary and proper clause questions (see, e.g., § 6.04), this defect in *Garcia* should become more plain.

It need not necessarily follow that *Usery* will be restored; for *Usery* itself also overlooked the distinction between the commerce and necessary and proper clauses, resorting therefore to the tenth amendment instead. That question-begging amendment (see § 1.01) is not a suitable foundation for any state immunity doctrine.

The language of the necessary *and proper* clause, on the other hand, arguably is. So also is that of the enforcement clauses; see "Sense and Nonsense About State Immunity," supra, at 115.

With unusual forcefulness, the four dissenters in *Garcia* expressed their conviction that its repudiation of state immunity from federal regulations would not endure. If, indeed, the doctrine does see a new day, it might be one indication of the gradually increasing awareness of classic fundamentals of federalism law.

CHAPTER FIFTEEN

INTERGOVERNMENTAL COOPERATION

§ 15.01 Some Methods of Federal-State Cooperation

Although the Constitution allocates governing power between the federal and state governments, this does not mean that they are to operate in isolation. Cooperation and accommodation help in adjusting the deliberate, but nonetheless artificial, constitutional allocation of power to the changing practical needs of society, without necessitating constitutional amendments changing the basic principles of power allocation.

Cooperation and accommodation frequently are achieved through the political process: Congress (or an administrative agency as its delegate) might exercise power less extensive than the Constitution allows, because of objections from states; conversely, sometimes it is the urging of states which prompts the federal government to act.

A prominent form of federal-state cooperation involves the spending power. Although states dissatisfied with the policies chosen by Congress and promoted through conditions on federal funds frequently complain of being coerced, very often in the formulation of those policies Congress consults with the states.

Congress' taxing power also sometimes has been used as an instrument of intergovernmental cooperation, Congress imposing taxes to reinforce efforts being made by the states (or by some of them) to deter certain activities. See, e.g., U.S. v. Kahriger, 345 U.S. 22 (1953) (gambling); U.S. v. Sanchez, 340 U.S. 42 (1950), and U.S. v. Doremus, 249 U.S. 86 (1919) (abusable drugs); Sonzinsky v. U.S., 300 U.S. 506 (1937) (certain firearms transactions).

Likewise Congress has exercised its power over interstate commerce to assist in implementing state policy. See, e.g., Kentucky Whip & Collar Co. v. Illinois Central RR Co., 299 U.S. 334 (1937); Champion v. Ames, 188 U.S. 321 (1903). Sometimes such action reinforces the policy of certain states while encumbering the policy of others; but it can also be designed to support whatever policy on a particular matter each of the several states might choose. For example, by the Webb-Kenyon Act of 1913 (before the eighteenth amendment was adopted) Congress prohibited the transportation of intoxicants into any state if but only if their sale or use would be in violation of the law of the destination state. Clark Distilling Co. v. Western Maryland Ry Co., 242 U.S. 311 (1917).

Also under the commerce power Congress has made it a federal crime to cross a state line to avoid prosecution or confinement for state crimes, or to avoid giving testimony in state criminal pro-

§ 15.02 *INTERGOVERNMENTAL COOPERATION* 393

ceedings; Fugitive Felon and Witness Act, 18 U.S.C. § 1073. The commerce power also has been used to require certain interstate merchants to supply state officials with information useful for the enforcement of state taxes, see Consumer Mail Order Ass'n v. McGrath, 94 F.Supp. 705 (D.D.C.1950), aff'd per curiam, 340 U.S. 925 (1951).

Cooperation and accommodation also are facilitated when Congress consents to state action on matters which otherwise would be foreclosed to them. See, e.g., Northeast Bancorp v. Board of Gov. of Fed. Reserve System, 472 U.S. 159 (1985); and see generally Chapter Thirteen.

§ 15.02 Miscellaneous Methods of Interstate Cooperation

Certain forms of inter*state* cooperation are mandated by the Constitution. For example, Art. IV, § 1, requires each state to give "full Faith and Credit" to the "public Acts, Records, and judicial Proceedings of every other State." Section 2, cl. 2 of the same Article imposes a duty of interstate extradition. In Kentucky v. Dennison, 24 How. (65 U.S.) 66 (1860), the Supreme Court held that it could not enforce the duty of extradition by mandamus to a state; but that old case was premised on dual federalism notions which long ago were discarded, and while the case has not been overruled it could not survive serious analysis today.

Beyond these *required* forms of cooperation, the Constitution *allows* many other forms of interstate cooperation, both formal and informal. Some mutual objectives are promoted by the independent enactment of uniform laws. Others are facilitated by reciprocal legislation, such as that for securing the attendance of witnesses at reciprocating states' judicial proceedings. New York v. O'Neill, 359 U.S. 1 (1959). Conferences and associations of various government officials—from governors and mayors to revenue officials and probation counsellors—are very important even though less formal means of facilitating cooperation.

Potentially more significant, however, and certainly presenting more serious legal questions and ramifications, are a variety of more formal interstate arrangements which are similar to instruments of international relations. To these the remainder of this Chapter is devoted.

§ 15.03 Interstate Agreements and Compacts: The Requirement of Congressional Consent

Formal interstate contractual arrangements called "compacts" were utilized from the earliest years of American history (even before the Constitution), most commonly to resolve boundary disputes. In the present century, they have been used for a growing variety of purposes. Some formalize reciprocal promises of aid, such as for fires or other disasters. Some create advisory commissions to recommend coordinated programs of legislation or administration on some topic. Some formalize regional approaches to common prob-

§ 15.03　INTERGOVERNMENTAL COOPERATION

lems, like disposal of low-level radioactive waste. Some create interstate authorities or agencies to carry on administrative functions, such as managing an interstate school district or an interstate bridge or even an enormous complex of port and related facilities (as in the case of the Port of New York Authority). One establishes the Multistate Tax Commission which wrestles with the difficult problems concerning state taxation referred to in §§ 11.12–11.15.

Were it not for certain constraints on vocabulary dictated by the Constitution, one might call these arrangements interstate "treaties;" for in nature, in function, and in variety they are comparable to international arrangements which go by that name. But Art. I, § 10, cl. 1 provides without exception that "[n]o State shall enter into any Treaty * * *."

Consequently, these arrangements must go by some other name. The third clause of the same section of the Constitution provides that "[n]o State shall, *without the Consent of Congress,* * * * enter into any *Agreement* or *Compact* with another State, or with a foreign Power * * *." (Emphasis added.)

The verbal distinctions given critical significance by these clauses do not conform to any differences given legal significance in twentieth century international practice. One can comprehend what the framers meant in using these terms only by reference to *eighteenth* century international law. That is fully explored in Engdahl, "Characterization of Interstate Arrangements: When Is a Compact Not a Compact?" 64 Mich.L.Rev. 63 (1965).

In modern usage, the term "interstate compact" generally is applied only to formal written arrangements approved by the legislatures of the party states. The "compact clause," however, applies not only to "compacts" but to "any Agreement" between states. This seems quite comprehensive; and indeed the Supreme Court said a century and a half ago that this clause reaches "every agreement, written or verbal, formal or informal, positive or implied, by the mutual understanding of the parties." Holmes v. Jennison, 14 Pet. (39 U.S.) 540, 572 (1840).

If that view had survived, the room for spontaneous flexibility and ingenuity in interstate cooperation would have been severely limited because of the requirement of congressional consent. On the other hand, had the terms used by the framers been recognized as terms of art taken from eighteenth century international practice, the clause could have been found quite inapplicable to most interstate arrangements, and certainly to the vast majority even of those to which the term "compact" is formally applied today. See the "Characterization of Interstate Arrangements" article, supra.

What actually happened near the end of the nineteenth century was that the Supreme Court recognized that *Holmes v. Jennison* could not be

§ 15.03 INTERGOVERNMENTAL COOPERATION

followed, and yet failed to recover the original meaning of the terms; and therefore it improvised. In Virginia v. Tennessee, 148 U.S. 503 (1893), it suggested that the only interstate arrangements reached by this clause and thus invalid in the absence of congressional consent are those

> which may tend to increase and build up the political influence of the contracting States, so as to encroach upon or impair the supremacy of the United States or interfere with their rightful management of particular subjects placed under their entire control.

Id. at 518; see also id. at 519, 520.

The "rule" of *Virginia v. Tennessee* actually was dictum; but it was reiterated as dictum in many succeeding cases. No interstate arrangement actually was held invalid for lack of congressional consent; yet negotiating states—and Congress itself—remained uncertain whether that "rule" could be relied upon. There also was considerable confusion over how to apply it in practical situations.

That "rule" was applied as a holding for the first time in New Hampshire v. Maine, 426 U.S. 363, 369–70 (1976), the Justices deciding 6–3 that a proposed consent decree in litigation over a state boundary did not require Congress' consent. Two years later it was applied again—the Court dividing 7–2, however, as to the rule's application to the facts. In United States Steel Corp. v. Multistate Tax Comm'n, 434 U.S. 452 (1978), the majority held that the Multistate Tax Compact (see § 11.15) neither "enhances state power quoad the National Government," id. at 473, nor "is an affront to the sovereignty of nonmember States," id. at 478, and therefore is valid notwithstanding its failure ever to secure Congress' consent.

The majority in the *Multistate Tax Comm'n* case so held notwithstanding the fact that the subject of that agreement—the impacts of state taxation on interstate commerce—manifestly is appropriate for federal legislation. (In fact, Congress wrestled with bills on that subject for more than a decade during the very period when the compact was being drafted and widely adopted.) Consequently it is incongruous and baffling that a 6–3 majority in 1981 found the Interstate Agreement on Detainers to be *within* the compact clause merely because "the subject matter of the [Agreement] is an appropriate subject for congressional legislation," even though it is manifest that the Detainers Agreement neither enhances the political influence of the party states nor interferes in the slightest degree with federal authority. Cuyler v. Adams, 449 U.S. 433, 442 (1981).

Four years later, in Northeast Bancorp v. Board of Gov. of Fed. Reserve System, 472 U.S. 159 (1985), the author of the vigorous *dissenting* opinion in *Cuyler* wrote *for the Court* (without any dissent) reiterating the test which *Multistate Tax Comm'n* and *New Hampshire v. Maine* had drawn from *Virginia v. Tennessee*. Thus it appears that *Cuy-*

ler's substantially different criterion for compact clause coverage was an anomaly, and is not to be trusted.

§ 15.04 How Congress' "Consent" Is Given

Congress' consent usually is given by act or joint resolution, after the party states have submitted for approval an arrangement they have agreed to which they believe requires (or which they believe might require) consent under the compact clause. Until the 1960's states sought consent routinely, even for arrangements which probably did not require it; more recently, there has been greater willingness to proceed without consent in arguable instances. When Congress consents to a specific arrangement, sometimes the act or resolution of consent merely describes the arrangement and sometimes it recites the entire text.

It is also possible, however, for Congress to give its consent in advance. On several occasions Congress has enacted prior expressions of consent to interstate compacts or agreements in particular fields, in an effort to encourage interstate cooperation which had not yet occurred. Some such prior consents have been unqualified; others have been made subject to various qualifications, the most common being that any agreement actually concluded be submitted for specific approval.

Whether given before or after an arrangement is concluded, Congress' consent ordinarily is express. The Supreme Court repeatedly has held, however, that "consent" can be sufficient under the compact clause even though it is neither explicit nor direct, and cannot be attributed to particular language in any act or resolution. The Court has been willing to *infer* consent, not only from some single legislative act, but even from a pattern of legislation over a period of time acquiescing in or conforming itself to the interstate arrangement in question. See, e.g., *Virginia v. Tennessee,* supra, 148 U.S. at 521; Green v. Biddle, 8 Wheat. (21 U.S.) 1, 85–86 (1823). See also *Cuyler,* supra, 449 U.S. at 441.

In perhaps the most extreme case of implied consent, the Supreme Court took an act which consented expressly to an *1879* arrangement as *implying* that Congress—either then or at some unspecified earlier time—tacitly had consented to a different, *1785* arrangement (entered into before the Constitution was even adopted)! Wharton v. Wise, 153 U.S. 155 (1894). One can easily imagine what problems might arise from so indulgent a notion of "implied consent" if the effective date of the arrangement were material. Was that 1785 arrangement, for example, valid in 1785? In 1800? In 1850? Or not until 1879? These difficulties inherent in the "implied consent" notion, however, have not yet arisen in litigation.

§ 15.05 The Consequences of Consent, and The "Law of the Union" Doctrine

The principal reason why states in recent years have been more willing to implement agreements without Congress' consent is that consent in the

§ 15.05 INTERGOVERNMENTAL COOPERATION

past has often entailed disabling inconveniences. Awaiting consent can delay for months or more than a year a cooperative effort important to the party states but of low priority to Congress. Even if an arrangement is not disapproved or merely neglected, Congress might condition its approval on added terms or changes, not the product of party negotiations, which none of the parties might find desirable. Moreover, occasionally the fact that congressional consent has been given has been seized as a pretext for intrusive investigation or oversight by Congress of operations under a compact, as with the Port of New York Authority. Certainly when a compact, or an entity created thereby, impacts fields of federal authority, inquiry and oversight is appropriate quite apart from the compact clause; but states understandably hesitate to invite federal meddling in other matters by submitting agreements which the compact clause might not cover.

One consequence, however, dwarfs in significance all the other troublesome and dysfunctional consequences of requesting or receiving Congress' consent to an interstate arrangement. In 1851 the Supreme Court declared that when an interstate agreement receives Congress' consent it becomes a "law of the Union"—i.e., a federal statute. Pennsylvania v. Wheeling & Belmont Bridge Co., 13 How. (54 U.S.) 518, 565–66 (1851).

In the generations since, this peculiar proposition has been alternately repudiated and reaffirmed in successive Supreme Court opinions; for a history and critique, see Engdahl, "Construction of Interstate Compacts: A Questionable Federal Question," 51 Va.L.Rev. 987 (1967). On even modest reflection, the proposition is bizarre and analytically unsound. It stands in stark contrast to the consequences accorded congressional consent in other contexts; see, e.g., Prudential Ins. Co. v. Benjamin, 328 U.S. 408, 438 n. 51 (1946), quoted in § 13.02. It is irreconcilable with the decisions as to how consent may be given, see § 15.04; no one would maintain, for example, that federal statutes can be enacted by implication, or decades in advance of their actual drafting. The proposition also is subversive of the doctrine of enumerated powers, since interstate agreements very frequently deal with matters of no legitimate federal concern.

This ridiculous "law of the Union" doctrine continues nonetheless to operate today. Justice Brennan and the majority in Cuyler v. Adams, 449 U.S. 433 (1981), gave this doctrine the most extravagant application in its history when they transmuted into federal law an interstate agreement for which Congress' consent certainly was not required (see § 15.03), for which consent never was sought by any state, and the purported "consent" to which consisted only of a few words in a federal statute enacted a quarter century prior to the interstate agreement, encouraging in the vaguest and most general of hortatory terms unspecified measures of

§ 15.05 *INTERGOVERNMENTAL COOPERATION* 403

cooperation among states for law enforcement and crime prevention.

The *Cuyler* dissenters pointed out some of the radical consequences which logically must follow from that "remarkable feat of judicial alchemy * * * transform[ing] state law into federal law," 449 U.S. at 450, and warned of a "judicial Midas meandering through the state statute books, turning everything it touches into federal law." Id. at 454. There was no dissent, however, when Brennan reiterated the "law of the Union" doctrine in Texas v. New Mexico, 462 U.S. 554 (1983). Perhaps that was only because the doctrine was not crucial to that decision.

This bizarre doctrine does indeed have disruptive and debilitating consequences for intergovernmental relations. The consequences would be even more severe if the doctrine really were taken seriously and applied consistently; but it is not. Its most troubling consequence at the present time, therefore, is that it renders the law of interstate agreements inconsistent and unstable, making the consequences of cooperation substantially unpredictable, and thus unnecessarily discouraging creative efforts to deal with modern problems.

It has been held that construction of the terms of a congressionally approved interstate compact raises a federal question for purposes of Supreme Court *certiorari* jurisdiction. Delaware River Joint Toll Bridge Comm'n v. Colburn, 310 U.S. 419 (1940). That case did not expressly endorse the "law of the Union" doctrine, however, and the holding is easily supportable without it (see "Construction of Interstate Compacts," 51 Va.L.Rev. 987 (1965), supra). Indeed, the doctrine had been expressly repudiated just two years before *Colburn,* in Hinderlider v. LaPlata River & Cherry Creek Ditch Co., 304 U.S. 92 (1938). If consent really made a compact into federal law, its construction should also invoke District Court federal question jurisdiction, but such jurisdiction has been denied. E.g., Rivoli Trucking Corp. v. American Export Lines, Inc., 167 F.Supp. 937 (S.D.N.Y.1958); cf. Port Authority Bondholders Protective Committee v. Port of New York Authority, 387 F.2d 259 (2d Cir.1967).

Jurisdictional premises aside, however, an approved compact has been said to be "a federal law subject to federal rather than state construction," *Cuyler,* supra, 449 U.S. at 438. In Petty v. Tennessee-Missouri Bridge Comm'n, 359 U.S. 275 (1959), the Court held the party states to a construction of compact terms contrary to that which they both agreed was intended, justifying this surprise to party expectations on the ground that Congress' consent made the terms' meaning "a question of federal law." 359 U.S. at 278–79. From the states' point of view, this means that no matter how well they understand one another the parties can never be sure what they are getting into.

If consent causes a compact to become federal law, it would seem to follow that any administrative body created thereby must be a federal, not a state agency. But logic does not operate here: It is held that such a body is a creature of the party states, and the acts of its members are acts done "under color of state law." Lake Country Estates, Inc. v. Tahoe Regional Planning Agency, 440 U.S. 391 (1979).

It has been argued that, because of this touch of Midas, the supremacy clause enables states with Congress' consent to conclude compact terms which violate their own respective constitutions. See West Virginia ex rel. Dyer v. Sims, 341 U.S. 22, 33–34 (1951) (Reed, concurring). Endorsement of that proposition, however, would not enhance the utility of this device for interstate cooperation; instead, it would make state legislatures less inclined to use it at all.

Obviously no state legislature can amend or repeal a federal statute; and it should follow (if one were serious about this inane "law of the Union" doctrine) that party states may not modify or withdraw from a compact, once consented to by Congress, without Congress' consent. But in *Lake Country Estates,* supra, the Court held that they may, 440 U.S. at 399.

Likewise, if consent makes the compact a federal statute, one would think it could be unilaterally amended by Congress, regardless of the wishes of the party states; the unacceptability of that proposition, however, seems to have been one reason for the Court's repudiation of the "law of the Union" doctrine in *Hinderlider,* supra, in 1938.

The law of interstate compacts provides particularly dramatic illustrations of the chaos that results from ad hoc and result oriented decisionmaking in realms of organic constitutional law. It is hoped that these closing paragraphs might puzzle and perplex the reader enough to persuade her of the importance of more systematic and careful theoretical analysis of questions of federalism law. It is that which the author of this book has aspired to encourage.

INDEX

References are to pages

ADMINISTRATIVE AGENCIES, 26, 351–352, 404–405

AFFECTING COMMERCE, 26, 29, 122–123

ANCILLARY POWERS, 17

APPORTIONMENT, 138–141, 142, 308, 309, 311, 318–322, 331–332

ARTICLES OF COMMERCE, 101–102

BILLS OF CREDIT, 200

BOOTSTRAP, 65–68, 198–199, 210

BURDENS, 287–292, 316, 322

CESSION OF JURISDICTION, 215

CLASS BASIS, 32–33, 38–39, 238

COLLISION, 252

COMPACTS, 212, 394 et seq.

COMPETITION, 114–117

CONFLICT, 251, 341, 344, 345, 346, 347

CONSENT, 357 et seq., 399–401, 402

CONTRACT, 84, 175, 185–189, 196–197

INDEX
References are to Pages

CONTRACTORS, 377–380, 382

DELEGATED POWERS, 8, 9

DIRECT, 22, 23, 25, 261–262

DIRECT TAXES, 138–141

DISCRIMINATION, 260, 281–287, 302–303, 309–312, 322, 323

DORMANT POWER, 248–249, 250 et seq., 362

DUAL FEDERALISM, 11, 53, 103–106, 111–113, 122, 258, 261, 278, 300, 324, 368, 387, 593

EARMARKED TAXES, 144

ENCLAVES, 213–217, 226–228

ENUMERATED POWERS, 8, 9, 11, 13, 17, 51, 53, 206, 217, 219–221, 230, 246

EQUAL FOOTING, 222–223, 231

EXCLUSIVE POWER, 251, 252–254, 256, 304, 334, 336–339

EXECUTIVE AGREEMENTS, 213

EXPORTS, 143, 212, 250, 326–330

EXTRADITION, 393

EXTRANEOUS, 18, 22, 53, 59, 60, 63–64, 77, 79, 83–84, 97–98, 135, 146, 170, 174–179, 180–183, 202, 370–373, 375–376, 382–383

EXTRANEOUS TO TAX NEEDS, 156–160

EXTRATERRITORIALITY, 217, 227, 256–257, 277, 303–304, 322

FEDERAL COMMON LAW, 75–76, 292–293

FILIATION OF NECESSITIES, 21, 237

INDEX
References are to Pages

FORMAL RULE, 279, 301–302, 309, 323

FREE TRADE, 277–278, 294

FRUSTRATION, 80, 180, 344, 345, 354

FULL FAITH AND CREDIT, 393

GENERAL JURISDICTION, 10, 27, 29, 67–68, 216–217, 220–223, 229, 230

GENERAL WELFARE, 162, 164–166, 184

HAMILTON, ALEXANDER, 17–18, 93, 108, 167–168, 169–173, 184

HOME PORT DOCTRINE, 306

IMMUNITY, 79, 191–195, 223, 368 et seq.

IMPLIED POWERS, 17

IMPORT–EXPORT CLAUSE, 212, 250, 326–330

INSTRUMENTALITY, 105, 369, 376–377

INTERNATIONAL COMMERCE, 135–137, 326–333

INTOXICANTS, 271–272

JEFFERSON, THOMAS, 17, 23, 167

LAW OF THE UNION DOCTRINE, 401–406

LEGITIMATE, 14, 19, 61–62, 68–69, 77

MADISON, JAMES, 12, 93, 166–167, 171, 184

MARKET PARTICIPANT DOCTRINE, 269–271

MARSHALL, JOHN (C.J.), 13, 20, 52, 94, 96, 234

MONROE, JAMES, 168–170

MULTIPLE TAXATION, 306–308, 323

INDEX
References are to Pages

NAVIGABLE WATERS, 128–135

NEGATIVE IMPLICATIONS, 103, 248 et seq., 359

NEW DEAL, 4, 22, 259–260

NEXUS, 50, 305, 307, 309, 312–315, 322

OBSTACLE TO ACCOMPLISHMENT, 343, 346, 347, 353–354

OCCUPATION OF THE FIELD, 337–338, 346, 347, 349

ORIGINAL PACKAGE DOCTRINE, 117–118, 328–330, 360

PARTICULARITY, 27–31, 49, 90–92, 157

PENALTY (DISTINGUISHED FROM TAX), 147–154

PIE-SLICE, 11, 53, 104

PLENARY, 53, 97, 127

POLICE POWER, 54, 58, 252–254, 258, 261

POWERS, 8, 10, 11–12

PRETEXT, 52, 56, 124, 146

PREVENTION, 237–238, 240

PRIVATE ACTION, 238

PRIVILEGES AND IMMUNITIES, 246–247, 297–298

PROBATION, 96

PROPHYLAXIS, 237–238, 247

PURPOSE, 39–43, 43–48, 150–154, 285

RATIONAL BASIS, 35–39, 238

RECIPROCITY, 281, 365, 394

REMEDIAL ENFORCEMENT, 233, 240

INDEX
References are to Pages

RESERVED POWERS, 9

SCARLET LETTER, 117–122

SHAM TAXES, 147–154, 160

SITUS, 303–305, 307, 308

SOVEREIGNTY, 203–204

STORY, JOSEPH, 168, 171

STREAM OF COMMERCE, 109–110, 279

SUBSTANTIALITY, 34–35

SUPREMACY, 74, 82–85, 185, 212, 224, 229, 334 et seq., 405

SWEEPING CLAUSE, 17

TELIC, 20, 24, 60, 71–72, 235

TENTH AMENDMENT, 9, 390

TERRITORIES, 218–221, 222, 224, 230

TREATIES, 74, 208–209, 210–211, 212–213, 395

TRIVIAL IMPACT, 34–35

UNIFORMITY, 141–143, 275, 290, 363

UNITARY BUSINESS, 313–314, 318–320, 322, 331

WILSON, JAMES, 7, 8, 12

†